For James O'Brien
with best wishes
Robert Epp

THAT FAR–OFF SELF

Maruyama Kaoru

THAT FAR-OFF SELF

丸山薫『遠い己れ』

the collected poetry of

Maruyama Kaoru

1994

Second Edition
revised and expanded

Second edition 1994.04
Revised and Expanded

Manufactured in the United States of America
Printed on acid–free paper by
Thomson–Shore, Inc., Dexter, MI 48130–0305

Maruyama [family] Kaoru [given] (1899–1974)
    [Poems. English. 1992 & 1994]
    That Far–Off Self : Poetry / Maruyama Kaoru;
    translated from the Japanese

    368 pp.   15 x 23 cm.
    Chronology, Contents of Collections,
    Indexes of English and Japanese Titles
    ISBN 1–880276–49–6

Library of Congress Catalog Card Number: 92–80812

Available from **Yakusha**
Post Office Box #666, Stanwood, WA 98292–0666
$35.00 (U.S. currency only) Hardcover (postpaid)

CONTENTS

INTRODUCTORY

THE POETRY

SUPPLEMENTARY

UNESCO COLLECTION OF REPRESENTATIVE WORKS
JAPANESE SERIES

The poetry of Maruyama Kaoru has been accepted by
the Japanese National Commission of
The United Nations Educational, Scientific, and Cultural
Organization

U N E S C O

Maruyama Kaoru——Summer 1973
Toyohashi Grand Hotel

丸山薫：昭和四十八年夏
豊橋グランド・ホテルにて

FOREWORD

I n the past, when Japanese interested in translating their country's literature into English have asked me what works would be appropriate, I have generally suggested that they try modern poetry. It has been my experience that the greatest difficulty for a person who translates into a language that is not his native one is the special rhythms of prose. Again, minor lapses in grammar or peculiar usage that would be glaringly conspicuous in a prose translation can sometimes, by their unfamiliarity, even enhance lines of poetry; nobody expects that poetry will observe the same rules as prose. I am not sure if anyone has taken my advice. I hope not. Robert Epp's superb translations of the poetry of Maruyama Kaoru have made me realize how irresponsible my suggestion was.

It is indeed possible to translate poetry into something that resembles poetry even if one is not completely fluent in the language into which the translation is made. The imagery and sometimes the thought pervading the original poem may be so compelling that it will survive the translation of the rankest amateur. Only when one compares such translations with those made by a poet in his own right does one understand how much can be lost by a "literal" translation.

Robert Epp's translations of Maruyama date at least to 1972 when he published a selection in the *Beloit Poetry Journal*. I remember reading them at the time and being favorably impressed. But, not satisfied with these entirely competent versions, which other translators would have been happy to acknowledge as their own, he has painstakingly gone over each translation again and again, in the effort to be as faithful as possible both to the meaning of the originals and to their specifically poetic qualities. A comparison of his earlier and newer versions of almost any poem will illustrate the nature of the changes he has made. Here is the 1972 version of "Song of the Sail":

> Gull wings beat the dark sky of the sea;
>   if I dip my shoulders
>   I think I might touch them.
> Gull cries shriek the dark sky of the sea;
>   if I reach out my hands

> I think I might catch them.
> I could capture them
>   but for the flickering lamp
> that dangles from my neck.
>   I'll blow it out and wait for the gull
>   to come and light upon
> the snuffed—out blackness of the flame.

The revised version is:

> Gull wings beat in the sea's dark skies;
>   if I dip my shoulder,
>   maybe I can touch them.
> Gull cries mew in the sea's dark skies;
>   if I reach out,
>   maybe I can catch them.
> But flickers from the lamp that hangs round my neck
>   keep me from seeing the gull.
> I'll blow out the lamp.
> I'll wait for the gull
>   to perch on the lamp's chilled, sooty wick.

I chose this particular poem as an illustration because I much admired it even in its earlier state. The new version does not change the meaning in any way—this is not a case of a translator who has had second thoughts about the accuracy of his version— but tightens and makes more effective the poetic expression by eliminating words that are unnecessary in English and therefore tend to dilute the intensity. "If I reach out my hands" became "if I reach out." Needless to say, even the earlier version was not batted out automatically on a typewriter while glancing at the original text; the poet in Robert Epp controlled that translation, too, though not quite so masterfully as in his new version.

The line in question reads in Japanese: "*te wo nobaseba te ni tsukame-sô da.*" A more literal translation, of the kind that many translators might make, would be, "If I stretch out my hands it seems as if I could catch them in my hands." It would be hard to explain to anyone who knows only words and has no ear for the English language what is wrong with this version; it is accurate but a betrayal of the original. I shudder to think of the translations of modern Japanese poetry that may have been made in keeping with my misguided suggestion.

The poems in *That Far-Off Self* are the product of the infiltration, over a long period of time, of the works of a major Japanese poet into the mind and spirit of an American translator. Maruyama Kaoru is not a household name even in Japan. His poetry, though in no way forbidding, lacks the familiar touch that is likely to endear a poet to his countrymen. The poems are filled instead with the loneliness of a poet who seemed happier when surrounded by the vastness of the ocean than when caught up in the concerns of modern society.

Maruyama was by no means indifferent to other people. His sympathies were naturally with those, like himself, who had known the sting of failure and neglect:

> No friend
> if he hasn't been defeated.
> No ally
> if he hasn't been deceived.
>
> Reject those and the standards of those
> who get ahead by elbowing others aside!

Many poems are moving especially because of their empathy with people and things that would be totally forgotten if they did not stubbornly linger in the poet's memory. Perhaps this nostalgia is what first attracted Epp to Maruyama and induced him later to revise his versions of the poems. Each change he has made in his translations surely reflects hours of beating out the rhythms and trying to capture the music of the originals in English. The translations not only do justice to Maruyama Kaoru and make him accessible to the English–reading world but are themselves enjoyable for their beauty as English poems.

Donald Keene

Professor Emeritus
Columbia University

MARUYAMA AS IMAGIST

... "In the soaring stance that is Poet."

One quality dominates the early poems of Maruyama Kaoru: their Imagistic aspects. As a poetic innovator, at least in his earliest work, Maruyama is best understood in the context of other Imagist poetry in Japan and abroad. Imagism suggests the direct treatment of "things," subjective or objective. Urging an absolutely accurate presentation without verbiage, Imagism emphasizes concentrated visual concreteness, avoidance of traditional forms and meters, and both clarity and impersonality. Maruyama did not abandon this Imagist "discipline" until the midpoint in his career.

F. S. Flint and Ezra Pound first set forth these principles in 1913. Western Imagists subsequently applied them to their poetry. They aptly fit Maruyama's early verse as well. At thirty three, his first collection, *Sail–Lamp–Gull* (1932) won recognition. These poems—which feature laconic, dense, concrete, and sharp visual imagery—closely approach the Flint–Pound ideals. They are, indeed, so close that one might safely call them Japanese versions of Imagism. Despite that, few Japanese critics have recognized Maruyama as the deservedly Imagist poet he then was. In fact, to my knowledge, the term "Imagism" did not enter the indigenous æsthetic vocabulary until 1940. That was when Hagiwara Sakutarô (1886–1942) first applied it to modern Japanese poetry in the essay "Protest to Miyoshi Tatsuji" collected in *A Traveler Home* [*Kikyôsha*].

Hagiwara's impact on modern Japanese verse is considerable. Not only do many scholars designate him "the father of Japanese free verse," but his work affected a number of major poets. All readily admit his inspiration. Aside from Maruyama, the most distinguished poets who came under Hagiwara's influence were Miyoshi Tatsuji (1900–1964) and Nishiwaki Junzaburô (1894–1982). All regarded Hagiwara their mentor, though Maruyama was the "master's" most congenial colleague. We are still awaiting an in–depth study of Hagiwara's impact on Maruyama. I suspect some identification exists. For example, in the 1965 "Foreword" he kindly wrote for a book of my poems, Maruyama reported a statement that Hagiwara once made to him:

> Even the utterly courteous gentleman, who
> looks unlikely to harm a fly, keeps a personal
> notebook flooded with the most defiant and acerbic
> expressions.

Judging from experience, Maruyama here describes himself.

This is the poet whose Imagism provides the topic of this essay. The trilogy of poems from which Maruyama derives the name of his first collection, *Sail–Lamp–Gull,* illustrates his Imagistic ingenuity. So does the following:

GUN EMPLACEMENT
Fragments yearned to snuggle together.
Fissures yearned to smile again.
The mortar barrel yearned to rise
      and be seated again on its mount.
All dreamed of transitory wholeness.
Each wind whip buried them deeper under sand.
The sea beyond sight——the flash of a migratory bird.

This initially appeared in the January 1931 issue of *Shishin*; it is a monumental work in modern Japanese poetry. How much meaning may be concentrated in six lines?

Here the poet presents a stark scene of ruin on a sandy beach. An inanimate thing, an *objet*, objectifies human yearning and frustration. As the figures sink into the mind, they invite an intense aftertaste: a sense of the gradual collapse of everything on Earth. Maruyama creates a microcosm of his frustrated desire to restore a long–lost original wholeness. This imagistically compressed metaphor achieves in artistic form a complete objectivity and impersonality. It is difficult to find anything comparable in the literary tradition of Japanese poetry and poetics.

A glance at two Imagist–type Japanese poets may help clarify trends originating in the decade or so following World War II. These poets are the Maruyama contemporaries Kitagawa Fuyuhiko (1900–1990) and Anzai Fuyue (1898–1965). Both were active members in the new wave of intellectual modernism, dating from 1928 and represented by the journal *Shi to Shiron* [*Poetry and Poetics*]. This movement marks the beginning of what we call "Modern Japanese Poetry" viewed as a reaction against the romantic approach. The following post–war remarks definitely qualify Kitagawa as an Imagist:

My primary concern has been to write verse using clear–cut imagery that rejects the ready–made diction and ideas informing most current poetry. (1951)

I have tried to grasp *busshô*, i.e., *objet*, directly through my senses without introducing [traditional] diction or abstract ideas. (1951)

A poet should present the poem as an independent physical object independent of the self. (1955)

It merits attention that he uses *busshô*, the same term Maruyama chose for the title of his 1941 collection. Kitagawa's celebrated short poem "Horse," read as a biting metaphor of militarism, imitates an Imagist experiment:

A horse bellies the naval base.

Anzai, the other Imagist–type poet, is well–known for his very brief poem "Spring."

A butterfly fluttered off across the Tartar Strait.

Both "Horse" and "Spring" are as remarkable for their typographical arrangement as for their Imagistic schemata.

Kitagawa and Anzai show that modern Japanese poets made the prosaic and the colloquial their landscape. Discontented with current verse, they earnestly experimented with new forms and new concepts. Born into the lyric tradition of Japanese poetry and confronted with novel influences both domestic and foreign, the "modern poet" faced fresh challenges. His primary—we can now say historical—role was to root himself in the modern consciousness by bridging mind and feeling, emotion and intellect. Kitagawa's handling of critical idea and diction was comparatively the more austere, forward, and revolutionary, if not headstrong. Maruyama tended rather to balance sentiment and intellect and so ultimately, in later years, attained maturity. All the same, in retrospect, the contributions these men made during their "Imagist periods" are estimable. They helped dispel the maudlin clouds that darkened the Japanese lyric tradition. The poet Yamamoto Tarô (1925–1988) stated in 1977 that Maruyama's poetry is a model of Japanese lyricism freed of its mawkishness.

This does not mean to imply that Maruyama dedicated himself to the original Imagist platform that flourished in England and

America just after the turn of the century. Much rather should we regard him a home–grown, self–made, and self–inspired Japanese Imagist. He danced to his own not to Pound's flute. Possibly he was not aware of the vigorous interaction of experimental English and American poetry the Imagist movement spawned during the first two decades of this century. The movement flowered especially between 1908 and 1917 but declined during the second quarter of the century. Maruyama's Imagist propensity was not an arty something stimulated by influences from abroad. It was innate. That's why it generated an objective and critical stance sufficient to turn him, early in his career, from the old Japanese poetry of easy idealism and emotionalism. In his own way, intellect tempered lyricism. At times, he did this to extremes: he adopted the heretical stance of viewing reality in wholly unconventional ways.

William Carlos Williams (1883–1963) presumably stands closest among American poets to the principles of the original Imagist school. It should be instructive to compare Maruyama's work to that of this non–Japanese Imagist. I cite Williams' well–known 1938 poem:

THE RED WHEELBARROW
so much depends
upon

a red wheel
barrow

glazed with rain
water

beside the white
chickens

Both Williams and Maruyama were image–oriented poets who sought hard and concrete analogies to immediate experience. They aimed to bring the word as close as possible to *objet*. Both excised every conventional and too–human association. Set beside Maruyama's "Gun Emplacement," Williams' treatment of "things" is raw and positive, his stance outward. The images in this poem emerge from the common, normal, simple, and therefore intrinsically human materials of everyday life. One critic notes that Williams' red wheelbarrow serves as a most useful and simple man–made implement, one upon which "so much depends." It is as familiar and as real an object as we can imagine, as well as a necessary part of our experience.

In his 1952 autobiography, Williams states simply, "no ideas but in things." By comparison, Maruyama's things or *objet* are, as it were, carved in relief. His negative, inward, and at times non-human stance casts shadows over his *objet*. The melancholy moods and tone of frustration possibly derive from his unsettled childhood. This, nevertheless, is where he begins. Maruyama then goes on to expand his *objet* somewhat beyond their original essences; contrarily, Williams was satisfied to present a poem of the raw *objet* exactly as it was. To him, the image itself was the only means of verbal expression.

This contrast confronts us with Maruyama's æsthetic. In his vital prefatory note to *Busshô Shishû* (1941), he exquisitely proclaims the concept and function of what he calls *busshô*:

> I perceive a forceful trend through my poetical works. It is the avid pursuit of and longing for *objet*....
>
> When I compose poetry, I marvel at those shadowy patterns emanating from the *objet*. They inspire my writing——the lamp of a ship quiet at anchor in an estuary; the crane–like cloud flying up from a pine tree the setting sun stains scarlet; a row of utility poles walking with me in silence like travelers. They exist always in my past poetry and will continue to exist in future work as well.

In his case, the *objet* serve as "prime movers"; they appeal to feelings that, seeking physical analogies, develop into images. The poet then clothes the images themselves in words.

The method of composition most congenial to him reflects this "prime mover" role. He makes the exquisite shading of external *objet* reveal internal yearnings. Human content is implied rather than stated. It might be pertinent here to cite Ezra Pound, who provides a one–sentence definition of what Maruyama was striving to create: "An 'Image' is that which presents an intellectual and emotional complex in an instant of time." Pound also declared, "It is better to present one image in a lifetime than to produce voluminous works."

We can distinctly trace Maruyama's imagistic continuity from the "fissures" in his 1931 "Gun Emplacement" to the "cracked roof–tiles" in his 1935 "Traces of a Butterfly." After that, however, in terms of their treatment of *objet,* his best poems of the Imagist type retrogress. His *esprit* becomes absorbed in and digested by more powerful and profound sources of poetic energy. We find fresh scope, degree, and diction. Certainly, Maruyama's 1945 to 1948 existence among common people in harsh northern land-scapes marked an important stage in his growth. These years mark a turning point. He discovered new answers to the problems of how and what to write; he moved from art and artifice to life and society.

Metaphors of embittered loneliness and frustration dominating the earliest collections gradually disappear. "Korea" (1937) moves us with its humanitarian sympathy. "Verdant Self" (1949) and "Atomic Balm" (1951) evince the poet's belatedly–restored youth. The title, *Lost Youth* (1952), in fact, sounds rather ironic because its poems so positively assert life. This collection is actually less a matter of youth lost than youth regained——though he never re-gains his imagistic approach to writing. By 1956, a work like "My Woman the Sea" acclaims a universal vital force. In retrospect, perhaps *Sail–Lamp–Gull* fully realized his Imagism.

At forty nine, he published his tenth collection, *Flowercore* (1948). It contains the poem "Ages" in which he reports the words of a young friend who had tragically died several years earlier:

> "Though poets have youth and old age,
> they know neither adolescence nor prime."

No doubt those years in the North had given Maruyama a new and more mature perspective on life and art. Referring to this verse, Inoue Yasushi (1907–1991) commented in his Introduction to Maruyama's *Works*, Vol. II: "Throughout his life, a young boy and an old man always sat side by side in him." He later turned his back on experimental expressions (those, for example, found in "Memos to Faces") derived from his modern consciousness and compiled in his first collection. These became completely super-seded by direct delineations of his mental landscape. Many critics comment on Maruyama's growth as a human being but generally overlook his decline as an Imagist.

This mental development is not difficult to trace. Notice Maru-yama's 1954 defense of Miyoshi Tatsuji (1900–1964), a lifelong friend and rival poet. He approved of Miyoshi's conversion from a French–style intellectual stance to a traditional Japanese approach in both idea and diction. He argued that scholarship makes no poet. Intellectual extravagance, he claimed, is rampant among contemporary modernist poets. They need not more learning but to lean more on innate tendencies, to develop a natural voice, and to tug more at the heartstrings.

What happened to his commitment to *bushhô*? At one time I wondered if Maruyama, suffering from its impasse, had finally accepted its finite limitations. It seems proper, in any event, to conclude that his Imagist period had been displaced by the next stage; this outfitted him as a maturing artist with wider range and profundity. Moreover, my reading of Maruyama's statement about Miyoshi is that it not only fully accounts for his own conversion but provides its justification as well. His art reaches its zenith when he ends "Tenth Floor Bar" (1966) with the words,

> I'm an old bird——motionless on its perch,
> highball fizzing vacuously in one claw.

Or when in "Mortified Figure" (1967) he describes that "enfeebled elephant [that] quit its herd" so it could abandon itself in "an unexplored grotto."

Referring to *Moon Passage,* the poet Ono Tôzaburô (born 1903) pertinently remarks:

> Maruyama's theory and practice of *busshô* [objet] proved it was no longer essential as the mold into which he poured and cast experience. Instead he finally attained greater human depth. When his craftsmanship preoccupied me, this escaped my notice.

According to the translator, Maruyama asserted that his long prose poem "Moon Passage" exemplifies a work with universal significance. The poet claims that this piece stands "as the finest example of his mature art." Had he found a way to accept his mortality and finitude after all?

Interpretations may vary. I presume, however, that the keynote of this poem is not the recognition, "my life, too, would soon return to space," but the poet's reaction to the shout, "Hey, Dummy! Get a move on...." That is to say, through his four decades of poetic activity, he never abandoned "the soaring stance that is Poet." In this way he could transcend and outgrow his starting point, Imagism. One can nonetheless hope that his Imagistic aspects might one day present historians of modern Japanese poetry with new frontiers.

In 1972, two years before he died, Maruyama wrote as follows:

> It was delightful to read Kuwabara Takeo's remarks on *Moon Passage*. He wrote, "I was entirely refreshed; it was as though poetic matter absolutely free of emotional slither had purified my every bone. I was pleased to notice the continuity with your first collection, *Sail–Lamp–Gull*."

> All my poetry appears to be an emanation of the loneliness that always parallels my existence. When I confront *busshô* [*objet*], life comes home to my heart.

Even after so many years, his formative *objet*—the theory of *busshô*—still quickened him.

Nagata Masao
永田正男

Professor of English, Emeritus
Seikei University, Tokyo
成蹊大学 東京都武蔵野市

INTRODUCTION

– I –

The title *That Far–Off Self* comes from *"Amanojaku"* [Perversity; 1936, page 88]. In this brief poem, Maruyama Kaoru (1899–1974) describes himself staring into a pocket mirror. He wants to look through the reflection and through his eyes to penetrate his innermost being. His true Self exists, he believes, beyond the self visible on the surface of the glass. This figure dominates my reading—and governs what I take to be the concealed center—of Maruyama's serious work.

More, it implies universals that place his verse in the mainstream of world writing. In folklore, looking into a mirror is tantamount to observing life's essence, the soul, which is said to be visible through the eyes. Some cultures regard the hand mirror an emblem of Truth——a magical means to view the past and the present banked in the psyche. Psychiatrists equally believe that data culled from the inner self can clarify both past and present. From ancient times, moreover, whether mirror or water, reflections have linked with the myth of Narcissus: an individual who probes his Self by gazing at the soul through his reflection. This may suggest but is not self love, for Maruyama looks into not at himself as he searches for universal truths.

Mirrors connect not only with the pool of water Narcissus gazed at, and so with the sea, but with the moon. Like the sun–reflecting moon, a mirror is passive. Like both moon and sea, it has long symbolized the soul and its complexity. Folk wisdom and alchemists have furthermore conceived of mirrors as "bridges" that connect to an unseen dimension. They facilitate respite from life's encroachments. That explains why the discovery of the protagonist in *Alice Through the Looking Glass* does not surprise. Alice finds herself free from entanglements with syllogistic logic the moment she passes to the other side of a mirror.

Studying one's Self reflected in a mirror implies a contemplative and observant mind. An artist who extends observation beyond feelings to understanding and analysis reflects a self–aware intellect. Some of Maruyama's best work aims to do just that. Indeed, his insistence on moving beyond emotions and his interest in

what triggers them combine to produce an æsthetic that chal-
lenges his poetic tradition. Professor Makoto Ueda of Stanford
University writes,

> Japanese æstheticians minimize the role of intel-
> lect in artistic creation. They are all intuitionists.

Intuition sustains a lyric impulse that has for more than a mil-
lennium given exclusive honor to feeling and subjectivity. This
culture highly values non–verbal communication. As Ueda notes,
poetry in Japan historically leans toward the emotional expres-
sion of experience. Those aspects of poetry preoccupy Japanese,
literary critics and scholars alike. Among them, the well–known
Cartesian formula, *Cogito, ergo sum*——"I think, therefore I am,"
becomes, *Sentio, ergo sum*——"I feel, therefore I am."

In the same vein, the poet–critic Ôoka Makoto writes, "In mod-
ern Japan it has sometimes been disastrous to be an 'intellectual
poet.'" The reason is clear. A people preoccupied with subjectivity
have little regard for brainwork. Japanese, Ôoka says, see intel-
lect in poetry an "obstruction, intrusive and suspect"; the deep–
seated indigenous intolerance of intellectuality in art makes it so.
Emphasis on emotions configures a poetic tradition that cherishes
every non–rational element that pure intuition supports. This
may explain why few read Maruyama's verse. He tries to put lyri-
cal impulse—his intuitions, and sentiments—under reason's con-
trol. In Japanese eyes, that makes him a "suspect" poet. In early
work, he often consciously compresses private feelings into flint–
like symbols. Throughout much later work, abstract problems
consistently fascinate him. Many hence find him detached, even
"cold." These qualities rarely endear a poet to the Japanese
reader. Worse, they make Maruyama come across as more cere-
bral than emotional, and, so, "non–traditional." A poet like that
stands in danger of distancing himself from critics as well.

Japanese readers of verse wish to feel intimately involved in the
poet's emotions. Involvement carries greater import than expo-
sure to brilliant imagery or metaphors. It means more than being
stimulated by profound poetic insights or sharing in the univer-
sality rather than the affective particularity of the poet's experi-
ence. Emotive engagement guarantees being touched or moved to
tears——the immediate reaction countless Japanese seek in po-
etry. For many, if not most, tears alone authenticate the poem as
a work of art. This helps explain why so few feel in the least
moved by intellectual verse and refuse to read it. Reason in Japan
is, indeed, a leaky ship on the sea of emotion. Japanese adamant-

ly choose to swim the sea rather than sail the ship.

The label "intellectual" is, to be sure, culturally relative. Saying he is no Wallace Stevens does not in the least belittle Maruyama. Nor does it demean his achievement to claim his work lacks the philosophical weight of T. S. Eliot's *Four Quartets*. The very gravity or weightiness that delights the Western critic distances a Japanese reader. Ideas or pensive musings appear often enough in Maruyama's poetry to cause such distancing. Below the surface of works that superficially treat a pure emotion, even the poet's widow feels certain he had a symbolic meaning in mind. Symbols channel meaning to levels beyond the superficial and ephemeral sentiment the Japanese reader so often expects. That level for Maruyama frequently ends up a concept or abstract idea he contends with. What is distance? What does it mean that experienced reality so often differs from what one senses it to be? Why do those who observe the same event or phenomenon perceive it so dissimilarly? Why do the past and memories impinge so relentlessly on the present? Concerns of this kind may recommend his work to Western but not to Japanese readers.

Rather than exploit sentiment to melt or buoy up his reader's heart, this poet uses sentiment to explore ideas. Although he often shares deeply–felt experiences, it rarely satisfies him to write only about feelings; he wants to uncover their source or significance. Of course, one obviously feels his experiences. Perceiving their meaning is an entirely different matter——one that relates to how the unreliable ship of reason might negotiate the vast sea of emotion. Reaching beyond visible surfaces for such meanings understandably causes some Japanese to perceive Maruyama as a poet of abstractions. For him, however, there is no other way to get at the intensely–experienced experience. That is exactly what fills his work with far more than flashes of feeling or insight. His probing lets the poem fester longer in the mind and thus burrow into the bones.

Most readers of English poetry have a higher threshold of tolerance for such probing than the typical Japanese. We accept cerebration and argument in verse; we reject treacle. Japanese welcome—no, they demand—sentimentality and emotion in their verse; they prefer tears to abstractions. Western readers may regard the scale of Maruyama's intellection limited. The mere hint of ideas in a poem, however, disenchants many a Japanese. By contrast, English–speaking readers show less concern over the extent of intellectuality than the extent to which they imagine the

poet profoundly felt his thoughts. It is not as likely in Japan as in
the West that those who want to express profoundly–felt ideas in
a moving way might turn to literature rather than philosophy.

Excessively intellectual or not, Maruyama has written many
excellent poems. Their excellence forces Japanese critics and
readers to come to terms with his cerebral aspects. Reacting only
to what they perceive in the poetry as interesting, as more conge-
nial to cultural expectations and taste, or even to what is easier to
handle, leads some Japanese critics to play up and concentrate on
a single aspect of this poet's work. They make much of his life–
long involvement with the sea, for example. The wholly romantic
notion of Maruyama as "poet of the sea" helps insulate readers
from his often self–conscious intellectuality.

To describe Maruyama's work merely as a product of his love for
the sea is limiting. Worse, it negates his achievements, artistic
growth, and range of concerns. Analysts praise the imagistic as-
pects of his maritime verse. They simultaneously ignore qualities
that lend his work far more depth than the one–dimensional sea–
poet description allows. This tag, moreover, disregards several
compelling facts. Maruyama never tried to merge with or roman-
tically identify with the sea. He rather exploited its images to
achieve artistic goals. Approaching fifty, he wrote that he proba-
bly would come to his end "writing poem after poem about the
fretful sea" ("Kaichô" [Sea Birds]; 1948, page 187). After writing
those words, however, he by no means produced "poem after poem
about the fretful sea." He instead wrote poem after poem about
his fretful Self. That has been the constant concern of his verse.
The "poet of the sea" sticker encourages critics to slight this and
other of Maruyama's most cherished concerns——including most
of his œuvre. Small wonder that during interviews the poet often
expressed considerable displeasure over such pigeonholing.

Part of Maruyama's production relates to the sea. He wrote
many poems about—and three of his fifteen collections relate to—
the ocean, so his work displays a deep love for the sea (thalasso-
philia). But when we consider a representative cross section of
Maruyama's entire output, we do not find a minstrel committed to
writing pæans to Neptune. Nor do we find a bard primarily con-
cerned with expressing his feelings about the Deep. We rather
discover a poet who exploits maritime imagery to examine issues
like perception, isolation, illusions, and lack of relationship.

That is to say, Maruyama uses sea images to realize his poetic goals. These reveal his self–probing more than his emotion or moods alone. In other words, beyond simply revealing an undeniable attraction for the ocean, these images serve as symbols for deeper concerns. Why the attraction? What are these concerns? Once we pay attention to these questions, we see a poet whose æsthetic quest far transcends maritime figures. Certainly Maruyama has deep feelings for the sea. At no stage, however, could dealing merely with his *feelings* for the ocean—or the sky, or whatever—satisfy him. As Santayana once claimed, emotions are not "about anything," for feelings have very little to say. Without doubt, Maruyama would agree.

Seeing how he expresses his nostalgia for the sea—and what his expressions symbolize—makes this clear. Considering a broad selection of works, we discover a poet in pursuit of the familiar ends of many modern writers: He mines loneliness to seek the whole self. He wants to discover his identity and life's meaning. He hopes to learn how an isolated individual might relate to others and to his innermost Self. To borrow a Mircea Eliade metaphor, Maruyama's concern is to penetrate the labyrinth of the Self. This will help him understand his lonely existence—and human existence in general. For all their commonality, these ends are never cliché. Such a poet writes much more interesting, far–ranging, intricate, and penetrating poetry than any simple catchword can imply.

– I I –

Maruyama believed he had reason to regard himself a loner. He spent most of his career removed from Tokyo poetry circles. This intensified the sense of separation and mistrust that unsettling childhood experiences created in him. The central government repeatedly re–assigned his father, a high–ranking bureaucrat. New assignments were so frequent that the poet's boyhood consisted of repeated uprootings and the constant need to make new friends. Maruyama had attended four different primary schools by the time he was twelve. He transferred to the fifth soon after his father's death. That forced his family to return to his mother's parental home in Toyohashi, a city less than fifty rail miles southeast of Nagoya.

Uprootings caused Maruyama to perceive himself a stranger. In Japan's tightly–knit, cliquish society, a transfer student always finds it extremely trying to make friendships. This was particularly the case in Maruyama's boyhood when families only rarely moved from one location to another. He longed for acceptance. A frail constitution often kept him out of school and doubtless increased his conviction of being separate. Bouts of high fever augmented an awareness of being different and provoked nightmares. These experiences led Maruyama to dream of the future. He would become a ship's captain——a man of supreme loneliness, but one in supreme control. In 1911, he visited the port of Yokohama with his elementary school class. Rain forced cancellation of the flying machine demonstration the class had gone to view. Instead, the teacher allowed his charges to look at ships in the harbor. There the haunting blue eyes of Scandinavian sailors astonished the young Maruyama. He dates his focus on the sea from that unforgettable experience. It is significant that eyes—windows to the soul and, in this case, blue like sea and sky—had triggered his interest. He, too, would become a sailor. So, when he graduated from middle school six years later, he sat for the entrance examination to the Merchant Marine Academy.

Strong opposition from his mother and relatives did not dissuade him. He could decide such matters because he was, after all, the pro forma family head. He failed the exam but promptly enrolled in a Tokyo preparatory school, hoping to pass the following year. As he studied, Maruyama chanced on books that stimulated his dream of going to sea. These included an English edition of Robert Louis Stevenson's *Treasure Island* as well as works by Joseph Conrad in Japanese translation. In April 1918, Maruyama passed the exam and entered the Academy.

From the outset, he dreamt of being master of his own ship. At the Academy, however, his terror of heights kept him from climbing the masts and working on the spars of the training barque. Inability to do so meant he could never qualify as a line officer. That left the engine room. Since an engineer could never become ship's captain, the dream was over. This bitter disappointment may have aggravated physical weaknesses. In any case, unaccustomed exertions during early months at the Academy caused his legs to swell. He received a medical release in September 1918. Still obsessed by unsatisfied longings to experience the sea, Maruyama briefly considered becoming a lighthouse keeper—— again, a loner in control. His mother managed to persuade him to choose another course. He decided to sit for the examination to the Third Higher School in Kyoto, a major route to the elite Tokyo University (Tôdai). After concentrated study, he passed the test and matriculated in 1921 as a French literature major. His choice of majors reflected both his vague hope to become a journalist and his aversion to becoming a bureaucrat.

Not long after entering the Kyoto school, Maruyama became interested in verse. Modern Japanese poets and French poetry in translation, as well as works by Edgar Allan Poe and Oscar Wilde, shaped his decision to become a poet. Writing consumed him to such an extent that he paid scant attention to the curriculum. He missed so many classes in Kyoto that he had to repeat the first year. Continued involvement with literary groups and writing resulted in more missed classes. That meant he had to repeat yet another year. Although this delayed his graduation until March 1926, falling behind enabled Maruyama to make lasting friendships with several who entered the school after him. The most notable was Miyoshi Tatsuji (1900–1964), who became a major poet. The two remained lifelong friends.

Maruyama entered Tôdai in April 1926 as a Japanese literature major. He didn't need a bachelor's degree to write poetry, so he paid little attention to courses or lectures. He sought instead the stimulation the campus promised. There, he met many would–be poets and discussed Japanese and European verse. He also helped edit a literary magazine in which he published his writings. His belief that his father's inheritance would allow him many years of financial independence gave false confidence. Not only did he imagine he might indefinitely devote himself to poetry, he furthermore figured he could humor his aristocratic tastes and enjoy a lavish lifestyle.

Involvement in writing brought Maruyama into contact with students from various disciplines. One friend from the Third Higher School in Kyoto with a shared interest in writing was the heir to the Ôtaniya——a well–known drapery in Toyohashi, a city in Aichi, the prefecture where Maruyama's mother was born. While visiting this friend in Toyohashi, he met the woman he would later marry. She was Takai Miyoko (born 1907), the daughter of a dyer who apparently had enlightened views. She received her secondary education at Christian schools in Yokohama and Nagoya. Spinal caries later forced withdrawal from the prefectural higher girls' school, where she hoped to earn credentials as an English teacher (☞ notes to "My Winsome Wife"). Following their marriage in February 1928, he rented a luxurious house in Tokyo. Six months later, he invited his mother Takeko to move in. Fortunately, Takeko got along well with Miyoko. In fact, she said that if her son ever divorced Miyoko, she would rather live with her than with Kaoru. The two women often went to the movies together, and Miyoko credits her mother–in–law with teaching her everything she knew about housekeeping and being a wife.

Economic hardships preceded the publication of his first poetry book. Shortly after his mother came to live with him, Maruyama dropped out of Tôdai to concentrate on writing. By 1930, the year of the financial crash in Japan, he managed to squander the last of his father's inheritance. Nobody had thought of putting even a single *sen* aside for the future. The underside of conspicuous consumption is that extravagance attracts leeches. Beguiled by what appeared to be boundless resources, freeloaders brazenly "borrowed" money or goods, neither of which they intended to repay. Over the following months, the Maruyamas found themselves presuming on one relative after another. However straitened their circumstances, Miyoko recalls with pride that they never missed paying their rent. Poverty, however, made it extremely difficult to concentrate on the writing Maruyama knew he must do. He had not yet properly launched his career with a well–received first collection.

In the autumn of 1931, his luck changed. Through a friend, the poet found Miyoko a job in downtown Tokyo. The couple promptly left Kyoto and settled in the capital. Miyoko's more than adequate income allowed Maruyama to concentrate on creating poems. His first collection, *Ho–Ranpu–Kamome* [*Sail–Lamp–Gull*], appeared in December 1932 when he was thirty three. The poetry's concrete, finely–honed, and unique imagery made a considerable impact on Tokyo poetry circles. He earned the reputation of promising talent. Despite the title of this collection, fewer than a dozen of its thirty–four poems plainly treat the ocean as ocean. All the same, Maruyama's initial reputation as "poet of the sea" stems from this work. In these poems, however, Maruyama neither explores the ocean nor life aboard ship. Metaphors derived from his idealized longing for the sea serve other ends. He employs them to delve into several ideas that use imagery related to the Deep. For example, he uses maritime images to probe his lasting concern for relationship.

The sail, the lamp, and the gull in the title refer to the book's third, fourth, and fifth poems. He published these at the end of 1931. These works form a trilogy that Maruyama never put in any other order, nor did he ever publish any of the three pieces separately. His trilogy assesses relationship in a single moment of time and space, using the conceit that two inanimate objects and a bird desire relationship. The way the sail, the lamp, and the gull view that moment reflects the poet's basic concerns. These include the difficulty of communicating and the aloneness that so easily prey on non–conformists in a close–knit, homogeneous society like Japan's. These ideas suggest the distance of the Self from itself. The trilogy also reveals the poet's impersonal, imagistic, and intellectual treatment of sentiment. It shows, too, his consistent approach to time, space, and perspective.

Sail, lamp, and gull perceive the moment of their isolated existence differently. They nonetheless equally share and suffer from the same stark realization of solitude. In *"Ho no Uta"* [Song of the Sail, page 67], the sail notes that it can hear the bird mewing and flapping. It can, however, neither catch the gull's cries nor touch its wings. The reason, the sail imagines, is the lamp's flickering. The sail decides to blow out the lamp because it thinks that darkness might entice the bird to approach. The lamp in *"Ranpu no Uta"* [Song of the Lamp, page 68] complains of the feebleness of its light. Unable to see beyond its own face, it can only sense the gull, invisible but by no means silent in the dark. The gull in *"Kamome no Uta"* [Song of the Gull, page 68] feels itself imprisoned, as it were, in the freedom of the night sky. It laments that neither lamp nor sail can see it. In truth, the skies are pitch black, so darkness prevents it from seeing even its own wings. The sail, however, reflects the lamp's feeble light and so allows the bird a clear view of both the lamp and the sail. Only the lamp makes the gull aware of its lonely existence. If the bird could approach the light, perhaps it could see itself. As though echoing the poet's innermost feelings, the gull feels distant and unrelated, doomed to fly unrecognized through the sky's icy blackness.

The moment Maruyama examines in this three–part poem bristles with ironies. To entice the gull, the sail would extinguish the only means the bird has to find and approach the sail. The lamp, so bright it blinds the sail and prevents its making contact with the gull, nevertheless imagines itself too weak to light up anything. The gull feels so invisible it very nearly assumes that the sail and the lamp it sees so sharply do not know it exists. If only the bird knew that they could hear it mewing above them, that both yearn for relationship! Perhaps the gull would then display more interest in the sail and the lamp. But even the free–flying seagull lacks adequate perspective of this moment. In the end, the chill of separation dominates. Each of the three stands locked in its own narrow, gloomy world.

This trilogy shows an important aspect of Maruyama's imagery. He makes an effort to create, according to Ezra Pound's definition of Imagism, dimensional figures. These will give readers "an intellectual and emotional complex in an instant of time." Far more than snapshots of reality, Maruyama's images compress disparate ideas, feelings, and insights into single moments that he expresses in concrete forms. These serve as metaphors for the persona's emotions, which in the trilogy reveal a penetrating awareness of separateness.

Sea also becomes incidental in a well–known poem presumably set near the seashore. This six–line work describes a dilapidated coastal defense mortar serving as a war memorial on Kudan Hill, near the Imperial Palace. Its scattered parts "yearned to snuggle together" again. Despite their dream

> of transitory wholeness,
> each wind whip buries them deeper under sand.

Scholars often cite "*Hôrui*" [Gun Emplacement; 1931, page 65] as an illustration of Maruyama's early imagistic style. Perhaps as well as any of his poems, "*Hôrui*" depicts man's inability to recover the past for which he longs. In Pound's words, he achieves the effect of lonely frustration "objectively——no slither." Maruyama's practice here certainly relates to that of Imagist poets in the West. He uses the exact word and maximum visual content. He avoids decorative devices or comment and treats images through sparse and intense diction.

In later work, the sea similarly provides Maruyama with raw material that he shapes to private ends. Two poems published some three decades after the trilogy and "Gun Emplacement" illustrate. Maruyama wants to deal with psychological insights that make use of sea figures. The first poem, "*Sonna Nagame ga*" [Such Scenes ...; 1968, page 271], deals with borderlines. Sea imagery provides metaphors that allow the poet to probe his concern for temporal or spatial boundaries. These he often interprets as harboring his far–off Self. No more obvious borderline exists than the horizon. This figure helps him explore hopes, dreams, longings for the unknown, and anything ambiguous. The sea represents ambiguity by symbolizing the eternal flux of life and death, safety and peril——the psyche itself. Sea meets sky on the horizon, blue merging with blue, at a spot that changes but enigmatically suggests the changeless. Similarly, both seashore and estuary serve as borderline images. Either implies the indeterminate. So does any transitional area that one can view from contrasting imaginative viewpoints. The poet adores places where

> Land breezes melt into sea breezes.
> Fresh water mixes with tide water.
> Skies over land merge with skies over sea....

These transitional areas alert the poet to the contrasts between appearance and reality. What appears fixed may be illusion.

"Omaezaki Tôdai Kairô de" [In the Corridor of Omaezaki Lighthouse; 1964, page 262] also spotlights the horizon. Here, using a technique of shifting perspectives, Maruyama describes the sweep of the lamp in the lighthouse. Light rivets the poet's attention to darkness, then to a faint glow on the offing——traces of daylight that darkness has yet to overcome. Almost the moment he focuses on that distant and almost indefinite line, he makes a discovery:

> griefs bearing the silhouette of a younger me
> unexpectedly drift my way.

This time a transitional area makes visible certain of the past's agonizing realities.

Several intriguing perspectives shape this poem. Instead of an eye searching the distance, Maruyama finds griefs searing his consciousness. Instead of eyeing a moment in contemporary time, shadowy past moments study him. He transforms a glance at the horizon (at the present or even at the future) into a glimpse of the past and the stunning way it can dominate one's present. Youthful griefs concealed in day's final glimmer refuse to quit the memory. The past invades his awareness in that instant, taking revenge on the present by merging with it. What was now is; one's past changes into an ever–present torment. On the horizon, dream turns to nightmare as harridans from experience absorb hopes for the future. Not content merely to re–create the mood of the moment, Maruyama typically hints at the mood's psychic meaning: what we are is, in part, what we were and are to be. These temporal and spatial images suggest the agonies, fears, and alienation that an artist's sensitivity can unleash. In a word, Maruyama here plumbs both intellectually and emotionally his awareness of that far–off Self.

Not long after issuing *Sail–Lamp–Gull*, Maruyama decided to join others in publishing *Shiki* [*Four Seasons*]. This decision influenced his entire career. The novelist–poet Hori Tatsuo (1904–1953) had started the magazine with two numbers that appeared in 1933. Hoping it might appear four times annually, he named

the journal *Shiki* [*Four Seasons*]. A year later, enlisting the aid of
Miyoshi Tatsuji and Maruyama, Hori decided to try again. The
three writers then revived the journal in the fall of 1934. From
the outset, Maruyama bore more than his share of the burden be-
cause his two fellow editors suffered from pulmonary tuberculosis.

Having played a pivotal role in each of its later reincarnations
meant that Maruyama's death in 1974 signaled the end of *Shiki*.
The magazine ceased publication in the spring of 1975 with an is-
sue that commemorated the poet's career–long connection with
the magazine as well as those who edited and contributed to it.
Reaching from 1934 through four decades, this activity kept
Maruyama involved in Tokyo poetry circles. It made little differ-
ence that he lived far from the capital.

Association with the journal also affected the development of
his æsthetic. He derived his poetic from several sources, all con-
nected with *Shiki*. Three merit attention. Hori Tatsuo's thinking
surely affected him. During student days at Tôdai, Hori trans-
lated several modern French poets. He had also become familiar
with contemporary European literary theories. A psychological
approach to writing appealed to him. His prescription for modern
literature stressed balancing intellect with lyrical perception.
This closely parallels the views of Hagiwara Sakutarô (1886–
1942), the poet Maruyama most respected. Hagiwara had written
about his approach to poetry in *Shi no Genri* [*Principles of Poetry,*
1928]; he later joined those putting out *Shiki*.

Finally, the ideas of Rainer Maria Rilke (1875–1926) stimulated
Maruyama through both Hori and other *Shiki* writers. Trans-
lations of Rilke's verse had touched several *Shiki* poets. Interest
in the poetry stimulated studies of the German poet's philosophy
of art. The Japanese became far more interested after learning
the details of Rilke's poetic, which challenged their tradition. As
they mulled over and discussed the issues, their reactions reached
the pages of their journal. Admiration subsequently led to imita-
tion——authentic flattery in Japan. Rilke wrote of the obligation
to use one's sensibilities to articulate the intellect. He talked of
uncovering forgotten psychological truths. He had strong symbol-
ist tendencies, too, and a penchant for personifying abstractions.
He struggled constantly to be impersonal.

Maruyama's æsthetic draws on these sources. The poetic princi-
ples he eventually forged for himself agree, in any case, with
ideas that Rilke, Hagiwara, and Hori espoused. These provided

the basis of Maruyama's æsthetic: the desire to harmonize sentiment and intellect. His idea of "intellectual lyricism" has two goals: to reconcile mind and feelings and to describe the process by which a poem comes to life. When an objective notion and a subjective image merge, Maruyama claims, you have the seed of a poem. This idea strikes a balance between ideas and feelings.

Thus, the key to Maruyama's poetic grammar is a lyricism that intellect tempers. Through this approach he hoped to control the indigenous penchant for indulging in purely lyrical or subjective feelings. He thought that intellectual control would result in poetry with two notable characteristics. It would have a more incisive impact on the reader than merely lyrical or sentimental verse; it also would reduce the chances of producing bathos. Not lacking in emotional content, such verse might nonetheless be "cool" and "dry" enough to transcend sentimentalism. As a bonus, it also might enable the poet to produce uniform results.

— I I I —

He continued to expand his reputation by applying this intellectual lyricism to his work. In 1935 he published two books: *Tsuru no Sôshiki* [*Funeral of the Crane,* May] and *Yônen* [*Infancy,* June]. The latter collection assembled works that, dating from college days, were nearly a decade old by then. He termed this verse a "bit sentimental" after it won the initial prize offered by the *Bungei Hanron* poetry magazine. The emotional poignancy of the verse—the collection's nostalgic evocation of boyhood experience—most impressed the judges. This may be why the book so embarrassed a more mature Maruyama that he preferred not to acknowledge the honor. More important than the prize money, the award brought considerable publicity and requests for manuscripts.

A short time before he learned that *Infancy* had won the Hanron Prize, Maruyama found that his sister–in–law Kunié had contracted consumption. After her March 1932 graduation from girls' school in Toyohashi, Kunié moved to Tokyo. She stayed with the Maruyamas and soon found work with the advertising and modeling agency that employed Miyoko. Seriously ill, Kunié returned home in January 1936 and died in March. She was only twenty four. The poet knew her before he knew Miyoko. Because his admiring sister–in–law had been as dear to him as a little sister, her death touched him profoundly. His fourth collection,

Ichinichishû [*Day by Day*, 1936], contains an entire section on her demise. These works stand less as monuments to Kunié's memory—the reader learns little about her as a person—than as records of how Maruyama tried as an artist to handle her loss. In his fifth collection issued five years later, he published several more Kunié poems. The length of time he struggled to express his feelings about her passing implies the depth of his grief.

Poems that feature Kunié's death both resemble and differ from earlier works. One similarity is the persona's doubt that poetry can effectively convey deep feelings. In "*Tôka*" [Elegy; 1936, page 89], Maruyama laments the inadequacy of mere words to express anguish:

> Sitting at the head of your bier, I mourn bitterly,
> yet my anguished cries fail to reach God.
> They scatter vainly into space....

A notable difference is that poems about Kunié's death derive from the deep–felt experience and associated memories of caring. This contrasts with much verse in *Sail–Lamp–Gull,* for instance, which issues from abstract hopes and dreams, or from the poet's failure to realize them. Indeed, verse dealing with Kunié's decease proves how difficult it is to extinguish memory or love. As he comes to grips with this difficulty, the poet shows, almost for the first time, a willingness to share private emotions. In many memorable pieces published before 1936, Maruyama objectifies his described pathos. Although this adequately controls his affective side, the reader remains a distanced observer of what the poet feels. The Kunié poems illustrate an inclination to involve the reader directly in private grief. Sorrow fortunately never crumbles into bathos. Conscious control of the impulses and ideas that fuel these pieces keeps Maruyama from losing the lyrical distance that makes the poems work.

Five years after Kunié's death, Maruyama finally realized his boyhood dream. Early in 1941, several months after he issued his fifth collection, *Busshô Shishû* [*Images,* literally, "poetry collection of object signs"], he went to sea. The *Chûô Kôron* [*Central Review*], a leading intellectual and literary journal, commissioned him a special correspondent charged with depicting the experiences of midshipmen training at sea. He left 4 May 1941 aboard the Kaiô Maru [Neptune], a four–masted training barque. He had by then already started taking medicine for stomach ulcers.

After returning in July, Maruyama began to convert his notes

into poetry——far from an easy task, for it took several years to
get the book in order. As he worked up his sea poems, he pub-
lished his sixth collection, *Namida Shita Kami* [*The God Who
Wept*, 1942], which contained only nine new works, none related
to his cruise on the Neptune. His sea verse appeared in 1943 un-
der the title, *Tenshô Naru Tokoro* [*Hear the Ship's Bell*, literally,
"where the ship's bell sounds"]. On the most superficial level, the
thirty–four poems in this collection provide an informative record
of life aboard an old–time sailing vessel. They also exhibit a style
much less reserved than any of Maruyama's earlier work. This
verse has an immediacy similar to poems about Kunié's death. Of
course, these works are less intense, but they likewise grow out of
concrete experiences, not from reading or dreaming about the sea.
Besides, Maruyama clearly intends this book for a more general
audience. Dense compression and lyric distancing, so characteris-
tic of pre–1940 efforts to control feelings, rarely appear.

Excessive compression or distancing would, in fact, have been
most inappropriate. Both starting point and aim relate, after all,
to the midshipmen's experiences. Two poems first published in
Hear the Ship's Bell illustrate. "*Darin*" [Helm; 1943, page 124]
begins by making clear that the ship is firmly attached to the
Deep. This leads the reader to imagine that the wheel itself
sprouts directly from waves——an attachment that requires

> two sturdy young sailors
> heaving together
> with all their might

to turn the "great helm at the stern." The persona then glances
"up at the mizzenmast." Suddenly his perspective shifts. He feels
that the helmsmen do not simply turn the ship. Their efforts sway
the sky, the sea, and beyond: "yes, [even] the world begins to
turn." The poet presents this lyrical experience in straight–for-
ward language. This much will satisfy most readers. Not Maru-
yama. He agrees with psychologists who regard reason a ship on
the sea of emotion. In this poem Maruyama implies that reason
can control feelings. The helmsmen's efforts to do so symbolize
human powers of creativity and imagination (feeble as they may
be) over nature's otherwise unyielding forces. "Helm" thus stands
as a metaphor for reason navigating the sea of emotion.

Until its final stanza, "*Sôtantei Busho*" [Lifeboat Drill; 1943,
page 131] looks like an account of a shipboard exercise. Maru-
yama, however, views the procedures and rituals of the drill as an
extended metaphor of his practice as an artist: to seek that far–off

Self. Disengagement from the mother ship stimulates his imagination. The sailors, who come prepared for the possible disaster of being severed from their source of life and sustenance, oar the lifeboat some distance from the ship. The poet then describes how fantasies suddenly snare his mind. Merely being in an exposed craft spurs daydreams; he fancies himself shipwrecked. That thought presumably did not occur to him aboard the safer barque; there he neither felt vulnerable nor questioned his safety. In the final stanza, he writes:

> I gaze at our steady–sailing four–masted barque,
> our stout, reliable ship,
> almost as though gazing at myself.

The waves that screen the ship's sides prevent him from viewing his cabin——his alter ego, the other self left in the "real world" when he boarded the lifeboat. The sea between his two selves is nothing less than the psyche, his unconscious mind. Once more, now dealing in plain language with a routine event, Maruyama endeavors to lace the lyrical with the intellectual.

Verse in *Hear the Ship's Bell* by no means consists of mere odes to the sea. Many do seem simple–minded ethnographic descriptions of life aboard a sailing vessel——but they are nothing if they are not more than that. True, most contain measurably more everyday language and relaxed imagery than we find in earlier poems. Yet Maruyama rarely reacts only on the shallow level of describing his experiences aboard ship. He continues to deal with issues close to his heart: shifting perspectives, illusions of time and space, the ever–present problem of the far–off Self and its needs for relationship, meaning, or stability. He remains the poet he was. He simply begins to use more relaxed language.

Japanese began to experience the war directly less than eighteen months after Maruyama returned from his Neptune voyage. By the winter of 1945, the Pacific conflict had touched the lives of common people in practically every major city but Kyoto. Firebombs forced tens of thousands to desert the metropolitan areas. The government urged people to have their children stay with relatives in the country where they would be safe from the hordes of B–29s and their incendiaries. Massive conflagrations caused shortages of merchandise in department stores; this forced many companies out of business. One casualty was the agency Miyoko worked for and had been managing for some years. Creating poetry was not possible in that environment. Nor were government censors supportive of frivolous lyric poems that failed

to spur the war effort. Maruyama, who could not have guessed
the war might end in another seven or eight months, therefore ac-
cepted an offer to teach elementary school in Yamagata
Prefecture. The school was in Iwanezawa, a hamlet in the moun-
tains of northern Honshu and far from firebombs. He headed
north in early spring and began teaching fifth–grade pupils from
the new school year in April 1945.

Maruyama's move to the snow country impressed him as start-
ing life afresh. This was the first time he had held a steady job of
any kind. Childless, this was the first time he had to associate
with small children. Aside from his Neptune voyage, this was also
the first time Maruyama had to live some months separated from
wife, family, friends, and literary colleagues. As he was adjusting,
he learned that a May B–29 raid reduced his Tokyo home in
Nakano to ashes. This made his experiences in Iwanezawa all the
more poignant; he had not escaped the B–29s after all. News of
this loss reached him several days later through a visitor.
Concerned for his wife's safety, he left for Tokyo on 1 July to
search for Miyoko; he found her at her parental home near
Toyohashi. Before Maruyama returned to his post in October, he
negotiated with school officials to teach third instead of fifth
grade. Apparently he found older children more difficult to han-
dle. This time, Miyoko accompanied him. His mother joined them
the following summer.

Life in the mountains was more than a fresh beginning. Every-
thing stimulated Maruyama's imagination. Everything was new,
including the local brogue he sometimes had difficulty under-
standing. Unlike Miyoko, he never tried to speak anything but
the standard language of Tokyo. At least he found no difficulty
writing. Never had he worked so feverishly as during those years
in the North. Deluged by inspiration and, later, by requests for
manuscripts, Maruyama produced a steadily increasing torrent of
verse. During their last two years in the North, Miyoko reports
that she walked almost daily the several miles to the post office
where she dispatched his manuscripts.

Those busy days gave Maruyama the opportunity both to stabi-
lize himself financially and to make several solid artistic gains.
The couple put most of the insurance money received from their
fire–bombed Nakano house into savings accounts. They did the
same with the greater part of the poet's salary, manuscript fees,
and the gradually increasing royalties that resulted from his bur-
geoning productivity. Fortunately, Iwanezawa lay far from the

many casual visitors and parasites who in Tokyo had so regularly undermined the family budget. Nor did circumstances in that remote hamlet allow Maruyama to cater to his patrician tastes. Significantly, these days in the North allowed—or, more precisely, they required—the poet to grow as a human being and an artist. That far–off Self never stood more nearly within his grasp. He had time to hone his skills through reflection, observation, and study. Those years gave him, as he constantly stressed during interviews, new perspectives on life and art.

Adjusting to the harsh environment and to the hardy northern people he grew to admire required considerable energy. Maruyama had long been accustomed to life in spacious, well–appointed Western surroundings. Only with conscious effort could he adjust to life in a single drafty, sparsely–furnished Japanese–style room——which for several months he and Miyoko shared with his mother. The required discipline helped give the poet fresh perspective. Iwanezawa enriched and leavened both his poetry and his life; years spent there were lessons in becoming human. These lessons affected his writing. He acknowledged that they made him a stronger person, a more versatile poet. During and after his "snow country interlude," his poetry shows an increasing range of interests and concerns. He found it much easier to write about personal and general human problems he had hesitated to face before 1945 ... unless he treated the material in a self–consciously oblique, distanced, or symbolic manner.

As for method, his postwar work displays a consistently direct and relaxed nature, at least on the surface. By then, he could—when he chose to do so—more effectively convey his poetic insights to the average poetry lover. The steadily increasing requests from editors of non–specialist magazines and journals, few of which appealed to intellectuals, make that clear. These requests at times enticed him to write about topics he would have preferred to avoid. That Maruyama confidently took on these challenges suggests his growing confidence. He had mastered fresh ways to order his materials and nevertheless maintain appropriate artistic distance from his emotions. He also learned to clothe his experience in simple and direct language.

Life in Iwanezawa inspired three books. Two concentrate on the local people, customs, and landscapes. The third reflects experiences with the school children. Few pieces in these collections treat directly Maruyama's personal problems or artistic concerns. It would be a mistake, however, to assume that his north country poems—any more than his verses about life at sea—show he had surrendered or compromised his poetic. *"Utsukushii Sônen"* [Lovely Notion; 1946, page 154] illustrates. This poem describes a daytime hike to a nearby hill where the persona peers into a deep, spring–fed pool. Well before dusk shadows the scene, he begins

> ... to see glimmers of countless stars
> coming from deep in the pond
> where sun had silently set.

The image suggests an attempt to apprehend during daylight hours the nighttime dreams buried in the depths of his unconscious. Stars shining brightly at the bottom of the pool may represent ideals, hopes, or dreams. This scene speaks of feeble starlight's resistance to the encroachment of cosmic Darkness. It also may imply the struggle that Maruyama knew he faced to keep from sinking into the snow country's shadows.

Much verse written in the North depicts the poet's observations of his radically new environment. Superficially, some of these works resemble depictions of experiences during Maruyama's two voyages at sea. But all confirm the poet's sharp eye and sure pen. He was an astute enough observer of life in the North that his descriptions make the locals marvel. People in Iwanezawa reported to me that they get no sense that an outsider, a "city slicker," had written this verse. We find many descriptions of provincial landscapes and customs, some of which he gets wrong, but Maruyama's better work always contains more than random descriptions. In "Lovely Notion," the poet projects psychological symbols onto his immediate surroundings: the pond reminds him of the sky and the unconscious. That, too, is how he views the north country snow that buries everything for half the year. This white blanket brings to mind the sea's engulfing power. He confides "In a Mountain Field" (1947; page 164),

> I can't explain why,
> but since coming to these mountains
> I've had the strange feeling
> I'm at sea.

No doubt existence in the North resembled life at sea. Whether in faraway Iwanezawa or aboard ship, the poet was on a journey. No more ancient symbol of distancing the Self from its roots exists. Journey and uprooting offer the traveler fresh perspectives. Being momentarily an alien releases one from the constrictions of the familiar. He had, in a sense, arrived at the mirror's "other side." The foreign context allows any who would exploit their freedom a unique opportunity to turn inward. There, if they care to—and Maruyama did—they can re–discover and develop the Self.

Iwanezawa's remoteness did much more than guarantee freedom from bombings. It allowed many worry–free hours to search for his far–off Self. Unfortunately, self–examination stimulated angst. Maruyama found that he was by no means free from doubts about his future as a poet. Troubling, too, was this indisputable reality of his existence: the more he wrote, the more requests he received for manuscripts. The more these requests motivated him to be productive, the more of a nuisance teaching little children became. Small wonder he longed for the stimulation of fellow intellectuals in the capital. Unfortunately, people living in Tokyo faced extraordinary problems. They suffered from shortages of housing, food, and jobs. They had to survive run–away inflation as well as damaged transportation and distribution systems. These conditions urged officials to refuse a rice–ration card to any returnee unable to prove that he had both employment and a place to live. Lacking either, Maruyama figured he could immerse himself in writing. He therefore resigned his teaching post effective at the end of the Japanese school year in March 1947.

Hoping to return to Tokyo, he decided to sit out the capital's reconstruction writing poetry in the North. He remained in Iwanezawa another eighteen months. In 1948 he published three books: his ninth collection, *Senkyô* [*Magical Country,* March], his tenth, a book of children's poems, *Aoi Kokuban* [*Blue Chalkboard,* May], and his eleventh, *Hana no Shin* [*Flowercore,* June]. Evidence of productivity aside, he knew his future as a poet obliged a return to Tokyo——or at least re–involvement in the capital's poetry circles. He had quarried the experiences of the classroom and the snow country. It was time to move on.

Government authorities continued to discourage people from flocking back to the shortage–ridden capital. Maruyama had no choice. If he wanted to leave the North, he had to go to where he had roots. That meant returning to where his mother and wife "belonged," so in 1948 he left Iwanezawa and settled in Toyohashi to write. Although he fully intended to return to Tokyo when possible, Maruyama became ever more firmly rooted there. In April 1949 he agreed to become a lecturer on modern Japanese poetry at Aichi University. This local private institution eventually appointed him a visiting professor of literature. In the end, as his plans to return to the capital just dwindled away, the poet increasingly came to regard himself a "lone wolf."

– I V –

Maruyama's move to Toyohashi marked an important stage in his life. In Jungian terms, this was a time to re–establish contact with his inner self, something he had seriously begun in the North. Maruyama had the energy to write many poems aimed at doing that. He published his twelfth collection, *Seishun Fuzai* [*Lost Youth*] in 1952 but waited a decade before issuing his thirteenth, *Tsuresarareta Umi* [*Hostage Sea, 1962*]. The title poem (page 249) grieves that man's irresponsibility to Nature and Self had taken the ocean hostage:

> A sea that in our youth breathed,
> once so very full of life,
> violated now,
> heartlessly polluted.

All new poems in this work date from his 1955 cruise to Australia aboard the Yamashita Maru. As with his Neptune cruise fourteen years earlier, he needed several years to shape these experiences at sea into satisfactory verse. Health crises impeded progress. In 1956, he had two–thirds of an ulcerated stomach removed; in 1958, intestinal blockage required major surgery.

Following another ten–year hiatus, he published *Tsuki Wataru* [*Moon Passage*, 1972], collection fourteen. He issued his fifteenth and last book, *Ari no Iru Kao* [*Face with Ants*], a year later. All the while, Maruyama continued to teach at Aichi University. Association with *Shiki* kept him involved with editing and poetry cronies in the capital, and that stimulated growth. His last two books contain many works that support Maruyama's claim to notable artistic development after leaving Tokyo for Iwanezawa early in 1945. Poems in these last two collections move with ease beyond the self that feels to the self that thinks. Throughout, the poet mixes poignant but relaxed diction and common experience with uncommon symbolism and suggestion. This results in verse that shows far greater depth and range than earlier works.

The verbal surfaces of most poems in the first collection, *Sail–Lamp–Gull,* were elaborate, the symbolic and metaphorical structures simple. Experience and maturity fashioned predictable modifications. The surface texture of his last published poetry is simple and direct, the symbolic organization complex. In earliest poetry, Maruyama examines, as he did in the sail–lamp–gull trilogy, plain notions of relatedness and detachment. He continues to write about cognate ideas, though with greater profundity. The best of his later verse also deals with far knottier interrelationships, multiple meanings, and complicated issues than we find in verse of his younger days.

Maruyama told me that *"Tsuki Wataru"* [Moon Passage; 1970, page 282] exemplifies a work with universal significance. He admired this work enough to use its title for his 1972 collection. In interviews, the poet insisted that "Moon Passage" stood as the finest example of his mature art. This prose poem is interesting for what it reveals about his increasing anxiety over life's transience. In "Moon Passage" he comes to grips with mortality by discovering a way to grapple with and overcome his death anxiety. By maneuvering the universal imagery related to the moon into fruitful associations, he finds a way to accept finitude: simply *be*.

"Kuma ni Atta Hito" [Man who Encountered a Bear; 1954 and 1972, page 245] shows a far greater skill and control of symbolism. The poet's description of an imaginary meeting with a bear conveys the pathos of a sophisticated person who faces a feral beast in a uncivilized place. Maruyama draws the reader into an intricate structure of confrontations by juxtaposing four (this number a homonym for death) elements: (1) The poet——repository of the urbane, the refined, and the cultivated. His function on the mountain suggests Wallace Stevens' jar on that rude hill in Tennessee. (2) A woodcutter represents the modest world of sweat and sinew. His job suggests mortality and evanescence. These contrast with the trees' constant seasonal regeneration and the hint of annual rebirth. (3) The bear serves as a metaphor for the savage, the coarse, and the brutal. It directly confronts the poet–persona, evoking his emotional and intellectual reactions. And (4) the mountain——symbolic intermediary between the cultured and the crude, space and time, heaven and earth, mind and feelings. It is here that this seminal and symbolic meeting takes place.

His brief encounter gives the persona an eerie feeling. It's as though he faced sudden death but managed to survive. The hunter had become the hunted. Again, we come across one of Maruyama's favorite devices, the intriguing perspective. A switch in viewpoint creates sparks of enlightenment that force the persona to imagine that for an instant he exists in an entirely different dimension. He "immediately sensed reality fade."

> No, no, not exactly——I sensed rather that Time
> from an entirely distinct dimension
> had crossed the Time where I existed ...
> an unknown Time breathing and pulsing ... like wind.

He perceives that moment as uncanny. After all, it allowed him to discover a dimension beyond even that far–off Self he so avidly seeks. Given his æsthetic, and his penchant for philosophical musings, it is not difficult to imagine his vision. He identifies himself symbolically with the mountain (recall that Maruyama means "Roundhill"), that mandala of integration. The poet himself spans the worlds of the raw and the refined, emotion and intellect, life and death.

Many works in *Face with Ants* echo the intricate and involved meanings that characterize Maruyama's confrontation with the bear. For example, poems describing a hunter and a fisher suggest the excitement of the quest for meaning. "*Nagare—Oita Ryô-shi no Hanashi*" [Stream—Tale of an Old Hunter; 1968, page 277] tells of a man stalking a stag. The buck has long epitomized pure beauty, grace, speed, agility, and potential. Its antlers serve as universal symbols of regeneration and life. Other hunters shoot at but miss the stag, doubtless because he runs so swiftly that his speed reverses the flow of the stream. This image Maruyama culled from the classical Chinese folk tale, the *Hsi–yu-chi* [*Journey to the West* (of China)], mentioned in "Moon Passage." Finally, the confident hunter–poet brings down the deer with his single–shot rifle. Then the magic:

> As it soaked up the fallen stag's antlers,
> the river again began
> flowing toward its mouth.

This work leaves the reader moved but exceedingly curious, even puzzled. There is no puzzlement in "*Kawa*" [River (ii); 1968, page 271], which describes an old man committed to fishing. He constantly casts for fish in the river's depths——an East–Asian figure suggesting the search for meaning and knowledge in the stream of life. The poet's search for his far–off Self echoes this act. It is not important that the old man ever catch anything. He must only be persistent. His mission is to fish. Thus, he sits "motionless [in space] despite the flow." The fisher–poet however finds himself swept into a realm beyond Time.

> One day the old man no longer appeared.
> A boy now drops his line
> at the spot where the man once fished.

Time and its passage also function forcefully in "Q *Hoteru Jukkai Sakaba*" [Tenth Floor Bar in the 'Q' Hotel; 1966, page 266], which also appears in *Face with Ants*. This work combines the sense of death's imminence with Maruyama's eroded dedication to his mission as artist. Here the poet lets us glimpse an overpowering angst. Perhaps Time has washed away his creativity, much as the stream of life has swept away the fisher. No longer does beauty or its potential significance so excite him that he feels compelled to capture or examine it in verse. The persona deplores his inability to stretch his wings and fly. The Chinese compound for prose resonates with the graphs for "walk" or "stroll," both of which imply pedestrian activities. Flying thus serves as a common metaphor to imply moving from the commonplace into the realm of poetry. Maruyama remains anchored to his perch in the tenth–floor bar. Without confidence in his poetic powers of flight, he makes a painfully unpleasant discovery:

> I'm an old bird——motionless on its perch,
> highball fizzing vacuously in one claw.

He remains inert and insensitive. By being inactive, he becomes untrue to himself and his mission. These thoughts occur to the persona at a bar, probably after alcohol has reduced his inhibitions. He now faces not only his impending death but an equally distressing recognition. His drive to create poetry may already have withered. As a poet, he may already be dead.

Hardening of the arteries curtailed most activities. After the spring of 1974, Maruyama spent part of each month in the Ogino Hospital in Toyokawa, a Toyohashi suburb. There he received the personal care of Doctor Ogino Akihisa. Ogino loved literature, wrote short stories, and had long been a dedicated supporter. Despite Ogino's efforts, Maruyama suffered a cerebral thrombosis. He died 21 October 1974 at home, aged seventy five, his only heir his loving wife Miyoko. On the following day, the headline of a Toyohashi news article described him as the poet "who loved the sea till death." The memorial program that the Japan Broadcasting Company (NHK) presented on 7 November similarly featured Maruyama as "the poet of the sea." Once tagged in Japan, escape is difficult. Death simply offers "taggers" the opportunity to reassert their appellation. This label persists even in Kôdansha's *Encyclopedia of Japan* entry on Maruyama.

Maruyama's poetic incisively illustrates his basic idea that intellectual control can create sufficient lyrical distance to enhance the impact of emotional expressions. The more intimate the statement, the greater the requirement to divorce oneself from its context and so gain perspective and objectivity. Particularly in earlier work, Maruyama creates such distance by focusing on the inanimate, on objects (*busshô*). It is as though he imagines that true poetry arises in the objective not in the subjective world——a heretical stance for a Japanese poet! That's why he sometimes gives human qualities to inanimate objects like a sail, a lamp, or a gun emplacement, sometimes to an animate creature like a gull. Doing so diminishes sentimentality, always Maruyama's nemesis, and keeps his work from becoming maudlin. In "*Kanashii Fûkei*" [Depressing Scene; 1940, page 103], for example, the persona describes his reactions to what he sees. He fears that

> without a single human being in the area,
> riders will naturally turn glum
>   and feel drawn less to people
> than to these gigantic, depressing arrays
>   of inorganic matter

that greet the eyes of those riding an elevated train through an urban factory district. Both the approach and the conviction suggest the distancing Maruyama sought.

"Bard of the sea" label or not, most regard Maruyama a major poet. He spent decades out of the Tokyo mainstream, yet he appears on almost any list of the dozen or so most important and representative modern Japanese poets. This although most critics tend to undervalue both his sailing verse or "regional poet" phase in faraway Iwanezawa and the influence these crucial experiences had on his development as an artist. Poems about his voyages or life in Iwanezawa consistently reveal the maturing artist. Experiences at sea and in the North contributed to the greater depth and breadth of later work. Maruyama expanded his appreciation of the universe, practiced his eye, honed his craft, and broadened his poetic—that is, his human—range. Beyond that, his Iwanezawa "period" especially reveals an independent-minded writer. For a brief time he shed the elite attitude that tends to dominate poetry circles in the capital. Given his aristocratic background, it is no small achievement that he could set it aside. Life in the North not only enlarged his perspective, it increased his ability to associate with and write for plain people. More important, it helped him stabilize his relationship with himself. All this occurred without compromising either his concern for intellectual control of his art or his passion for symbolic statement.

His poetry and his person could have developed in different directions. Both would doubtless have done so had he not taken the "road less traveled by" to the North. If Maruyama had never dared to be a "lone wolf," he might not have so persistently examined his Self, nor have done it with the insight, intensity, honesty, and growing openness visible in pieces published after 1945. Experience out of the mainstream, in short, helped make Maruyama a poet for all readers. Being separated from the special environment of Tokyo writers, with its peculiar forms of isolated togetherness, in no way kept this poet from his work. In fact, being isolated made it easier for Maruyama simply to be himself. Through those years, he realized he must never give up reaching for that far–off Self, always just beyond his fingertips.

The 462 poems translated below include all 410 works in Maruyama's fifteen books of poetry. I rendered them from Volumes I and II of the five–volume *Maruyama Kaoru Zenshû [Works]* (Tokyo: Kadokawa Shoten, 1976–1977). The remaining pieces consist either of published works that the poet did not include in these collections or verse published after his last book. Most of these appear in Volume III of the *Works*. Maruyama methodically destroyed all unpublished verse and drafts, so nothing unpublished survives.

To aid the appreciation of Maruyama's development as an artist, I arrange these works in rough chronological order. The position of each work depends on the earliest known date of publication. I differentiate works that appeared in the same month and year according to their location in the *Zenshû*; a poem on an earlier page appears first. Those who wish to investigate how Maruyama arranged his works for publication may refer to the appendix containing the collections. There I list the order he assigned new poems in each of his fifteen books.

ACKNOWLEDGMENTS

Crediting everyone who has contributed to these translations and to my study of Maruyama Kaoru would require many pages. Even the shortest list must, however, begin with the late poet and his lovely widow, Miyoko. Maruyama graciously responded to many questions that, on the whole, surely seemed peculiar if not downright dense; Miyoko favored me with endless kindness, cooperation, and hospitality.

Several years before he died, Maruyama introduced me to Professor Nagata Masao, scholar of English literature, published poet, and translator of English verse. No amount of gratitude could adequately acknowledge his input. I have shamelessly exploited his intimate knowledge of Maruyama's work and accepted many suggestions for improving the accuracy and aptness of these translations. Nagata Sensei was also kind enough to write for the 2nd edition the essay, "Maruyama as Imagist."

I am much indebted to Professor Donald Keene for allowing me to use the Foreword he wrote for the 1st edition.

In Toyohashi, the late Ms. Takahashi Noriko, and in Iwanezawa both Ms. Watanabe Hanako and Mrs. Katakura Fujiyo responded over the years to frequently bothersome questions. I sincerely appreciate their patience and thoroughness.

Mr. Inoue Yûji of Yamagata also deserves many thanks for corrections in the chronology; he furthermore provided vital information on plants native to the area.

Mr. Haraguchi Saburô tirelessly researched—first from Toyohashi and later from Seattle—a myriad problems that cropped up. Not only did he help improve the Japanese index, he made major contributions to the reliability of the Notes.

I owe boundless gratitude to Professor Iida Gakuji and Professor Ben Befu for so often and so persistently untangling mysteries of syntax and meaning. Dr. Donald Brannan, the late Dr. Elva Kremenliev, Professors Arthur Kimball and Enno Klammer, and the poet Thomas Fitzsimmons suggested numerous improvements in the Introduction, the translations, or both.

Special appreciation to Professor Erhardt Essig—to whom I dedicate these translations—for many years of understanding, support, and warm encouragement.

Taihen arigatô to Mitsuko for endless labors on the manuscript, for proof reading and help in preparing the indexes, for the unpleasant drudge of checking and re–checking countless dull details, as well as for ferreting out bushels of oversights.

Responsibility for the final form of poetry, notes, and all supplementary materials is, of course, solely my own.

Finally, when I began making these translations, I cherished the hospitality of the late Iida Kakuyoshi and his widow Aya in Kodaira, of Tamesada Nobuyuki and his late wife Yukiko in Machida, and of Shôji Toshio and Toshiko in Urawa.

*   *   *

The *American P.E.N. Review*, the *Hiram Poetry Review*, and *Poet Lore* published earlier versions of several poems.

In the summer of 1972, *The Beloit Poetry Journal* issued a chapbook of some sixty works in different form. In 1987, the *Journal of Asian Culture* XI included four works on the north country.

Slightly over 100 of these poems appeared under the title *Self–Righting Lamp* (#12 in the series *Asian Poetry in Translation: Japan*, 1990), edited by Thomas Fitzsimmons, published by Katydid Books, and distributed by the University of Hawaii Press.

*   *   *

Aside from adding Professor Nagata's essay and several paragraphs explaining Maruyama's sea symbols, the second edition makes numerous revisions. These correct many mistakes, particularly in the augmented notes, add two inadvertently omitted poems, and enhance readability by changing margins, fonts, and spacing.

CONVENTIONS

Names of Japanese nationals appear in the indigenous order, family name first. Kaoru is thus Maruyama's given name.

A raised asterisk (*) following a title indicates that a note on that poem exists in the appended materials (page 295 ff.). Many italicized Japanese words in the poems appear as separate entries in the notes (in ABC order; articles ignored).

A bullet or raised period (·) after the last poetry line on a page advises that the first line on the following page begins a new stanza.

I add (i), (ii), and (iii) to poems with the same English titles. Maruyama added numbers only to the two poems titled "Bar Song" and to two poems dealing with Nakatajima. In either case, he used I and II.

Special symbols in the Notes include a pointing finger (☞) and a down–slanting arrow (↘). The ☞ urges the reader to refer to the note or poem following. The ↘ breaks the text; it may signify added, related, or—most often—gratuitous information.

Poems generally follow the order in which Maruyama published them. For the way he sequenced the uncollected works in his books, see the Collections (page 335).

Japanese write poetry from the top to the bottom of the page. This tends to produce very long lines, a fact that accounts for the need to break many translated lines to fit the space. In 95% of the poems, the translations are nonetheless equilinear; that is, if the original has ten lines, the English will have ten lines (counting those flush to the left). From time to time, I combine two lines to preserve the poem intact on a single page.

Nearly every stanza break remains as the poet intended it. In prose works, however, I make new paragraphs when it seems appropriate.

SYMBOLS

Profound interest in metaphor characterizes the æsthetic of Maruyama Kaoru. Symbols intrigued him sufficiently to become a primary element in his verse. The following sketches may nevertheless represent less the poet's conscious meanings than my idiosyncratic readings of his work.

SEA——Oceans, sources of the primordial material from which life emerged, are unfathomable and awesome. The sea resonates with the symbolism of the mirror and has long stood for the collective unconscious, the psyche, and the conscience. Sea represents not just time and eternity, life and death, freedom and loneliness, but the restless emotions. Few images are more complex, multi–faceted, or as charged with potential meanings.

SHIP——The claim of psychologists that "Reason is a ship on the sea of emotion" I regard the primary symbolic weight of this image in Maruyama. Seeing a ship as reason struggling against the sea of feelings readily connects with the various symbolic dimensions of sea, anchor, and helm. Since ancient times, ships also served as metaphors for living beings. As feminine symbols, their hulls suggest the womb and thus fertility. More obviously, ships imply a journey, adventure, the perils of the unknown, and the pains and joys of isolation from human society.

ANCHOR——From the Greek vocable for "hook," this word suggests a means to link the ship to the seabed and fend off sea's (the psyche's) power. By restraining the waves, an anchor offers stability, reliance, and safety, even as it implies steadfastness and patience. Since the time of the early Christians, the anchor has furthermore been a sign of hope and salvation; people can rely on its solidity. The top side forms a cross and so reminds the faithful of Christ's sacrifice for them. The bottom forms an arrow pointing unambiguously to the depths of the mind——or even to Hades. Anchors imply steadiness and rootedness, both of which suggest things hoped for.

Ambiguity and dualism distinguish this symbol. On the one hand, the anchor's ability to secure a vessel allows sailors to depend on it to keep the ship from drifting; this puts the mind at ease. But an anchor plunging into the Deep is a metaphor of probing the unknown, the unconscious, the spirit (psyche)——the Self. As a figure of fathoming the soul, an anchor implies dis–ease.

At the same time, an anchor promises the "ship of reason" a chance to ground itself in something firm like the seabed, and so promises psychological steadiness. Ironically, however, the anchor's figurative plunge into the psyche intimidates reason by threatening to chain it to the "sea of emotion." It is not trivial to add the obvious: dropping anchor implies the end of a journey, arrival in port and its pleasures, return to solid land and family. Weighing anchor implies adventure, hardship, and the threat of loneliness or isolation.

The anchor's dualism derives in part from its shape. Shank or shaft and stock bring to mind the mast and yardarm—frames for the sails that let the ship run before the wind. At the bottom of the shaft, the arms with their pointed flukes hint at the shape of the hull. Freud, moreover, sees the anchor as a phallic symbol: the shaft suggests the male member, the ring the female.

HELM——By controlling the rudder, the helm keeps the ship on course; it functions to augment man's leverage against the ocean's potential powers of destruction. The helm serves, then, to help man deal with the formidable power of the sea (the psyche). It also reminds of the vulnerability of reason in the face of the emotions' overwhelming power. Though the helm cannot conquer the sea, it helps bring the ship home safe.

Shaped like a wheel, a helm shares the circle's symbolism, particularly the notions of perfection and calm. Round, too, like the eye, the helm implies sight as well as insight. But circles are static while helms and wheels move, and both follow commands determined more by intellect than intuition. Indeed, the controlling function of reason (and the helm) best imitates perfection. Reason can most effectively "see" when it remains calm in the face of feelings. Here the helm hints of essentials that ancient Greek thinkers taught Western man: be aware and intentional, choose goals and strive to reach them, and—if you're an artist—control your material, don't let it control you.

MIRROR——The Introduction explains the significance of the mirror and its relation to the title of this collection. All mirrored graphics (reflected parts usually imperfect), whether on the title page or between poetry sections, connect intimately with the title.

PART I

POETRY PUBLISHED BETWEEN

1923 and 1940

Fountain (i)

In an imposing public plaza,
I once saw
a marvelous fountain
spewing water high into the sky.
Or——thought I saw it.

Skies there
——a celadon blue vessel.
The fountain spurting water beads
——transparent grapes
flung at the vessel ...
the celadon–tinted grapes
soon falling
in radiance.

I say, Indian gentleman
shrinking on the bench——
Remove your turban!
Are you thinking of that fountain back home
where the holy man lives...?
Two elderly lovers walk by
on the other side of the fountain.

The fountain's ceaseless water
then resonates in my garden of fantasies....
Oh, those echoes of ardent love....
Even now, however,
the figure of my illusion past sight,
fixed forever in the dark.

Troubled Yard

Early on a quiet afternoon, Father roosts like a bloated balloon
on a rattan chair at the edge of our *engawa*.
My aging mother knits beside him.
Not even the spring warbler has come to sing.

This listless scene, so afflicted with affluence
——who moved it to weep?
    cutdowndaddy
    cutdownmommy!

Invisible from here, the quavering voice of melancholy
cries out again in a flood of tears
as it plucks those yellow rose petals
blooming behind the little hill in our yard.
    cutdownthatdaddy
    cutdownthatmommy
    cuteveryonedown!

FABRICATIONS

Charged with sundry and singular dreams,
a boy's fabrications
have the adroitness of white–winged sea birds
    stitching the waves.
Only when he beguiles Father and Mother
do parents become noble in the boy's eyes.
But who can say he feels no regret?
When something too lovely wings in from afar
    and lodges in the lad's heart—
as when flowers burst abruptly into beautiful blooms
or when twilight on sky's distant edge
    sparkles the world pink—
who can claim he never sheds tears into skies, into clouds,
saying, "I'm the only one beguiled" ... ?

FISHER

One day   a fisher's son dreamt
his father shouldered the bronze–bowl sun,
rolled up gorgeous sea–crowning clouds into his arms,
and from beyond the dazzling sea
plummeted like an anchor toward him.

One night   a fisher's mother dreamt
her son tried to snare stars from dawn's fish–scale skies
as he rode a shoal of sharks and the Black Current,
then streaked like a lightning bolt to a distant seashore
less peopled than a palace of ice. •

One morning   a fisher dreamt
his son's and mother's white hands
peeled open twilight's petaled clouds,
then closed them like roses in the skies
over hometown shores beyond his sight.

INFANCY

I was born long ago——in a lovely old spire
     under flitting bird shadows,
hemmed in by sweets and maids,
my father a blue–bearded marquis.
Asleep in my cradle by that window framed with evening clouds,
I recall having heard pensively in my dreams
someone singing lullabies of a faraway magical glen.

I was born long ago——in an isolated glen
     that soaked up even starlight.
I struggled day and night with deer or wolves
hunting Mother through mist–boiling mountain heights.
Dozing in that wind–rocked treetop cradle,
I had the vague impression that I mournfully heard
someone singing lullabies of that faraway magical spire.

LION

"I have but a single hope:
When this child becomes man,
may he have that lion's strength."

"I just ask one thing:
Let that lion with his strong fangs gobble up Mommy,
squat as a sponge cake."

FATHER*

Father comes from within the house——the castle lord
driving our hearts into gloom.

Our demented father goes back into the house,
depriving us ... of Mother.

CROW*

In the hills, a fellow wearing a black shroud
constantly caws for chilly winds.
In the hills, a fellow never turning his cheek
constantly dribbles tears into evening's glow.

WHEN LIGHTNING STRIKES

Striking from beyond the clouds,
lightning pales the entire sea,
then vanishes in a flash.

Striking from beyond the clouds,
lightning instantly illuminates a sailor's life,
then blots it out.

SHIP'S CAPTAIN

Always attired in well–pressed, luxurious dress blues, the cap-
tain clacked aimlessly over the coconut–polished promenade deck.
   The beard on full cheeks always neatly trimmed. He grimaced
as though the world were a polarity between leisure and languor.
   Nevertheless, if ever a loquacious passenger sprawled on a cane
chair addressed him, his reaction was predictable. He hurriedly
climbed the ladder to the soaring bridge—where his private pro-
cedures and perceptions of cruising ceaselessly affected the heav-
enly bodies—trailing the words, "I'm sorry you know, but...."

PANTHER*

The panther paces back and forth,
as though to squeeze through the invisible bars of space,
as though to leap through wind–flared rings of fire.
He twists his body,
flicks his tail,
kindles his golden coat.
Padding silently,
the panther paces constantly ... back and forth.

DEEP IN THE CASTLE*

Prostrate outside the tightly–shut *shôji*, the loyal retainer
    mentally drafted prudent counsel.
In the room, however, only a toppled armrest.
A human form had slipped from behind the reed screen,
    sauntered over the stepping stones, and now sports
    in moonlight beyond the garden's chilly mock hill.

    – I –
On the moon–bathed *engawa* last night, did the maid bounce
the ball or bounce the moon? Did the moon bounce the maid and
the ball? Or had the ball bounced the moon and the maid?
    moon and ball
    ball and moon
    moon and moon
    moon and ball
    ball and ball
    ball and moon
Even at dawn the lord, confused by carousing, could recall no
more of the song.

    – II –
At dawn,
for the first time, roses in the inner garden
scatter their scents everywhere.
Cranes in the pond uniformly stretch their necks into space.
The lord's every shutter sealed.

    – III –
The castle has fallen.

    – IV –
Watchtowers burn.
Flaming masses of ceiling boards fall to the *tatami*.
In one room, the pages ritually slit their bellies.

BY TRAIN

I'll take a train
to an Irish kind of countryside.
I'll go to an Irish–like landscape
where rain streams through sunshine,
where people twirl festive parasols.
Traveling with my face on the window,
I'll cross lakes and thread tunnels.

I'll go to an Irish–style countryside
where fine–faced girls and cattle roam.

Training barque*

Young fellows who love the sea
may one day sail a barque.
They'll soar with outspread wings
to southern isles where bananas grow.
Forgetting love,
they'll spend a lifetime with waves.
Grizzled like Robinson Crusoe,
they'll then marry doll–like girls.

Views of the harbor

Evening sunlight from China
shines on hotels, on funnels, on rickshas,
on sailors' caps.

Wind from America
whips through masts, through flags, through smoke,
through poplars by the road.

Waves from the offing
ripple against launches and small boats, against anchor chains,
against even the red buoy by the jetty.

From every vista,
sailors' whistles pipe the sunset in.

Aeroplane*

Something glowing in the sea–like air
since early morning ...

delicate, aspen–like alloy tail
glimmering immobile in the sun,

it darts bolt quick
through sweeping skies.

WIND

In the thicket, a cow lows——once.
Branches rustle in chorus as if to drown out the lowing,
    then as one fall still.

In the thicket, a cow lows——once.
Branches crackle in chorus as if to silence the lowing,
    then giggle raucously as one.

In the thicket, a cow lows——once.
Branches jabber merrily together,
    then, as one, soon laugh their leaves off.

In the thicket, a cow lows——once.
Branches banter merrily together.
    Their banter conceals itself in twigs.
Hidden bantering breaks then into a chorus
    of titters jiggling every twig.

Adding to the laughter, the cow again ... lows.

MOUNTAIN*

Kenkichi said I was chunky, looked like a mountain. Ever since that night, when in a dream he climbed a round hill shaped like me, a mere glance at my face and he's sure to compare me to one. He enjoys saying such things as, "Hey, the hill's walking this way." ... "The hill's lying down." ... "Gads, it's smoking!" ... How annoying! Though I crack a grim smile, despite myself I get the feeling I'm a colossal, immovable hill that doesn't think. It feels odd that chilly clouds wreathe me from time to time.

BECOMING WOLF*

She laughed when they told her, "Say, if you go too deep into the mountains, you'll run into wolves!" "No wolves there. Besides, I'll not be alone. It happens I'm taking Jon along." So the girl went over the swaying suspension bridge to the other side of the gorge. For a while one could hear her whistling through the trees' dense growth, but foothill breezes soon carried the sound away.

Then, twilight. Unusually pale, the girl returned alone from the mountain. When they asked her, "Where's Jon?" she replied: "Just now on my way back, when I got to that rocky cliff over there, something unexpectedly pounced on me from behind. My dog Jon, I was sure. Well, the creature jumped up on me and bounded around, romping playfully. I had the eerie feeling I'd be gobbled up...." Then she said she fled, leaving behind shoes that had tumbled down the precipice.

The girl repeatedly glanced at the scrapes on her bare knees. Then the old caretaker of a country estate snickered. Looking away from her he mused:

"Hmmph, that damned wolf's gotten quite classy."

Eaves

Beating the air with a distracting noise, a bird dropped something on our eaves at night. What could it be? I picked it up——the bird itself, dreadfully blackened by fatigue. Well, then, what had fallen, and what had so quickly fluttered off again?

Bullets' path*

... Yes, I'm terribly envious: Of those who lose their life to bullets. Of those who become lotus pips mowed down by machine gun fire——and people who instantly disappear in the blast of a forty-centimeter shell.... Expectantly, I choose the bullets' path and meander through the battlefield. If I go to the left, however, bullets miss me to the left. If I climb to a high place, they hit the sand round my feet——I just can't manage to get hit.

By contrast, rigor mortis fetters those countless corpses in the bunker. Each certainly had a private appointment with an enemy bullet. If not, there's no reason slugs that missed others so casually hit their marks.... The bullet to do me in doesn't exist in any enemy ammo clip. That keeps me from sleeping through the night. No doubt the war left me behind——me alone. Fellow soldiers meanwhile swiftly go where they were fated to go....

While talking I suddenly call out, "Oh, you've come!" Then, when I turn, my knees dissolve and I mash my sparse beard against a rock ... innocent as a child just returned to its mother's breast.

Street

Gear–snipped
ratchet.
Belt–polished
ratchet.

TWILIGHT (i)

Matches that never light.
Empty, antiquated hopes.
Cloth–wound neck.
Bare knees.
Wind and rain scattering the blighted leaves
of my beard.

TWILIGHT (ii)

The river flows black——lighting a white flower on its breast.

TWILIGHT (iii)

Heavy current.
Scull sounds wearing out poles.

MEMOS TO FACES*

☆ Hands too short. Clock face constantly bored.
☆ Ears small. Voice surprisingly loud.
☆ Beard dangling the hem of its gown to the chest.
☆ Features glimmering like a traffic light.
☆ From behind the face of "A" another "A" peers;
    "A" stares back, then both again merge.
☆ The face smoking into sunset becomes sunset.
☆ Sand smudges lips imprinted on the sand.
☆ Ecstatic eyes swim deep through a pool of tears.

GUN EMPLACEMENT*

Fragments yearned to snuggle together.
Fissures yearned to smile again.
The mortar barrel yearned to rise
    and be seated again on its mount.
All dreamed of transitory wholeness.
Each wind whip buried them deeper under sand.
The sea beyond sight——the flash of a migratory bird.

WORDS ON DRIVING RAIN*

☆ Driving rain pricks the eyes. Eyes pierce the storm.
☆ Driving rain discharges driving rain. Driving rain crumbles
  then scatters over the spine of driving rain.
☆ Driving rain breathes into a chest from which I pick a flower
  shriveled by driving rain.
☆ The forehead chokes up lightning. Elbows hinder mud.
☆ Countless grains spill from wrinkles in sand–smeared faces.
☆ I never saw anything wetter than driving rain.

SPRING (i)*

On the beach where I recalled a plum tree in bloom——no tree
now. A crane. The crane's eyes flare as I near. It dashes round
and round, eager to fly off. Stretching its neck, it tries with both
wings to embrace the air. But its legs only drag along the flats
like bamboo poles. That's what one expects when tail feathers—
now visible, now hidden whenever wings flap—had been cut like
teeth from a comb. Scant drafts from those wings lifelessly brush
my shoulders.

SPRING (ii)

Later on——I no longer had those mud–scraping sensations.
Was someone there? I thought they'd all left by now. I looked back
to make sure. Oh, just angled sunlight tinting the ice.

RIVER (i)

Tugging at memories of lamps about to dim, rows of houses me-
ander dreamlike under dawning skies.
Driving dreams, the river's invisible breath oozes from mist,
nestles close to the road.

MIST

A woman of the street sleeps with an unlabeled beer bottle. The
bottle sanctions sleep. Comforting each other through the night,
street woman and unlabeled bottle fraternize with mist–clogged
alleyways.

NAUGHTY TARÔ

Penetrating my dream, that naughty Tarô seemed only to weep plaintively. Back in the real world, however, he'd instantly resort to ghastly giggles. Poking a stick–like finger at me, he said with a smile, "You're the one who was crying, right?" Turning the tables on me, he tried to bowl me over....

FRAGMENTS*

Crows nested in a mortar barrel.
Bats skulked in its ruined mount.
Sand piled up.
Each exists in rust–coiled thoughts
that jumble day and night.

CRANE (i)*

What but a broken wing belongs to a crane
stretching its broken wing?
Tilting your broken wing as full as a sail,
crane!——What would you shield from wind?

DARK SEA

Flocking gulls swallow cries spilt over the dark sea. Soon they'll wing up from beyond the distant murk.
A lamp lights only the prow–pelting rain.

SONG OF THE SAIL

Gull wings beat in the sea's dark skies;
    if I dip my shoulder,
        maybe I can touch them.
Gull cries mew in the sea's dark skies;
    if I reach out,
        maybe I can catch them.
But flickers from the lamp that hangs round my neck
    keep me from seeing the gull.
I'll blow out the lamp.
I'll wait for the gull
    to perch on the lamp's chilled, sooty wick.

SONG OF THE LAMP

Anchor chain disappears into sea's dark depths
———beyond the reach of sight.
Rigging flees into the mast's dark heights
———beyond the reach of sight.
My meager rays light only my sightless face.
Eyeing me, the gull mews from the distant dark
———beyond where I can see.

SONG OF THE GULL

I can't even see myself.
How much less could the lamp see me
———or the sail reflecting its light?
Though I clearly see lamp and sail from here,
I merely circle through the distant frozen dark.

PAIN OF PARTING

A gull whispers into the anchor's ear.
Suddenly the anchor slides wordlessly down.
The startled gull leaves.
Instantly the anchor sinks pale into the blue.
What the gull had fondly cherished
turns to plaintive moans sprinkled through sky.

SEA LION

The sea lion has a whistle in its throat———a whistle stuffed with sea's frozen detritus. Suddenly he blows it, husky as a steam–venting safety valve, then leaps from the crag.

His flippers leave a wake that bubbles briefly. Like alcohol. Ripples glow on the surface, as though he's still swimming. But he's gone. The sea lion caws in the distance like a cold crow.

ESTUARY

The ship drops anchor.
Sailors' hearts drop anchor, too.

Gulls from the river greet the halyards' groans;
fish gather at the bilge holes.

The captain goes ashore after shedding brine–scented blues.

Each night he stays in town.
How many more barnacles bond by now with the hull?

In dusk's progressive deepening,
his sailor son solitarily lights the bow's green lamp.

LAMP AND ALBATROSS*

Albatross soaring over blue seas
becomes a mast lamp ... at dusk.
Navigation lamp on the darkened mast
becomes an albatross ... at dawn.

Neither albatross
nor lamp
knows whether the albatross is a lamp
or the lamp an albatross.

What if——the navigation lamp on the dark mast
never returned at sunrise to the sea?
What if——the albatross soaring over blue seas
never returned at sunset to the mast?

The immense ocean would lose but a single albatross.
But how might the barque's unlit mast
navigate the night?

ANCHOR*

The captain sips his rum.
As he drinks, he sings a song——
his hoarse chanting plaintive as a halyard
     wheeling slowly through its block.
Gulls' muffled wingbeats whisper through
     the faint dimness at the stern.
Over the estuary, moon will soon rise.

The captain's breast has also reached the high tide of his red rum.
Tonight again under tide's flow,
his tattoo anchor quivers blue.

GLIMPSES OF THE CIRCUS*

The big top appears patched together from scraps of sail.
The name of a ship stretches and shrinks in the wind.

Horses trot off. An elephant appears.
Brandishing his hook, the trainer leisurely positions the beast.
(How precisely the elephant performs.)
What next?

Winking lamps slide in concert down the ropes.
The brass band fades away. Only a piercing trumpet lingers on.

DIRGE

Scatter petals in the coffin.
Cover the petals with a lid of sand.
Nail the lid shut with tears.

FOUNTAIN (ii)*

The moment it would take wing, beads of water welled up
through its throat. Ever since, the crane has looked up——won-
dering, Why?

WINTER*

As I left the glass enclosure where the anteater naps, I recalled
the bear cage I saw just last summer. I then observed the bear be-
hind his north–facing steel bars. He used a paw to sweep the leaf–
scattered floor. He raked the leaves incessantly, then moved
away. After standing back, he raked them together again. As I
watched, he seemed to push them deep into a kiln–shaped hole at
the front of the cage——as though kicking a large ball a bit at a
time.
The fountain shriveled into my cigarette.

DAYBREAK*

A   In one dream——I looked at an elephant through his nose.
      In skies over the black box–like prairie inside twinkled a
      distant star, wee as a tiny lamp.

B   In my dream——I passed first through several living rooms,
      their chandeliers glaring ... then through work places with
      machines raving like gales. Surprisingly, I emerged in a
      whale's inky mouth.

C   I had another——I connected the tails of the elephant and
      the whale. Before I knew it, I'd become a towering ginkgo

tree drenched in sweat.

A　How odd! Whenever at dawn it's muggy, we dream incredible dreams.

ELEPHANT AND SHADE

The elephant looked for shade from noon's glare. He found none. There was shade. He was just too gigantic to fit under it.

"Why am I the only one so hot?" His trunk wiped the sweat from his trunk. He then plunged into thought.

Glancing at his feet, he felt he'd partly unraveled his riddle.

"That's it!" He was quick to admire his solution. "That's it! That's my shadow, isn't it? I cast a broad roof–like shade. I mean, I am the shade. Well, well——how about that...?"

Shortly afterward, a kangaroo ensconced in his shade began to annoy him with its cool snore.

EVENING SKIES

Kenkichi silently shinnied down from the lowest branch. "The bird?" He grouched that he'd suddenly lost sight of it. Pointing to a high branch, Shôta asked, "Isn't that it?" Kenkichi looked carefully through the branches. The bird was indeed sitting on its tall perch, lapis blue wings glistening vulnerably among the leaves.

Next Shôta's turn to climb and catch it. As Kenkichi looked up from below, a dispirited Shôta came back down. He repeated how when he got near he lost track of it...it'd likely flown off...and whatnot.

"But isn't it still there?" Kenkichi pouted. Once on the ground, Shôta could see it clearly, too. The bird waited at the same spot, facing the same direction as before. Silent, one might guess it felt lonesome.

Looking up, Kenkichi shouted in frustration, "Dummy!" Shôta looked for a pebble to fling.

The pebble bounced from a fork on the branch and fell with a snapped–off leaf. The bird didn't flinch. As they stared at it, they lost it little by little to shadows. Soon it melted into lush leaves. Baffled, Kenkichi again and again cocked his head.

Suddenly the bird changed from lapis blue to an eye–smarting madder red. At that moment, Shôta broke into laughter. He realized that layered leaves had formed a slit. There, peek–through evening skies had scooped out what had resembled a bird.

DAWN*

A drake took wing from a reed clump
where a tube lamp had been swaying through the night.
The drake's beak smoldered black,
its face the vacuity of spent oil.

LAMP

The corner arc lamp unaccountably fell still
as I drew near.
Pretending not to notice, it let me pass,
then started shrilling raucously again.

NIGHT

Squeaking up grief's staircase,
saké cheerfully lit a lamp in the garret of despair.
Unfurled sighs began bowing a viola of smiles.
Tears listened mute.

DRINKING BOUT

Rain's grumble stops.
Wind begins its chant.
Crowflaps.
Soon ... sunup.

SUNDOWN

When I lit the lamp,
it promptly shouted,
——"I can't see the darkness over there. Can't see it...."

When I placed it in the darkness,
the lamp shouted louder,
——"It darkened where I was. Turned dark...."

A bat snickered.

EPISODE

A bat tangled itself in sails
still strapped to the yard——
windless,

never unfurled.

"What happened then?"
——the running lamps whispered,

SUPPER

Setting sun innocent
——melting, smudging.
Clouds finally erase it.
Its smudges warble briefly on.

ALL DAY LONG

A sightless fountain
plucks its strings.
A deaf flower
tilts its head.

WAVES AND FOAM

Sorrows, go ahead
and sink to the bottom of the cup
——the way an anchor plunges into waves!

Sighs, go ahead
and hang yourselves in saké bubbles
——the way a sea gull drowns in foam!

BAR SONG I*

When I hurled my saké bottle into the sea,
the bottle did not sink.
It floated off cheek to cheek with waves.

When will you return to me,
sprouting wings of poetry, singing to clouds?

REMINISCENCES OF LAMPS*

In my childhood, when electric lights were not yet the wonders
they are now, shabby antique fixtures still enjoyed high regard.
To mention several I recall: bamboo lamps, hanging lamps, port-
able lamps, bantam lamps, lanterns. These at least were surely
used in every home.

People as a rule set the bamboo lamp, fashioned from a thick bamboo tube, on their living room *tatami*. The barrel touching the oil stood nearly as tall as a child of four or five. They attached a balloon–shaped frosted glass shade to keep the glow from fleeing its long, slender chimney. In the daytime, families with large houses stored several of these bamboo lamps in such places as the north–facing family Buddhist chapel or at the dark ends of hall-ways. These lamps gave me the chilled feeling that mushrooms or some such had sprouted profusely. When I think back, I recall that among all those fixtures now vanished—rapidly overtaken by the electric light—this lamp was the quickest to disappear. I felt especially sad to see it go.

Portable lamps. This type had the broadest use, probably best representing the notion of what we today call the lamp. Since they came in various shapes, and since they were handy to carry around, portables inevitably come to mind when one thinks of lamp light——that "friendly lamp light in autumn" flickering ele-gantly near the face of one at work, on desks, at the meal table, on book cases. I remember that Anzai Fuyue's portrait in his po-etry collection *Warship Mari* showed him carrying one. I think I also saw one atop a bookshelf in Murô Saisei's study, which fea-tured a sunken hearth in the north–country style.

Hanging lamps. These are lamps in a cylindrical frame that, as the name suggests, hang by a wire from the ceiling. Because they have neither handle nor stand like a portable lamp, the shape of the weighty bottom reminds me somehow of a sluggish sea bird. Solitary hanging lamps sway in wind that on winter afternoons dribbles through *shôji* screens. When I look at the saffron light partially screened by jam–packed eaves over fisher households that darkness from the sea is about to enfold, I figure that when dawn comes those lamps will surely turn into cormorants and fly off singing beyond the waves.

I long for the flame of the strawberry–colored bantam lamp. You can never quite be sure it's lit. These lamps still flicker in the bathing areas of country homes where crickets sing.

Lanterns——wick lamps with that squarish look. From the old days, set out at roadside construction sites, next to manholes, etc., they displayed faces turned scarlet as if by a shot of brandy. But I suspect it will be difficult to forget the dim flame that flickered faintly under the circus tent near the elephant's ear.

Aside from these, I recall acetylene lamps lighting the evenings of temple festivals. And bicycle lamps. The glowing mist of those pale lights makes it hard to resist nostalgia for childhood days.

In any event, during the fitful transition period of illumination, hallucinations rose up at night from those now discarded lamps.

Now, more than ever, something in them tugs directly at the heartstrings of people who even briefly experienced those times. That's because of the lamps' artless function, because of their plain soot, their round, compressed shapes, their diffident rays. When I catch a glimpse somewhere of one of those lamps, I naturally feel a fondness for the old days. It's like chancing after many years on an honest and ingenious servant, or like gazing at a vintage picture of that tender–hearted girlfriend who, for some reason, went her own way. Those with the experience know what I mean. Even the complicated cleaning of those lamp chimneys becomes a touching recollection. Trimming the wick was as painful as cutting a bird's tongue. It was nevertheless agreeable and endearing to gaze wide eyed or to squint, depending on how you adjusted the wick. In contrast to civilization's modern convenience, where with a flip of a switch we instantly douse the electric light glowing above our heads, I find these lamps very much like meek animals who sleep and blink as they breathe. So I'd like to be kind to them and pet them....

Ship lights that conceal themselves in sea's curvature——as in the lyric, "Sailing lamps sparse on the offing." Mast–top mooring lights that reek of the sea. Beacon buoys, for example, that morning to night whisper to sea gulls provide an air of romance ... everything on the sea outfitted with self–stabilizing devices, thanks to the billows' constant and tireless agitation. The giant lamp that revolves high atop a lighthouse. Signal lamps along the railroad tracks. A train's tail lamps that soak into the traveler's lonely eyes ... if you try to list them all, there's no end to it. For most of these, their shapes alone resemble lamps——their essences replaced by the electric light.

If there's a land where lamp flowers bloom, I'd like to go there. I'm no Mérimée, but as he enjoyed reading letters by starlight, I adore the rare pleasure of perusing a poetry collection by lamp light.

AUTUMN (i)

Rain falls on the shabby shutters of mind's inn. Pounds the slant of sentiment's pointed eaves. Surges through grief's downspouts on cracked walls. Stains the boot tips of vagrant solitude— no one to turn to. Fills the handle of oblivion's cast–off walking stick with chills. Plaintive lamps over the pavement, their brows hooded by spray. Recollections' tattered and blighted leaves flutter down ... a tear trace glitters through the glooms of my meditation. I hear their lone lament merging with my mind.

WINGS

A gull careened through the window,
leveled the lamp,
lay unconscious in the dark.

Once Hopes perhaps,
those tide–tarnished wings
glow lustrously now ... like remorse.

WATER'S SPIRIT*

Though water is clear, its spirit teeters fiercely,
wavering with bewilderment.
Water would be still, yet often cries out.
Water sparkles and heaves,
its will lashed, emotions unruly.
Feelings crushed and agitated, it loses hope.
Water wakens from nightmares
     where it careened and somersaulted,
     where it screamed and scattered.
Then, all the more tinged with vacant sadness,
water prays fervently to regain its soul.
Its prayers unanswered,
water seethes, yearning to protest.
Indeed, its senseless words prattle about this and that.
Water ponders it origin.
What misery in being without form!
Rage soon surges and overflows; then, unable to contain itself,
water yields to despair.
Still troubled, it hopes to forget its face.
For a moment it believes it has.
Water hasn't yet opened its eyes.
Sun gently strokes its lids.

OUR HOUSE*

On the wall hangs a chiming clock with Mother's face.
We children became adults looking up to it.
One by one our maids left that mansion with its surplus rooms.
Those days   Father already as still as sunset.
Before long   the crane in our yard had left as well.

Funeral of the crane*

Sunbeams swelling its eyes with tears,
   at dusk a single cloud finally sank
   behind the little hill in our yard.
Apparently awaiting a breeze, soon it lifted long–stiffened wings
   and stole off through the back gate.
From the pine–covered slope, I caught a brief
   chilled glance of it in the western sky.
For some days since ... still no sign of rain.

Steam launch

Moored to the wharf against the wind ... a steam launch. Here and there smoke had smudged its snow–white awning and the rim of its funnel. Smudges quite as impressive as the stained shirt and cap of a lad at his most mischievous age. The toy–like compass on the bridge. The gleaming helm. An anchor and a life–saving float on the deck. The cheerful clock in the cabin appears and disappears from the porthole. That, too, pleases——as when we discover that elaborate wisdom inherent in the schemes of boys who love to dream. And the bow that never stops bobbing, the stance of air ducts and masts leaning into the stern.

These imitate the emotions of those lads whom even small hopes and disappointments readily fluster. Each so lovely to note.

Spring (iii)

Wind's howl erases every recollection.
Sand beats on windowpanes——I shield my eyes.
Suddenly the clock responds with cheerless chimes.

Summer

A lily had been walking with me down the steep slope.
Singing memories of the peak, she wilted under sun.

At sunset, as we stood on a bluff over the stream,
she at last fell haggard from my fingers.
Swirling into mist, she vanished in a trice.

Dusk*

For a time, water writhed in pain.
Writhing turned to screams.
Bent and crushed, water turned to quills of honed light

and soared away on flapping wings.

Water yielding to tears. Water without griefs.
Water that shadows nearly blotted. Water no longer visible——
perhaps no longer existing in the gloom beneath the bridge.

In dusk skies, far beyond the river,
    the candle in a pointed spire kindles a cross,
    turns it the hue of crinkled leaves.
Bits of water's wings apparently still cling to the spire.

PALISADES

Swooping in from the sea
with gloom–numbed wings,
a gull smashed the lamp in my lodge.
Now desolate sea winds pummel my cheeks.
I'm entangled in profoundly–exhausted wings,
in onshore winds balmy with storm.

MOUNTAIN PASS

The locomotive whistles warnings
as gasps and grinding gears prod it on.
The engine no sooner scales the zigzag to the heights
than a yellow lily behind the grade marker
    that looks off after the train
shrinks beyond the tunnel's arch——a painful blink.
Looming ever nearer, pointed peaks
exchange intimate greetings with sunset silhouettes.
The dim lamp makes even my face by the window another shadow
roaming sadly over the gorge's distant slopes.

SORROW*

Face scorning the world,
a gargoyle perches on the tip of the temple's tiled roof.
On hot afternoons when clouds burn brilliantly,
a crow often swoops from the core of the blaze,
lights on the gargoyle's ear, pecks its eye.

FIRE

Fire and smoke have fled me now.
I'm but a wretched clinker.
Yet in the furnace I blaze more fiercely than before.

Shaped only as I am with neither sorrows nor smiles,
I rage more, I flash more ... than ever.

SONG OF THE CRANE*

Beak clogged with dead leaves,
its water spray beads, forks, then re–forks.
Finally it becomes a trickle of sobs
transformed at night into icicles edging the crane's wings.

With each stab of dawn's honed light,
the icicles twist, then shrink——
ruefully transformed.

ROOF*

I stand high on the ridge of the roof
this heart–struck midday ... isolated.

Burnished by glows lurking in mist,
roof tiles radiate sun–dream glints
as cloud shadows mirror deep tints.

Now and then I feel nuts reject their branches
and tumble nimbly into gutters.
Then the gargoyle near the eaves
	exchanges glances and whispers with the one next door.
Nearby, a crow about to touch down gently
(could it have seen me?) flaps its wings, flies off.

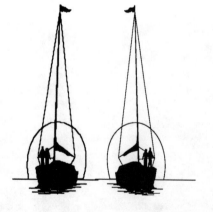

ORISON*

Swelling through twilight, the hues of repose sadden.
I'm the bow of a ship rusting at berth,
my anchor casting weighty shadows into the cove of regrets.
In the gloom of breast's yardarm, ready now
    to glimmer with hope,
a lone sea bird——tattered wings of yearning folded,
golden beak shimmering intermittently on the crossjack.

BEDROOM

When it forgets its flame, even the lamp knows moments of hush,
blinklessly enraptured,
wick kissing oil.

I, too, sang of life–glittering nights similarly gone——
long ago when her scarlet beak innocently pecked
    the finger in her hand.

DAY-LONG DREAMS

My studio awash in morning sun,
I hurriedly take a carpenter's plane
and confront that rose–tinted pillar.
I scatter those scraps of dream
that threaten again to glitter my day.

NEW YEAR SEASON*

Carpenters wedge dovetailed timbers together,
shoulder the assembled framework with a shout,
and set it on a foundation of firmly–tamped black soil
exorcised by sacred leaves.

Hammer pings echo sharply.
Studs wrapped in morning sun
——burning candles.

STARRY NIGHT*

Farmers quarreled
about that "god" tethered in the stable.
Folding forelegs on misty straw,
the god listened ... straining wise ears.

CRANE (ii)*

Looking up,
the crane stretches its wings.
Stained scarlet by sun——the bird ready to flame.

In a moment ... gone.

Already smoke,
the crane flutters elegantly in the sky.

SONG OF THE SPRING BIRD

Not even oats will sprout from such barren soil,
nor does the glow of a single dandelion dress it.
A bird wonders what those gravel lumps have in mind.
Tentatively he claws at one, breaking it up.
When he pecks at the obstinate core,
sparks that sadden twilight scatter faintly into his eyes.

VOICES

Lamp's glow liquefies the gull's eyes.
They flow down its cheeks.
Wings glaring blind
stagger through flame.

SHADOWS (i)

When at sunset
sounds spill from the harmonium,
a lily strolls over from the distance,
peers into the lantern's face.

NOSTALGIA

Sharpening the spine
of a feather plucked from your tail,

I make a quill pen and sketch you flying off.

Since I captured neither eye nor beak,
once more my sketch, alas, resembles an oil lamp.

Bar Song II*

Adorn the canvas tablecloth with kelp flowers.
Drain your shell cups dry.
Sun drops ... wind drops
——sour recollections of tear tracks.

Cove

Stained gulls soar back and forth.
Discarded bottles drift along the strand.
At night in that narrow dune–lined cove,
a cluster of engined fishing craft align their anchor chains.
Husky voices counting the catch
    and the fumes of distressed anchor lights
cloud the serenity of dawn's Milky Way.

Earth and Heaven

Pecking at the sun and sucking up rain, a crane tried to be as
white as that cloud. Failing, it melted deplorably into hunger——
its feathers vanishing again into diluted sunlight and rain.

Sun–shouldered rainwater retreated straight into sky. There it
might at least become a crane–shaped cloud.

Early Spring (i)*

Light bathes the grove. A clearly visible tree nymph sparkles.
Naked, her hair dancing, she again and again scoops water from
under fallen leaves, then tosses it high into treetops. Brutally
heavy, water resists every effort to elevate her strength. Resistant
chest and back bend delicately. Apparent weariness wrings her
arms, glows the tips of her fingers white.

Tale of a Butterfly

He caught it in grass in the woods and gently put it in a card-
board tube. There it made soft, tender sounds.

Closing one eye, he squinted through the little window he'd carved with his pocketknife. On the bottom, where a beam of light leaked in, he saw a tiny princess sitting. Her airy skirts puffed out like a rubber ball. She spent the entire long spring day stitching the curious cloth spread over her lap. This spectacle the boy saw as a scene in a distant castle.

Before long those faint sounds ceased. He took another peek. No trace of the princess. She no doubt had finished her work before he was aware of it. He saw the dim, seductive outline of a mosquito net hanging in a gloomy corner. It looked like an upturned bottle gourd. Well, then, was that the net that she had been diligently stitching? If so, the boy felt quite relieved. He couldn't see the princess, so he figured she'd perhaps crawled under the net.

Already time to waken. Whenever he thought of it, he took a peek through that window he'd made. She was apparently quite sleepy, however, so she never appeared. Since she slept on and on like that for three days and three nights, he finally became bored and soon forgot about her.

Soon, the gleaming summer. One day the boy at long last remembered the tube. He peered in through the little window. What did he see? In the pitch dark that filled the tube, no trace of the mosquito net that certainly should have been there, not to mention the princess. Well, then, he figured, they got away. In a fit of spite he hurled the tube down....

Rolling with a clatter, it hit the edge of the bookcase. The tube's cap popped off. Apparently a being on the inside of the cap had for a time been holding its breath. Something like a pair of postage stamps fluttered off. It flew out the window, into the yard, then disappeared beyond the fence through a gate of gleaming colonnaded clouds.

MONK HILL*

No pines on Monk Hill,
no crags either,
only the rustlings of bamboo grass.
Whichever direction you turn,
rose winds rub your chilled face.
Abdicating to assembled sunbeams,
skylarks fly up from under violets.
Have the larks returned?

One lost its way in the field.
Soon, as night's ring of stars begins its glisten,
I hear the banter of water drops——
bells tinkling in the breast.

Brothers

A streetcar and a locomotive collided. Clutching each other, they tumbled down the small hill in our yard. One fell into the pond. One stopped under the azaleas and whirred its spring.

Two Behinds

Both he and I were children. One day I took a castle–shaped piece of candy from his hand and ran off. He chased me relentlessly. Finally he caught me at the bottom of the stairs. Worse, my bare behind ended up getting paddled with a slipper. After that, each time he met a friend he told him that the blue mark on my behind came from greed for what belonged to someone else. It was terribly embarrassing that others knew my behind was blue. Besides, I rued being the only one in the world with a blue behind. One day when he filched my toy sailboat, however, the tables turned. When I cornered him standing on the fence around our yard, I pulled on the bottom of his shorts. Well, well! He had a large apple–sized black–and–blue welt on his behind——just like me.

After that, neither of us said a word about behinds.

In Praise of Morning Sun*

As he rose,
Sol sliced through daybreak branches
and granted me a cool pillar.

Swinging my mallet, I put my chisel to work.
I shape that rose–pink pillar
into bird forms glittering with life,
into time forms beating wings of hope.

City Awakens*

What lovable chimneys!
They line up, glittering intensely at sunup.

They stretch stoutly and start their chorus now,
chanting day–long war songs ... chanting empty thoughts
into skies with neither chirrups nor wing beats.

GOD*

Suddenly screaming,
he ends up engraved in rock.
Never–ending shrieks rise
like light to heaven.

Then ... the hush.

AT THE BEACH

Blades in a grass patch sprout buds.
Water collects as though struck by light.
Sun backlights the clouds.
A bird glances back in passing.
I genuflect fervently to my heart.
Yes, I weep on this indulgent quilt.

AFTERNOON

On a cloudy urban afternoon,
crows scurry off
through the space over harried roof tops,
through skies over the river where a whistle shrills.
Their footfalls tangle instantly with space.
The crows' willowy receding figures
momentarily float into the telescope of my nostalgia.
One speaks to the other with a misty voice.
Its partner's reply ... unheard.

LIGHT'S PATH

Buds sprout through the pale grass patch
like the weeping eyes of a dirt clump,
like the leaping core of a dirt clump.
As sunlight falls in threads,
a crow flutters delicately from the sky,
folds its wings, sparkles its head.

TRACES OF A BUTTERFLY*

I look at the awning
where the figure of a butterfly had totteringly ascended.
I trace her path
up the roof slope, where the glow of her bewilderment
    became chalkily entangled.
I hunt through my heart
for the height of the roof ridge where glimmers of her prayers
    quavered then vanished.
Oh, I look longingly into my heart
for the poignant griefs piercing sky's lone eye——
the way summer grasses jut like swords
    from cracked roof tiles.

AUTUMN (ii)

A rock in the yard harbored as much light and heat
    as strength allowed.
Finally it shrieked with an unseen and distressing crack.
At sunset, a cricket floated up from the fissure
and long sat still——a printed word.
At midnight the rock began a lusty song.
Melting its identity, the rock overflowed itself and split.
Then, like wretched water shadows, the rock's voice
lapped even against the cheeks of one asleep and in dreams.

JOYS OF SNOW (i)

Skies pour plumage. Bundled in white,
Earth stretches still as a patient asleep.
Now her every aching inequality
sees wondrous dreams.

MYTHS

These tiny drop–like bits falling from the heavens——
wisps of rain? ... mist? ... dust? ... pollen? ...
    soot? ... volcanic ash?
Bits with unidentifiable shapes,
without murmurs, with no scent——
bits that leave no image on eyes that strain to see them.
Plainly, nothing falls.

Branches nevertheless stretch out thin finger nets.
Birds extend short tarnished tongues,
intently receptive.

MAKING A LIVING

Humble hands again today, rake dead leaves,
gather wood scraps, burn rags, send smoke

toward stars....

PERVERSITY*

Ah, I stretch out on this vast, this dreary,
this shadowless clump of chalky emptiness.
Taking out my pocket mirror again,
I gaze at it hard enough to plunge through it ... into my Self——
into that far–off Self deep within eyes gazing at my Self.

CAMELLIA*

The yard behind my house, quiet as usual today.
While I was out and my doors locked,
two or three cranes dropped by.
They flapped off the moment I returned.
Ah, puddles of rain water frown mournfully,
drops of wept sunlight.
I imagine someone calling me
from behind shrubs where breezes rustle.
Whoever is it? A tittering *otomé* camellia!

CHERRY BLOSSOMS*

I wonder if cherry trees bloom even there?
Pallid, bursting with light,
full of flame——beneath them a thousand,
ten thousand prancing demons.
Now and then their queued–up heads stare and jeer.
Today, a train lumbers through the world's depths
on rails of twilight rays and weary dust.

HER REMAINS

You were so still,
stretched out like smoke,   speechless,
dwindling like a treetop,   not a stir.
Back from seeing you laid away,
my grief threadbare, only memories quicken.
I remain with the throb of your single bloom that seduced
the scent in your clothing, your bells, the ornaments in your hair.
Breezes come, settle down, rise, leave.
Sunbeams shine, bend, crumble, thaw.
As though they loved me.
As though I loved them.

BELL SONG*

I live through the day with your photo.
I tinkle the little bells you loved,
trying to call the soul in your picture back to life.
Your likeness—startled—opens its eyes wide
and silently comes to lean on me.
Ah, soft black hair shedding light.
Wind lips whispering a thousand echoless words.
I shake the bells harder ... I shake them ... I make them sing.
But their thin string slips from my fingers like a shriek,
and they land on a rock in my crane–forsaken yard.

ELEGY*

Your kimono, alas, reversed in death.
Your young dreams already in heaven,
only a shell of what you were, prayer beads in hand.
Why is your hair as still as a stretched–out beam of light,
your lips as mute as the redolence of trees?
Sitting at the head of your bier, I mourn bitterly,
yet my anguished cries fail to reach God.
They scatter vainly into space,
merely beguiling a bird at the edge of the roof.

TO A PINE

Pine   Play the organ in your limbs!
Branch tips   Blow wind's flute!
Sun   Rain stray needles and cones!
I'll sweep her gravestone clean.

DREADFUL DREAM*

I bought a baby goldfish from a vendor on the street. In a pinch
for a container, I filled a glass tumbler with water and set the fish
free in it.

The tumbler's curved side mirrored the fresh leaves on the
maple in our yard, reflections from our *shôji* doors, other shadows
still thronging everywhere. When I raised the tumbler to light,
fins and eyes and gills split into fragments. And those white,
those golden colors simply swirled round and round, white and
gold, away from the world of the fish. Exquisite!

A friend stopped by. After we talked a while about the goldfish,
we gingerly transferred it from the tumbler to a washbowl. After
rinsing out the glass, I used it to drink some beer. I fell asleep
feeling slightly tipsy.

Near dawn I had a dreadful dream. I was a goldfish swimming
in the wash basin. Water dripping from the leaky tap gradually
spilled over the basin's wide flange. Buoyed by the water, I
couldn't tell from one moment to the next whether I'd be flushed
out of the basin. Striving in vain, I was finally swept over the
flange and found myself on the metal sink. It had a small opening
in one corner for washing potato peelings, rice grains, and such
from the sink. Once caught in that, it'd be curtains for me. I
flipped. I jumped. As I was leaping around, I awoke. Heading
straight for the kitchen, I returned the goldfish to the tumbler;
relieved, I then went back to sleep, this time dreamless.

Sometime during the day yesterday, I realized the goldfish was
gone. It disappeared while I was occupied with something else.
Had it melted into the water? Had the cat made off with it? Cer-
tainly it could not have climbed into the clouds on its own.
Despite my certainty, I stared into a corner of the sky. Then I
stooped down and poured the tumbler's lonely water over the
roots of a rose bush, its buds still asleep.

DIGRESSION ON A SOLAR ECLIPSE

I couldn't figure out what to do with that fragment of smoked
glass. Peering through it, the depths of the pond and woods along
my way looked as melancholy as a moonlit night.

A cuckoo wailed incessantly from those depths.

NIGHT BELLS*

"Oh, those bells. Has my dead little sister returned?" •

Eyes welling, my wife rushes to the window. I get out of bed,
    open the shutter.

Only tree roots brightening the late–night yard.
    Leaf scents whisper to me.

As I strain my ears, the bell sounds stop. Then I hear
    snatches of someone's whistle.
"Ha! Somebody calling his dog."

I close the shutter, lie down in the dark, douse the light,
    and a dog once seen in the neighborhood comes to mind.

Its skinny silhouette runs gray as smoke.
    On its collar, tinkling bells....

ROSE

Rose!
Prick yourself with thorns,
scratch your cheeks,
swallow your blood——glare white,
if only in the instant day dawns.
That's best ... yes, in days like these.

DOVES

Standing on the pavement,
I plan to watch doves drop from sky.
Scarlet rays illuminate me
as though it's time for griefs to sidle up.
Fanning its tail feathers, one descending dove
beats violently on my brow,
blanketing the scars in my mind with a chill.

SUN TO LOVE——FLOWER TO LOVE

Sun shines through the day——
    enamored of the sunflower's looks.
Proudly raising her face, the sunflower bathes
    the whole day in sun's glare.
The flare of sun's fierce desires intensifies moment by moment.
The flower's sentiments successively stir.
Yes, in this noontime hush
the vital frenzy of sun and flower ... fulfills itself in grief.

JOURNEY ON A CLOUDY DAY

Jostled in a country buggy,
mother and son once traveled a road paralleling the sea.
Spinning through the day on its rounds,
sun—now on the offing—
listened to shifts in joyous chats.

Sunset. We reached a village of fading sunflowers.
In the house a woman the image of Mother greeted us,
patted me on the head, slept with me in her arms.
The next morning from a stone step by Granny's grave
I watched ships in the fishing port below.
I saw a crow nonchalantly about to perch
on one boat's hat–pin yardarm.

IN SUNSET'S GLOW

I can't believe that such a colossal chimney towers into sky.
I can't believe that such a ghastly whisp of smoke menaces skies
beyond ruddy roof tiles that blacken the horizon.

Am I dreaming?
Do I gaze into sad dream scraps
     that twilight's terrors reflect——
or into the unplumbed hollows of my mind?

DECEMBER TWENTY FOURTH

God sends snow.
From Earth the echo of bells, of bottle caps.
Smoke from countless turkeys
rises into sky.

SACRED FLAME

Ah, I see the back gate
through darkness hugging an off–plumb stud.
Wasting in the shed   a lonely cow.
In distant skies   a lonely star.
Is someone lighting a fire on the dirt floor?
Crimson dust musters ... ready to beset my eyes.

DREAMS

Cold boughs sweeping the sky
have snared two or three stars——
like dust specks,
like chips of glass.

BELOVED TOMB*

Though I search everywhere for one I love, she's no longer here.
Deserted, I engrave a low stone for her in my heart
and shower fruitless regrets over the little bells in her hands,
    the ornaments in her hair.
Day after day I count the steps to her grave.
Yet under the lilies——only chilled and broken shoulder blades.
Pine needles wheeze indifferently on forked treetops
and sun now displays, now veils its smiles.
Grins soon transform into dumb black beads,
whirl the light—wing like—then fade.
Look! Just as I thought. Today again
    a shadow from her grave marker slices through evening mist,
flees toward the real–world train that clatters the trestle.

STANDING BY THE GRAVE*

Mustard blossoms shimmer.
Purple vetch radiate brightly.
Under a flickering Venus,
a train moves along the levee——
engine scattering shreds of smoke,
whistle windless...
a stringy shadow gliding into Sheol.

SELF–RIGHTING LAMP

I love the lamps they lit on sea voyages in the old days. You
know, those self–righting lamps that always returned to the ver-
tical despite being swayed endlessly by swells. ——As a boy, I of-
ten dreamed of going to sea.

Years later.... The winds of this world tease the sails of life.
That lamp spinning under my ribs nevertheless still keeps the
silent flame of my poetry perfectly plumb.

Autumn Impression

Coming home at twilight, the child said breathlessly——"What a big red sun just now sank behind the grove!"

I stared at the child's face. Indeed, something round and red still burned vividly in those tiny cheeks.

Drifting Penguin

His land of ice crumbled.
Riding an ice floe,
he drifted out into the sun–bright sea.
His luckless floe narrowed by the day.
One morning it barely fit his feet.
In the end, the floe melted away.
For a while he floated on the brine.

A merchant ship saved him from drowning.
A gentle bearded captain cuddling him,
he sailed to a temperate land he'd never seen.

Now screened in at the zoo,
he stands on an isolated isle in a leaf–scattered pond.
One wing raised, he imitates that well–known pose
of Napoleon greeting his troops.

Sea Darkens*

I told him about the burial service at sea ... the canvas coffin that grated as they lowered it ... the three volleys ... our ship circling the spot thrice, its triple wake marking the grave.

I also told him about a romantic crane that, defying high seasonal winds, flew off toward a foreign cape.

I even told him about the strangely intoned commands I had heard during daily drills aboard the training barque. And, imitating the bugle that echoed so long, I told him about the giant helm in the fantail——one that took two men to wheel.

Glare from the table tinged my young friend's cheeks. I stopped talking——only the hand holding my saké cup continued to move.

Recalling that my engagement had fallen through saddened me. I suppose that even now she presses to her breasts the youthfulness of those days! Nevertheless, when twilight gathered beyond drapes framing the window behind me, she removed the ornament, let down her hair, slipped out of her clothing, and retired into nightfall without a word——forgetting to douse the lone riding light on the horizon.

Korea*

I don't know how long it'd been going on, but a princess was in flight. A demon desperately chased her. As she ran, she pulled a comb from her hair and threw it down. The comb turned into a conical mountain with a spear–like peak. With the demon on the other side of the mountain, the princess got well away from him.

Soon the demon came dashing down the mountainside. Little by little he gained on the princess. She tossed away the purse that dangled from her waist. The purse turned into a pond, lush with lotus blossoms in full bloom. The demon, who had started to cross from the opposite bank, apparently had difficulty wading through the mud. Once again the princess could escape.

The demon easily closed the gap. Next, the princess removed a slipper and threw it. The dainty shoe hit the demon on the nose, fell to the ground upside down, transformed into a cliff. Clicking his tongue nervously, the demon began climbing the cliff. The princess once again eluded him.

The tenacious demon closed in on her. The princess ripped the blue cord from her jacket and threw it down. The cord turned into a meandering river. The princess once more escaped as the demon searched for a raft.

Midway through the tale, the storyteller heard his master call. Mr. Han took the long–stemmed pipe from his mouth and dashed from the shed.

Thirty years have passed since then. Indeed, the items that the pathetic princess discarded as she wept survive on the soil of that country through which my childhood memories have been grop- ing. A barren phantom crag blocks one's path across the rib–like field. A pond abruptly appears to dry up, its mud bursting into flame. A cluster of spotted crows caws from the tip of a lonely, leafless tree. Hidden by rocks that resemble people, a stray *nuku- te* wolf howls, its mouth a "V."

The princess remains fated to flee through her land. Nearly dis- robed, having abandoned everything, she continues to fly, scream- ing. The demon constantly reaches out cruel claws trying to clutch her flowing hair.

One year, at her most luckless moment, she discarded the thin cloth over her privates and sadly stretched prostrate on the ground. The cloth fluttered in the breeze, then sank into a nearby riverbed. There it turned to water. Overflowing the banks and breaking dikes, it became a furious flood that buried the plains.

Water flooded cabbage fields, entombed horses and cows, in-
undated grave mounds at the foot of a hill ponderous with Confu-
cian wailing. Countless village houses—thatched roofs heavy with
hands that bid good–bye to this side of the grave—bob on water
swirling off slowly toward the sea.

FREIGHT CARS

When I lived in a small provincial city, I longed for Tokyo's
skies. At the end of the day, I crossed the square and often headed
for the station.

Many gathered there, pointing to the schedules. Mingling with
one such group, I, too, hurried off toward the wicket. I leaned
against a niche in the wooden barrier by the ticket puncher and
gazed off beyond the overpass.

Inbound and outbound trains slipped in like avalanches of
light——their lamps more dazzling than those on the platforms.
Inbound lines stopped at the far platform, so I could easily see
boarding and detraining passengers.

The spectacle exuded bewilderment. Congestion spread as
though driven. Sounds of feet and the crowd's bustle melted to-
gether in apparent disarray. The cries of hawkers shrilled from
every quarter. Then the commotion instantly died——as though
smothered. An almost mystic hush gripped the scene.

In but a few moments an entirely different spectacle. A train
with only a few cars had stopped on the siding. Now the face of an
old woman, now of a child or a sailor, peered as though bored from
one of its windows. Glinting in the light, a beautiful flute–like
train then slipped into the station and screened out my view. Just
when I thought this train would be staying, it moved out. The
waiting train appeared again, then departed as though it had re-
membered something.

I loved those moments in the wake of a departure. Sometimes I
aimlessly scanned both ends of the long platform. Sometimes I
listened to the solitary ticking of the clock that echoed from the
wall of the waiting room——as vacant as an empty box. Or,
standing under the clock, I thought back on that wondrous hub-
bub, now absolutely still, that had till this very moment eddied
about me. Like detritus from the eddy, a group of two or three
people was certain to remain. Somebody sitting idly on the edge of
a bench, face in hands as though in tears, suddenly stands up and
goes off. Such dreamlike events invariably grew in my memory.

Each reminiscence was likely a miserable phantom haunting
my mind. In those days, I burned fervently with the hope of going
to Tokyo. My fettered life nevertheless drove me day by day and

month by month farther from that hope. I wandered into the station only to cool my heart's painful simmer.

In the end, however, even those recurring scenes palled as I looked on. Or, rather, I found it unbearable to watch travelers and trains head for the place I longed to be ... but, of course, couldn't get to.

The station bizarrely attracted my wandering feet. After a while, however, I no longer headed for either the waiting room or those wickets where passengers bustled by. I began instead to observe a different, somewhat detached part of the train yard. I watched from a wooden fence that enclosed the baggage–handling section. It faced the station exit, an area usually devoid of people. Away from incoming and outgoing passenger trains, it was an extensive, desolate place, dark and reeking of smoke. The crowded roofs of storehouses and the uncanny water supply tank or the switching tower tinged its space with shadows. As though from a distant land, light from lamps at the end of the platform drifted somberly over the ground. Numerous rails glowed there like abandoned, oil–soaked ribbons. Two or three scattered locomotives constantly belched smoke like anchored ships. Beyond them, rows and rows of overlapping boxcars stood dead in their tracks as though riveted to the rails.

Each boxcar string looked to me like a mere line of rectangular shapes. Blacker than night, they had neither windows nor canopies. Handcar–like flat cars—most fitted with bulky, water–repellent oilcloth or canvas—for some reason had been mixed in with them. Roofed cars were either stuffed full of heavy goods or appeared empty. I couldn't tell when the freight had been off-loaded, when it had been on–loaded, or why the cars had been sitting there so long. They were like files of dumb tethered cattle unaware of where they were or where they headed. It seemed only that those files were proportionately of equal length. Since these cars occupied the same amount of space, I figured they stood there eternally motionless.

Depending on the time I watched them, however, I knew that leisurely adjustments gradually took place. The signal man's vibrating lamp moved here and there between given locations along the tracks. The lamp turned now fluorescent, now strawberry. A locomotive plied back and forth, aiming at the lamp. The switch engine cut several cars from the tail end of boxcars lined up on the readying tracks. It sent them back to a given intersection of the tracks. The shoved cars rolled sluggishly down a different siding near me. Then, sounding like the odd cries of someone sightless, they coupled with one end of the file of freight cars standing in their way. Some hauled–off freight cars didn't come back. They had been shunted down another readying track and only the engine returned. The switcher then cut off the next several cars, hauled them away, gave them a push. They rolled off down the tracks. This process invariably resulted in the formation of two long freight trains. When locomotives hooked on at the end of each line, the trains departed at their appointed times. They left almost simultaneously in opposite directions.

They got underway at a lonesome time not listed on the passenger schedule. By chance, I often showed up when they were leaving, so I remembered the hour. Soon I began timing my visits and stood by the paling as they left.

One line of freight cars began from around the spot where I stood. Another ended near that spot. The engine apparently coupled to the far end of the line heading away from the capital. The reverberating sounds of the cars banging into each other carried through each boxcar. They gradually turned to lethargic creaks and eventually stopped jiggling the taillights in front of me. Soon the train departed.

The in–bound locomotive furiously began spouting steam as I watched. Checking his watch, the engineer—bathed in firelight—looked dead ahead through the cab window. Finally the train began to move. Dragging the woolly tail of its whistle, it slowly and ponderously snaked off to where that signal dimmed. There it joined the passenger line.

Each night, the same boxcars as the day before formed the same line. They departed when their unannounced time arrived. I alone saw them off.

THE GOD WHO WEPT*

The troops accomplished more
than one could expect of mortals.
Some of the wounded
had now returned to the land of their birth.

I visited a friend
lying on a white pillow by a window
in the Second Army Hospital in Tokyo.
He stared from between hospital gown and bandages
at winter sun fading on the wall.

I reached out,
intending to pat that close–cropped head
where once a god had dwelled.
His charming stubble prickled my palm. •

Instantly his eyes watered.
"That tickles," he said smiling ... and turned his head.

DOG WATCHING HORIZON*

A dilapidated western–style house
stands on the shoulder of a dune.
Does anyone live there?
Every balcony window
tightly shuttered.

Breezes flutter a shepherd's purse
growing from the rickety handrail.
In the afternoon,
a dog lies motionless
under sun's glitter.

He rarely raises his head.
Tensing pointed ears,
he gazes steadily at a sea empty of yachts.
Soon, apparently bored by that as well,
he lays his head back on forepaws.

At that instant,
beyond infinitely swelling wave caps,
a single prominently–towering breaker
comes into view...
then gleamingly crumbles away.

SEA WIND*

A swell surges from the distant offing.

It touches the shore and crumbles.

Someone stands there.

He comes up on the beach.

He lacks form.

Only foam for eyes.

He heads straight over the crest.

Its eulalias glow.

TOUCHING YOUR TOMBSTONE*

You told me before your lungs rotted and you died:
"Take the lane by the graveyard in dusk's gloom!
Inexplicable warmths will dangle from your back.
Glints of butterflies and moths will prickle your cheeks.
It looks but isn't really eerie
because those ranked stones stand through the lengthy day
holding banked warmths."

This evening I happen to be out strolling
and by chance pass the gate of this familiar temple.
Visiting your grave, I touch your tombstone.
Still warm, as I imagined——
        the way you were when you were here.
Out of nowhere, several winged shadows
flicker up my kimono sleeve.

JOYS OF SNOW (ii)

When snow piles up, boys love to tumble into drifts.
Mother's arms will come
to enfold them and help them from the snow.
This morning, too,
impression after impression in the snow
where boys and their mothers
had tenderly embraced under blue skies
on the way to school.

CHEERFUL BOOK*

I'm on a train.
Midday cloudless on the Suruga Plain.
Mt. Fuji stands out
as though painted on the sky.

A clump of white clouds
moves across the peak.
The clump leisurely
casts shadows over the mountainside.

The young girl sitting next to me
reads a book.
Light from its pages
brightens innocent cheeks. •

As the train dashes ever on,
pear orchards whip past like flipped pages,
yet Fuji stands majestically still.
Nor does the cloudscape move.

I now take a book from the coach window
and open it——
a cheerful, pageless tale
titled, *Japan*....

ⓄUR UNSHOD POOCH*

We were all on the *engawa* one day
when my eyes unaccountably watered.
Mother asked if it was a speck of dust.
My wife eyed me dubiously.
Smiling, I feigned indifference
but couldn't hide what tracked my cheeks.

Don't nag me about being syrupy!
The fact is, a trivial thought depressed me.
I couldn't tolerate seeing our precious pooch
—bristling with cottony fur,
his little heart more honest, more wise than ours—
always looking up at us unshod from the yard.

ⒹOG AND OLD MAN

I have a purebred spitz puppy.
I walk him mornings and evenings.
The dog's coat a profusion of snow–white tufts,
his eyes exuding mellow purple gleams.
I dare say he has the look of a polar bear cub.
Because he's such a curiosity,
people we pass always stop and comment on how cute he is.

One day when I was taking the dog to the field,
an old man clad in shabby western clothes came down the hill.
He, too, took note of the puppy and stopped.
"Say, fine dog there. Cost a bit I figure."
Without turning to face him I responded,
"Somebody gave him to me."
"Really? A rare breed, right?
What's he eat? Costs a pile, I bet."

"He's a poet's dog. He eats only leftovers."
"Really? Well, well now.
Anyhow, giving him goodies'd be a fault.
Same with people, too."

Squatting down, the old fellow stretched out his hands.
In a flash the dog laid back his ears and assumed a pensive pose.
Then he jumped up on the man and furiously wagged his tail.
The old man's palms were gnarled and gigantic,
one hand missing a finger.
That hand vigorously pet the darling pup.
For a moment I thought the dog might vanish
      into that uncannily shaped hand.

"At my age," the old man said
suddenly sighing irrepressibly,
"a simple creature like this, you know,
      would comfort me more than anything.
My wife's in her grave.
The children raised and in no need of me.
Life only misery.
After working the day long, if I had something like him
      to fuss over me,
that'd be enough to put weariness out of mind."
His words exuded a marvelous savor.
The puppy sniffed busily through the grass.
He then leapt up on the oldster's patched pants and shirt.
Bending down, the old man stretched his face toward the dog.
The dog began licking the wrinkles on that brow
      glistening from toil.

The old fellow stood up.
"Raise him well. He'll be a good dog."
Then, for some reason, he took a quick look around and said,
"But he could be stolen——stolen.
There's the risk anyhow that rarities draw attention.
Best take care."

The old man left with a lightness of step belying his appearance.
Both the puppy and I looked off after him.
For some time we could see him
      on the hillside road at town's edge.
He then blended into a factory chimney in the distance.
At that moment, smoke belched from the old man's well–worn cap
and fluttered for a moment in evening sky.

SCHOOL FROM AFAR*

I've come about a dozen years since finishing school.
Looking back, the school glitters tiny as a carved medallion,
far beyond recall.
In the carving, classroom roofs merge their tiles.
Poplars twist and tremble in the wind.
The teacher discusses something
as young faces listen absorbed.
Someone near one window looks off,
staring vacantly in my direction——as I did then.
Ah, I see him so clearly from here.
Can he see where I am?

DEPRESSING SCENE

Riding a train or the interurban,
suddenly I find myself passing through
    a curious quarter of the city.
An enormous compound–like area
with one deteriorating factory wall after another,
    discarded piles of iron,
mighty brick chimneys standing abreast
    and silently spewing smoke,
a gas tank abruptly closing in on me.
As though sketched onto an empty sky, a radio tower
    appears faintly ... then disappears.
I no sooner imagine that waves of roof tiles gradually recede
    below my window
than I find the tracks crossing above another viaduct.

At such times I invariably sense that,
without a single human being in the area,
riders will naturally turn glum and feel drawn less to people
than to these gigantic, depressing arrays of inorganic matter.

RHINOCEROS AND LION*

The rhinoceros runs.
The lion clings to its back.
He bites the rhino.
Blood spurting, the rhino twists its tortured neck,
gapes into sky.
A daytime moon hovers.
Sky hushes pale. •

This a painting,
one instant in a far–off jungle,
the landscape mute,
the two animals always as they are.
But in that grave silence,
second by second the lion kills,
timelessly the rhino dies.

INTO CLOUDS ON THE HILL

I pet my dog
neck to back,
back to tail.

Ears lie flat.
Coat glistening,
belly bent in a bow.

Ah, my petting hand——wind in motion.
The dog's stance bends into my strokes.
The dog dashes through its stance.

I unleash him into clouds on the hill.
He bounds off full speed
like the flung stone you can't call back.

MY PRESENT PATH

My cheeks have roughened.
Somehow my hairline recedes.
I've actually caught up little by little with the pace of adults
        once well ahead of me.
Now I travel with them.

Is it that we cannot bear each other?
Not even our faces ever meet. We cough
        as though uttering a courtesy.
We affect sighs without feeling distress.
How dreary my present clouded path!

A silver head walks briskly ahead of me.
Distant scenes visible where a gourd belly mirrors plum buds.
Reflections clash sharply on the tombstone.
Yes, all the more delightful there!

PLUM TREE*

Granny's hard of hearing.
She never relates to what we talk about at home.

All day long, Granny sits beside the brazier.
She just moves her knitting needles lethargically.
Only when the lad cries into her ear
does she respond loudly——Yes! Yes!

Worn out, she now or then falls asleep,
apparently taking a journey to some far–off place.
When she wakens, she starts talking vividly about the old days.

I wonder if Granny's partly in another world.
No, no——she certainly seems to be here still.

One night I dreamed of Granny.
As she stooped down in the garden,
      she turned into a knurled plum tree.
At bloom near her elbows——several buds reeking of India ink.

ON THE ROAD

My dog stops in his tracks.
Sitting down, he glances up at me.
How splashed and wet with mud his paws!
In the disordered illimitability of our world,
I suppose he can see no more
than quite simple scenery:
this utility pole bathed in a brush of light,
or, beneath the pole, this small sagging house,
and me under its eaves.

He sits quite still
so I, too, stand still,
searching his eyes.
Suddenly, I feel deeply moved,
not by the dog's shabbiness
but by my solitude.

DECADE

I went back home. •

In the living room a wall clock. Its pendulum had ticked
   slowly, ever so slowly, through my fleeting decade.

Under the pendulum, Mother's face had slowly, ever so slowly,
   ticked wrinkle upon wrinkle ...

yes, ticked old–age wrinkles no one can smooth.

SWALLOW (i)*

I catch a swallow. She breathes softly in my palm,
   as though still in flight.
I squeeze gently.
Distressed, she opens her bill, her soft body ready to melt away.
I bring my hand closer to my face figuring I'll study her carefully
and fix her features in my mind.

    ——This her tiny head.
    ——These the bottoms of her little feet.
    ——This her white jacket.
    ——Here the familiar mole on her jaw.
    ——Shiny satin wings, just so.
    ——Stylish tail as well.

I stroke her gently. I print a clear picture of her in my mind.
Opening our second–floor *shôji* doors,
   I then free her into far–off hills.
The swallow melts immediately into the green breeze.
Then, that figure in my memory vanishes, too.
Her subtly uncanny color and shape cling even now to my mind.

WHITE FLOWERS

One spring morning
as my train dashed along a water channel,
I noticed a tree behind a bamboo hedge on the opposite bank.
Its branches burst with white flowers.
I wondered what kind they were.
They resembled magnolias——crucifer blooms I'd never seen.
Shadows of those flowers, mirrored even in the water's depths,
cheered me momentarily as I passed.
They put me into a serene and buoyant mood——
almost as though I'd just chatted with someone
   back from the dead.
That fixed my resolve never to deny the world
but joyfully to affirm it.

CALMER THAN THE FLOWER*

When that girl I so adored passed on,
I sat through the night by her remains.
Because of their extreme stillness,
I lapsed more and more into bizarre hallucinations.
Her shut eyelids fluttered like moth wings.
Shadows suddenly sprang from hands folded on her breast.
Her face turned at times to the side.
Each time I sank into my own thoughts,
some part of her sent off spark–like signals.

To compose myself,
I placed a single lily at the head of her bier
and tried to concentrate on it.
Her body stilled then,
but soon an even more pathetic illusion bewitched me.
The lily clearly looked alive.
The bud slowly opened as it sipped water from the vase.
Toward dawn it drooped heavily over her brow.
——Death ... calmer than the flower.

DARKNESS

When the boy lights his lamp,
squirrels scamper up the tree.

He shines his lamp on the tree.
The squirrels hurry to hide in the treetop.

When the boy points his lamp at the treetop,
squirrels flee into sky,
turn to stars.

PART II

POETRY PUBLISHED BETWEEN

1941 and 1946

昭和十六年から昭和十八年の間に発表された詩

INTO THE FUTURE

The father said,
"Look at this picture:
dashing sleigh,
wolf pack in pursuit.
See, the reinsman frantically whips the reindeer.
Look at the rider steadily aiming a rifle
from behind his luggage.
The muzzle's scarlet flash."

The son said,
"One wolf's downed, right?
Oh, another sprang at the sleigh
but tumbles over backward, covered with blood.
It's night. ——
Snow buries the endless steppes.
Can the rider hold out?
How far has the sleigh to go?"

The father said,
"The sleigh dashes on like this till dawn.
It slays yesterday's regrets one by one
as it rushes like Time into tomorrow.
Soon, beyond sun's path,
streets of the future will glimmer into view.
Look!
Sky on the hill whitens now."

JAPANESE SKIES*

A cloudless morning early in May.
Standing on high ground,
I look toward the distant town.
It's roofs and walls gradually shrink from me.
Roof tiles string together those nostalgic cameo–like shadings

in remembered picture books.
Far and near, poles for the boys' festival are up.
No carp swim on them yet,
only arrow pinwheels attached.
Each arrow emits a golden patina and,
as if by caprice,
here and there a pinwheel gently creaks.
Finally (swirled by wind … ?)
they all begin whirling furiously in unison.
Ah, how elegant those artless flashes!
Born and reared in Japan,
I marvel the more that the glare of her skies
still makes my eyes smart so.

ⓄLD POETRY COLLECTION*

Using a soiled goose–quill pen,
I once wrote some boyish verses
and gathered them into a poignant collection.
Winds of the world scattered the book,
leaving me no copy.

Years later
I went searching for one.
Yesterday, in a dismal second–hand bookshop,
I chanced upon that nostalgic Self.
Sitting on a dusty shelf,
he sold for fifteen *sen*.

I figured on paying a *yen* for him.
Holding the book and turning his pages,
I saw sunset on the corner where I used to live.
A faded dog came out barking,
leapt up on my shoulder.

ⓁONER'S DOG

Being a loner,
I have no friends to love or be loved by.
Because I'm a loner, however,
I ache with yearning,
wanting to love everyone,
to be loved by all. ·

I have a shabby mutt at home
that I constantly scold, shoo away, or pet
with the tenderness I crave from people.
Unaccountably,
my dog takes to one and all.
Everyone dotes on him.

MINING

Man first made a scrap of iron by hand.
He learned to forge iron with that scrap
and turn it into steel far stronger than iron.

Today, man's tender hands can't refine iron.
He must smelt it in the fire and beat it with iron.
Both the furnace that heats the iron and the hammer shaping it
are themselves nothing more than iron.
Did the iron that makes iron come first?
Was the manufactured iron first?
Whichever, man fashioned the first iron by hand.

Long ago, man resourcefully rubbed sticks together
     and made fire.
He hand–polished stone tools that broke hands
and used tools and fire to make iron that shatters stone.

One day I raised my hands to the sun.
From the delicately spread webs between my fingers,
I saw layer on layer of hands that gush heartbreaking blood——
     the hands of countless distant forebears.
Like gears scattering green and purple sparks,
those hands began a tumultuous gyre.

MUD–COLORED PAINTING

I painted a soldier:
steel helmet cocked to one side,
pack, canteen, and a cartridge belt across his chest,
feet spread out in the Parade Rest stance.
One extended hand grips a rifle with fixed bayonet.
He grins now as if to greet someone.

Then I added the setting.
No shreds of cotton clouds, no lonely rampart.

No meditating crow, none of the horizon's countless swells.
Instead, I smeared the background solid with a deep mud color.
In the end I daubed out those two chilled marks
I'd hesitantly left unfinished under the rim of his helmet
——those lashes now shadows over shut eyes.

HORSE AT DAWN

Sounds of hooves gallop at me from beyond dreams.
They stop before the house.
My horse already come for me.

I recall that I'm going out today.
I leap at once from bed.
I must get ready fast.

Ah, as I dress I hear him
impatiently kicking the gate,
vexatiously neighing shrill volleys.

Then I see his golden wings
burgeoning like the sun
in the frost–frozen dawn.

SPRING SCENE

As I stand on the edge of the pond
and watch its tranquil face,
a bird flies up from the surface;
a drop of water wets my brow.

Startled, I look up into nearby trees,
into branch nets full of ripening red globes.
I gaze at the copse around me,
every treetop vivid.

Though the globes' redness pales,
though branch nets blur,
they are clearly visible, even in the far–off hazy sky.
Incomprehensible!

LIKE MUSIC*

In a day or two I go to sea.
I'll sail with young mates on a four–masted barque

to southern isles with glowing, underwater reefs.
Then westward, through bands of trade winds,
I'll head for harbors in the Philippines and along the China coast.

Ah, think how joy
will billow my sails the entire cruise!
That'll coax into song the tackle taut on my breast
and make me run true under constellations of dream,
rolling and pitching fiercely.

I'm busily ordering my feelings now.
I lash my flapping sails;
take a careful fix like the ship's officer;
inspect the compass, plot my course on the charts;
stream the chip log, ring the ship's bell.

Setting sail! What spectacular days to come.
Just now the season at the peak of its dazzling gala.
May flowers in my tiny yard vie for color; since dawn
summer butterflies as well have fluttered
        effortlessly over the hedge.
My heart, too, like music——*forte*!

Winds*

Our barque sails——
the wind its life.

The mate watches the wind.
Noting its direction,
he changes the tack of the yards.
Sailors tug at the sheets and braces,
now unfurling, now furling the sails.

Winds touch more than masts;
they affect the crew.
Sailors begin buffing decks leeward.
Sailors climb the rigging windward.
Sailors lower lifeboats leeward.

One young face,
called "Leeside Watch" after the wind,
rings the ship's bell, delivers orders.
Two winds stand aft:
"Weather Wheelman" and "Lee Wheelman." •

Weather Wheelman wheels the helm.
Lee Wheelman lends a hand.

On land one cannot discern the wind's configurations
so clearly as at sea.
Today again barefooted winds bellow
as they bustle under cumulus clouds.

"Three points starboard. Right on! Right on!"
"All hands on deck. Secure the sails!"

Feet of Sailors

Sailors walk barefoot
over slick decks.

Each morning they polish the decks
with sand and coconut,
wash them down with brine,
sweep them with brooms,
dry them in the equatorial sun.

No dirt in sea wind.
That keeps sailors' feet
cleaner than if they'd walked on waves.

Once
sailors on the foot ropes
worked on a high spar.
All eyes looked up at white soles
that seemed almost to mirror the seven seas.

Be a Tiger!

As a child I loved playing with my cat. After all, he somehow
resembled a tiger....

I pulled his soft ears. At times I grabbed his tail, stroked his
whiskers, tied his feet together and dropped him upside down. Or
I turned him on his back and relentlessly tickled his throat. I saw
a certain unassuming ferocity in the demeanor of this animal I
treated like a rubber toy. That somehow exhilarated me. I felt I
was having my way with a tiger cub.

But, I wondered, what if this creature had been an enormous
tiger? He would have ripped me apart in an instant. Simply be-
cause he was so small.... The moment that thought came to me, I
took pity on him.

I picked up this cat I had tormented and put him on my lap.
Stroking his back I whispered:
Be a tiger! Be a tiger! Be a tiger!

I stood before its cage at the zoo. This actual tiger was beautiful,
far more dignified than my cat. As you might imagine, however, I
felt that a kitten lurked somewhere within him.
Surrendering to my fantasies, I approached him——apprehen-
sively. I ended up on his back shouting, as though mine to decree,
Be a kitty! Be a kitty! Be a kitty!
I felt unaccountably sad.

POET'S WORDS*

The late Nakahara Chûya said,
"You find no mermaids in the sea.
In the sea
are only waves."

For some strange reason,
these words linger vividly in my mind.
If I chant them thrice,
mermaid faces peer from between the sounds.
If I mutter these words to myself
while thinking back on my recent cruise through southern seas,
countless mermaid arms and tails appear from
and disappear into high blue swells.

Or if under overcast skies
I dreamily recall these words as I stand on a rocky shore,
splashes of foam dashing against crags
sigh like mermaids.

The late Nakahara Chûya's legacy to me:
He transformed the word *wave* to *mermaid*.
He transformed *mermaid*
to *wave*.

DAZZLING SPRING

Leaves already bathed in gloomy shadows,
rows of cherry trees spread their branches
along the fence by the intersection.
During the day, wind stirred, shadows whitened, then flickered.
A thorny caterpillar fell to the road.
Shoes and wheels continually trampled it,

charging the place with a savage stench.

Passersby knit their brows
thinking, "Ah, it may happen this year, too."
Cheeks quivering, girls dash through at full speed;
they titter shrilly and cling to each other.
Old men and boys walk through
    intentionally feigning indifference.
Each soon pulls up
and squeamishly brushes off his sleeves and cap.

Half shutting my eyes as I walk by,
I, too, pass through that place.
Deliberately I duck under the eaves
    on the other side of the street.
To imagine that caterpillar not yet become a butterfly
somehow saddens even this dazzling spring day.
Just then a stormy blast stirs overhead,
raining on my shoulders objects that gleam.

BLOSSOMS IN SOUTHERN SEAS

The moment we enter the trade–wind belt,
air turns refreshingly cool.
Each day gentle southeasterlies blow.
Sea——ready to dye my hands
the way it melts the ink of its ultramarine.
Like gigantic white blossoms,
our ship blooms on southern seas,
all twenty–six sails swelling.
Caught in reflections on those dazzling petals,
we laugh together,
squint through the sextant,
wheel the helm.
We all shake with mirth
at every slack swell.

CLOUDS BILLOW ON THE OFFING

What a pleasant view of the harbor.
Many ships ride at anchor,
bows high, masts leaning,
each set to sail off.

Ships tell me about

coral reefs in southern seas, northern lights,
towns and ports in distant lands.
Their invitation:
> *How about it, little boy——*
> *Won't you sail the boundless sea with me?*

Clouds molded into the world map
billow on the offing.
When will I become a ship's captain
and sail from Japan?

SEA BIRD*

An unfamiliar, solitary bird
flies over swells
along our beam.
It leads, then falls behind us.

Neither an East China sea gull
nor the common South Sea albatross,
but an ashen shadow
shaped perhaps by the nostalgia of a drawn–out cruise.

"Been with us since day before yesterday,"
my friend the Third Mate said.
"Seems to rest somewhere on the mast during the night.
Before moon was up on my watch last night,
the bugger—still drowsy—flew right into my face
as I walked through the darkness opposite the chart room!"
Laughing, I said,
"No doubt come from Nagasaki to welcome us.
Or perhaps a love letter courting us from Amoy."
Somehow I thought of the galley hand
     ——deathly sick below deck.

Kyushu's mountains loomed into view
after noon the next day.
When our windlass echoed through the cape's sunset glow
and the anchor slid down with a sigh,
I unconsciously looked for the bird.
It no longer flew with us.

BACK IN PORT*

By the time we anchored in Nagasaki Bay
after four thousand knots under sail,

winds that had wailed through our rigging,
the dazzle of southern seas,
sea–stained albatrosses, and
illusions of porpoise–shaped waves
had all disappeared——who knows where?

Weary of unlearnable English nautical terms,
weary, too, of the stench of pitch,
deafened for fifty days by sea's lavish lays
so abruptly concluded now....
Sunset's glow
tints Japan's quiet capes and coves,
shines into emptied minds.

Coming across the water all night long
to visit us like girls from back home——
voices from fishers' huts against the bluff,
squeaks from sculled fishing boats,
misty land breezes bending trees and grass.
Even crickets begin their serenade
at the gangway near my porthole.

Changing into heavily–starched *yukata*,
we lie on our below–deck bunks,
wide awake till late into the night.
How well I recall hearing someone
stealthily sit up in bed then
and light up some Ayamé.

YOUNG MEN SHOULDER THE SAIL*

At twilight again today several young men
haul a sailcloth across the poop deck.
They carry the weighty mainsail as they chant,
    Hefty! ... Hefty!

They'd furled the mainsail,
then fastened it securely with ropes.
Sea breezes and rain made it limp and damp:
a veritable serpent up from the Deep.

This sailcloth serpent crawls through the hatch,
slowly descends to middeck.
Belly and tail dragging here or there,
it goes once round the base of the mizzenmast. •

There it loiters a bit,
hangs on the narrow ladder to the lower deck,
then glides into a dark storeroom in the hold
as though suddenly infatuated with Sheol.

Once the sail lies safely stashed,
the ship's bell rings four times from the bridge.
Say! ... Isn't that sunset glowing on horizon?
West–facing broadside portholes scorched scarlet.

The young men remain in the hold.
What could they be doing?
Only moments till sunset.
Time for the lamp man's rounds.

In MY PORTHOLE*

For thirty days
my porthole mirrored
skies over the Pacific
and the harsh glare
of billowing clouds.

For ten days
my porthole framed
Ku–lang Hsü Island's verdure
and the cool sail silhouettes
of countless junks.

For seven days
storms on the East China Sea
hammered my porthole——
dashing rain
and prodigious gray waves pummeled it.

For fifty days
this porthole clouded up
with the cares of my cruise.
Mermaids glinted through seas
beyond my misted glass.

STARRY SKIES*

Jirô finished making his airplane
late at night,
the entire family in bed,

only Mother at his side.

Before turning in,
Jirô wanted to fly it just once.
Ignoring Mother's objections, he opened the front door
and went out.

The night cold,
the street hushed.
Jirô wound the propeller tight,
held the plane steady with outstretched hands,
gently launched it.

The plane flew up,
higher and higher into the night sky....
——Then he saw it glance off the second–floor eaves
and abruptly return on a crash course.

The flight lasted no more than a dozen seconds,
but Jirô saw several scenes:
Stars shining throughout skies
he thought were black.
Snow–white frost
on every neighboring roof.

Jirô continued to shiver inside.
He felt he'd seen the dreams of people throughout Japan
now sleeping soundly under stars, under frost.

DESTITUTE FRIEND*

He sat under a pear tree.
As he talked he scooped water from the ewer
and let it dribble from his palm.
He scooped it up and let it trickle away.
The drops made rings on the water,
ring on ring on ring——
serene as a *koto*.

These sounds conveyed
as gracefully as possible
the sense of his edged words.

MOORED IN AMOY*

Chalking up three thousand knots,
we enter Amoy Harbor
and drop anchor off Ku–lang Hsü Island,
some distance from a battleship queue.

Every morning at five–to–eight,
a flourish of bugles
rises from the fantails of scattered naval vessels
as they raise their sunrise banners.

The colors on our stern
sparkle as well.
Two young men at attention on the afterdeck
intently play our national anthem.

Just then a gentle land breeze
flutters every battleship flag.
The colors of our square–rigged four master
flutter toward the Pacific, too.

WAVES

In my imagination, I see those swelling, seething waves
wet the palm
I reach from the bulwark ...
then curl and slip from me——
huge laconic swells
sending off neither foam nor spray.

Beyond our heaving sailcloth and rigging,
waves stand on tiptoe so they can steal glances of us
over the ventilators' shoulders, over the heeling helm.
Sometimes swells suddenly raise their heads nearby,
then slowly pass, looking down at our deck——
mammoth waves shaped like deep blue hills.

One day, quite unexpectedly,
a chunk of one dolphin–shaped wave
leapt up on deck.
I tried immediately to stop it with my foot.
For some reason, my head began to swim.
Ah, that dream–like instant. •

He vanished.
Sun promptly dried the puddle
he left behind.

Birds (i)*

They call it "the fo'c'sle."
Washed by those crisp shadows
    the jibsail casts along the bowsprit,
a young man takes his post every hour
in that wondrously isolated spot jutting over waves.
He looks dead ahead.

Whenever I weary of our long cruise,
I take off to the forecastle,
walk up to the young lookout
and ask——always the same question,
"What do you see out there?"
He answers always,
"Only waves. Only clouds."
"How many more days by now?"
"Hmmmm...."
For a moment I imagine he's counting.
He then falls silent, eyes fixed on distance.
I say nothing, either.
We're quite like two birds lost in thought.

That's right.
It's as though we're two birds lost in thought.
Yet we watch nothing in particular.
Nor are we thinking of anything in particular.
The ample, the constantly heaving and sinking horizon,
the boundless glare of clouds,
only make us look as though we are.

Helm*

The great helm at the stern,
weighty as something sprouted from waves.
Two sturdy young sailors
heaving together
with all their might
turn it round and round. •

I glance up at the mizzenmast.
The ship turns.
No——the ship doesn't turn.
Pivoting on the royal sail,
clouds silently begin to turn.
Little by little the sky, the sea,
yes, the world begins to turn.

SONS OF THE WINDJAMMER*

Young men——callused palms
reeking of manila rope.
Young men——frayed dungarees
pungent with paint and pitch.
Sea breezes constantly
billow your jackets, flutter your pants,
strip away your odors ... scattering them
distant and aimless beyond the ocean's breadth.

Young men——your palms still reek
of manila rope,
your frayed dungarees remain pungent
with paint and pitch.

It's as though an endless manila rope
had been coiled into your callused hands.
It's as though you'd stowed your dungarees
in casks of pitch and paint.

Sons of the windjammer——young men!
Day in and day out your palms, your pants,
glow with the scents
of new manila rope, of pitch, of paint.

CRUISE DUTY CHART*

Names of young seamen,
refreshing as a view of night skies in June:
　　　Hoshide.
　　　Tsukihara.
　　　Katsura.

Tsukihara climbs to the compass bridge.
Katsura stands under the ship's bell.
Their silhouettes blend with the rigging

to make the deck seem deserted.
Only our four pagoda–like
full sails
cast twisted shadows over broadsides
running over deep swells
... moments from the afternoon watch.

Hoshide crouches in the well deck
sneaking a butt.

SLOW SAILING DAY*

A white bird
floats on our bubbling wake.
It bobs slowly, ever so slowly.

Suddenly it flies
high over our masts
and flaps off shrieking toward the sun.
It heads for who knows where.

Soon afterward,
another like it bobs on the identical spot,
rising and falling gently, ever so gently.

Drawing in the log line,
young fellows at the stern
read our velocity:
"One ... Two,
Three ... Four,
. . . .
. . . ."
I feel sure, however,
that it's the same bird.

DAYTIME SEA

Such a dazzling day.
Time to hear wondrous songs on the sea.
Time when mermaids rise from waves
to cut past sailors
who drowse against the rigging.

Waves dart quickly.
Waves sport fins and tails.
Waves swim. ·

What swims is a mermaid!
She rides the waves.
She scampers instantly into distance.

In the blink of an eye,
sea's colors change
as though day has ended and dawn has come.
Scores of shadows sprout from waves.

Five minutes till sundown*

Our training ship sails
from off Uracas Island
toward Balintang Channel.
Southeastern trades blow daily at a set velocity.
They raise swells of identical height
on an ocean burning like magnesium.
Seeing neither ship nor landfall
for an entire month
makes us feel we're stripping pages
from a dreary blue calendar.
Morning   sun rises from the stern.
Evening   sun lies on the horizon under our bow.
Then the young fellow on leeside watch
dashes past my cabin crying:
     Five minutes till sundown!
     Five minutes till sundown!
Sailors fold up the windsail,
secure portholes and hatches.
Our lights come on.
Time for a pleasant evening at sea.

On seas not far south of where we sailed——
our foes.
I now hear
those very words that the world's radios and newspapers
send to hostile East Asian lands
     that long made the sun their own;
I hear in its plaintive sense the shout:
     Five minutes till sundown!
     Five minutes till sundown!

At sea*

When I finish supper,
I lug a deck chair and small table to the hatchway

sandwiched between middeck cabins.
Basking in trade winds that slip through the hatchway,
I talk with the young Third Mate.

How gorgeous the sunsets at sea!
Like stands of fir on an extensive plain,
wondrous cirrus clouds glow in pink tiers on the horizon,
change shape before you're aware of it.
Then, when sea spreads out blue at dusk,
they abruptly vanish.
The Third Mate stands up, stating adamantly,
      "Say, it's dark already.
      'Bout time for my watch."

We hadn't finished talking about
back home, families, parents, siblings,
voyages to ports in Australia, India, China,
visions of younger days.
Or present dreams for the future
including the marriage
for which he so longed.

I'll never forget his telling me
about that girl behind white *shôji*
      in a rainy town on the Inland Sea.
She waits calmly for him to come back home.
Burning as fervently as the Southern Cross,
      just then beginning to glitter beyond the waves,
the eyes of that unaffected young man
riveted on mine....

MEMORIES OF MASTS*

Four masts too thick to reach around
stretch from floor to ceiling on lower decks
and tower well over a hundred feet into sky.

Foremast	before the crew's quarters.
Mainmast	through the center of the midshipmen's hall.
Mizzenmast	between the officers' head and bath.
Jiggermast	through the stern workshop.

During leisurely breaks each day,
men gather round the various masts.
Sitting by the foremast, I heard an old salt

tell of a galley hand buried at sea off South America.
Under the swaying oil lamp on the mainmast,
those unable to sleep talked deep into the night of home.
I went to the head by the mizzenmast any number of times.
Oh, yes, the jiggermast.
That's where when it rains tranquil sail repairs begin.

On stormy nights
all four masts became virtual antennae
that sent my bunk the groans of rigging or tackle.
Mingled with them——the wind–scattered shouts
of frantic lads on high yards.

NEWS OF RAIN*

More than fifty days under sail
on our sultry cruise through southern seas.
The wireless
receives news of rain in Japan.
That dredges up reveries
from far beyond the sea
that I so weary of staring at day after day ...
reveries of my tiny yard at home:
——The stimulating patter of summer rain
falling on my palm–sized pond.
——The charm of our scant plants,
those blue flags, lilies, and morning glories,
all stretching tall under the drench of rain.
I wonder how they'll bloom this year.
I visualize my wife shouldering her parasol each morning,
likely chatting with Mother by the fence.
As I think such thoughts,
fantasy waves
break high beyond the spray
where porpoise leap.

SEA TRAVELERS

Porpoise break water on the windless sea,
their numbers increasing as I watch.
Swimming playfully, they surface then plunge
round our sluggish headway.

I lean against the boom. If I look off the bow,

I see them dive deep, then rise to the surface.
Sometimes they glance up at me
with the look of a traveler met on the road.

I return to my cabin and try to nap.
Outside my porthole——sounds of breathing, sounds of fins.
Like stirrings in an adjacent room at an inn,
they keep me from sleep.

DOLPHINS' VISIT

The sea—like peering into a blue mirror—
transparent to the bottom of our hull.

Two dolphins visit.

They turn green, then glow yellow
like twisted neon tubes.

Someone on the railing says,

"That's 'cause they change color in the warmth."
"No. I bet the light causes it."

Burning like phosphorous,
the dolphins suddenly dive deep into sea.

CATCHING BONITO*

Longitude   131° east.
Latitude   18° north.
Near sundown, all sails aslant,
our ship runs at eight knots
before rising southeasterlies.
Young men not on watch cluster astride the bowsprit.
There they cast bonito lures.
Looking at the sea they cry,
   There they are!
   There!
Countless deep mauve shadows braiding golden waves
overtake us with blinding speed.
Sometimes a shadow leaps through foam.
Sometimes we catch one.
Shuddering sharply,
its mauve transforms to lead.

LIFEBOAT DRILL*

Scurrying through the ship, the leeward watch calls out,
    "All hands on deck!
    To your lifeboat stations!"
Chilling winds blow, swells rise ponderously.
Wednesday morning——sea and skies so blue they look dyed.

I hurriedly don my coat,
take my life jacket from the rack, tie it on.
I put on shoes, my cap, grab a blanket,
scurry off through the officers' hatch to the afterdeck.
Mine is boat No. 5 in the stern.

Some hold the cork fenders.
Some come armed with rifles and bayonets.
Some carry semaphore flags, the boat compass, lamps.
Some shoulder tins of sea biscuits.
Falling in, the crew awaits the captain's command.

    "Boat No. 5——Two officers, seven midshipmen,
        seven seamen, one passenger.
    Lower away!"
Like locusts we bound over the rail into the boat.
Davits swing out——pulleys sing——
    lifelines slide through palms.
All six boats glide down as one.

Swells support us gently.
Oaring furiously for twenty minutes,
we move like runaway children from the ship.
Once we set the mast, hoist flag and triangular sail,
we join the column running abeam our distant ship.

Giant waves shake and drop us.
I stretch out my hand and smack one.
I lean back on my seat and gaze at far–off clouds.
What boundless joy!
At this moment, I'm more intimate with the Pacific than anyone.

Spray constantly dashes our brows.
Our boat sinks deserted into the abyss.
Ah, relentless fantasies
of shipwreck——being adrift——landing
    on an uninhabited isle!
At this moment, I'm more engrossed
    in youthful adventure than anyone. •

I gaze at our steady–sailing four–masted barque,
our stout, reliable ship,
almost as though gazing at myself.
Ah, waves screen her sides,
my porthole, too.

MORNING WATCH*

Early morning, all hands still deep in sleep.
Down from the poop deck, the leeside watch on his rounds
knocks at each officer's middeck cabin:
"Second Mate! Fifteen minutes till all hands on deck."
"Third Mate! Fifteen minutes till all hands on deck."
"Doctor! Fifteen minutes till all hands on deck."

Soon he descends to the lower deck,
pounds on my door,
dashes off toward the midshipmen's forward quarters.
I hear his voice and footsteps in my slumber,
then doze off to enjoy the rest of my dream.
I'm thinking, Ah, this morning it's Midshipman "X."

He promptly comes by again.
This time, with urgency and a fairly loud cry,
he announces it's only five minutes till we hit the deck.
Lie–abed that I am, I spring from my bunk,
slip on some clothes, dash up on deck,
eyes half shut till sea wind wakens them.

Sometimes we're roused from sleep beastly early.
I glance then at my porthole in singular protest
and find that night has painted it shut.
Shaking my drowsy head I ask myself,
Has the morning watch misread his clock?
Is this because of a shift in ship's time?

I drag myself out and climb the companionway.
Once on deck, I see immediately why we're up so early.
Such mornings are sure to be stormy——
rain soaks the shadowed deck, licks the rigging,
wets the helm, drips from sails,
from the rain gear of young men at work.

The sea dim and choppy,
thunderclaps near the invisible horizon.
Eyes bloodshot, young men raise their hands

in greeting with that odd, "*Yo!*" "*Yo!*"
They then file one after the other past the officers, past me,
and muster opposite the mainmast.

No leaves scattered over the sea,
yet——oh, that desolate morning watch!
Inspection done, I waste no time
sprinting straight for the middeck head.
The lampman comes by dripping wet,
blows out the lamp, leaves.

Apples*

Time already for dessert.
Before taking his place at table,
the watch officer down from the spar deck
never fails to report,
　　"Our course——southwest by west.
　　Winds shifting now.
　　We're doing around six knots."
The captain takes note and responds,
　　"Well done."
Sunset clouds pitch in the portholes behind them.
All at table
silently pick up their knives.

Plates go *clinkety–clinkety.*
Fourteen apples halved.
For an instant, air thickens with a heavily sweet–sour scent.
Air thickens with the chokingly heavy sweet–sour scent
of grass,
of trees,
of land.

Sea Impression

Thirty days out of Japan
yet my porthole somehow remains securely shut.
That below–deck porthole the Captain sternly told me,
　　Never open it!
wouldn't budge. Given the summer heat
　　of 18° north latitude,
I just get more and more seasick.

One day I concentrate every ounce of strength

and wrench it open,
painfully skinning my knuckles....
Once open, I spit at the trade winds blowing in
and harshly curse the sea.

Then, a sudden broadside roar.
No sooner does a blanched blue fellow peek in
than he soundly whacks my cheeks,
soaking me from head to toe.
Bunk and writing table drenched as well with stinking brine.

Into my astonished ears
comes this gent's faraway chortle.
Joining in gleefully,
sounds of countless thrashing fins.
Even the belly of our heavy–heeling ship shakes with mirth.

WATCHING A WHALE

I saw a whale in the Pacific.
It swam boldly through swells off port,
morning sun tinting its ashen back.
Soon after we'd been alerted,
it dove.

After a bit, it surfaced leisurely
on the opposite side of the ship.
Excitedly we went to the starboard.
Once again we saw it
sweep up its tail and dive.

No sooner had it disappeared
than it re–surfaced near our port side,
so we returned to port.
For some reason, it suddenly dove again
and surfaced off starboard.

It dived and surfaced again and again,
each time raising a mighty spray.
Sea resounding like a cannon,
we scattered over the deck
before a solid wall of brine.

Finally we broke into laughter.
Both the baffling behavior of this mastodon,
survivor of the Deep,

and the enormous and bottomless depths
     of the dreamy sea delighted us.
We held our bellies and roared.

ISLAND*

When that tiny island came into view,
a microscopic drop on the horizon ahead,
you knew all hands would gape at it.
Those not on watch scurried topside with a clamor
and gathered in the bow.
Those on watch stared
from their posts:
the helmsman holding the helm fast;
the officer checking the compass;
both the young fellow tugging at braces
and the seaman who rings the ship's bell;
even the Captain, who'd stepped out of the chart room ...
all stood nailed to the deck, gaping.

No more than a pile of rocks
on which nobody lived——no trace even of a bird.
Something pale green did, however,
sprout from the islet's sharp crown.
Like a lonely traveler the tiny drop approached
from three points off starboard.
Once it lay directly off our starboard beam,
even those who fussed about the island fell silent.
The entire ship quieted to a hush.
Only waves murmured against our sides.
Only wind hummed through sails.
Hums and murmurs merged
with the crash of waves on rocks.
We caught a whiff of green–scented wind.

Visible for some two hours,
the island gradually faded off our stern.
Soon only a faint dot,
it melted into sea.
Those who had come to watch dispersed
and returned to their tasks.
Now and then someone gazed through binoculars,
as though he'd just thought of something,
but quickly looked away, resigned.

Then before we knew it ... twilight.

When night enveloped our ship,
the sailors felt in high spirits.
Whether at table or in their bunks,
carefree that evening till taps.
An island no bigger than a millet grain,
on which nothing lived, not even a bird,
had released a whiff of chlorophyll
into the minds of these mariners who for a month had reeked
    of sea breezes and brine.

Reckoning the Compasses*

I learned about the four compasses on board——
the standard compass,
the steering compass,
the boat compass,
the gyrocompass.
Let me tell you about them.

The standard compass on the bridge
is the general manager of all on board.
Next, the one that determines our course
stands before the helm.

The third, as its name suggests,
will be transferred to the lifeboats.
Fated for use in disaster,
this compass, is, as a rule, stored in the hold.

Well, the last one's below deck,
next to the engine room:
the incomparably precise master of them all,
an electric spinning top——the gyrocompass.

No, wait. I forgot the fifth compass,
that odd one in the captain's cabin.
It's on the ceiling directly above his bunk,
a companion the master can talk to
as—stretched out in bed—he puffs a cigarette.
Even its name is disarming   the *telltale compass*.
Even its name disarms   *telltale compass*.

CAPSTAN*

Sailors turn a halyard
on the capstan,
then push round and round.
    Heave around! ... Heave around!

Brandishing his capstan bar,
one cracks
the head of a shark
just hauled in.

Half crouching
on the capstan,
the salty old boatswain
chants again today:

    Capstan!
    Way back when,
    some imported butts
    bore your name!

SWALLOWS OF AMOY*

Swallows flit back and forth
under second–floor balconies.
As they skim—now over seamen's shoulder straps,
now over marines' caps—
I suddenly find myself longing for home.
Swallows abruptly flutter into the crowd.
One Chinese gentleman, cane in hand,
strides leisurely over them.

BREEZES FROM LAND——FROM SEA*

Ten days at anchor.
Each morning I open my porthole
and land breeze slips in
with a cheery, "Mornin'!"

Land breeze comes to visit my waking.
She's laden with the aromas of vegetables and fruit,
like a Chinese girl returning from market,
shopping basket on her arm. •

Spending time with me on board,
walking all day with me through port,
returning with me at sundown to the ship,
land breeze acts the sprightly wife.

It's good–bye now to her, as well.
Listen! The anchor winch silent now.
Our ship turns her bow.
The stern already tugs its whitish wake.

The coast fades into distance bit by bit
and you also quickly pale.
Farewell Amoy! Ku–lang Hsü Island! Lighthouse!
So–long, breezes from land!

We soon reach the gateway to the East China Sea.
Time now for our ship to pitch.
Indeed, time for swells to peer
into below–deck cabins.

I descend the companionway
and secure my porthole.
You no longer visit my cabin.
Now I'm with breezes from sea.

ABOVE OUR VILLAGE*

I hear summer has come to the foothills.
In this village atop a high mountain,
however,
cherry blossoms are not quite ready to fall.

And yet ...
in higher hills above our village,
wild cherry trees still bloom.

Amazingly, the snow there
continues to shimmer sporadically in hollows
among the groves.
Though sun shines fierce, as you'd expect,
breezes remain slightly chilled.
Somewhere the muted songs of spring birds.

Are the children thirsty?
Now and then they scurry out to dig up white chunks.
The hard snow
painfully sets their teeth.

NOBUO WEATHER——LAMENT FOR

TSUMURA NOBUO*

When you asked me to go somewhere with you,
we sometimes ran into downpours.
Sometimes the train broke down.
The friend we went to visit was out.
The coffee shop closed.

Wringing out drenched clothing
in a beech grove at Sengataki,
I lit into you.
Looking at the skies you sighed deeply
and roared, *Luckless! Oh, luckless!*

When it's rotten weather
I tell my wife,
"Say, it's Nobuo weather again."
Then your footsteps approach
as though invited by my remark.

A cheerfully carefree misstep
always stood waiting beyond your boyish self,
your boyish ways.

Crape myrtles radiant this midsummer noon!
But chilly winds already.
Frigid autumn winds come the way we parted——
far too soon.

HELMSMAN OF THE WORLD*

I wheel the helm
but the bow does not move.
The sky, the sea, the world
move round and round our mast. ·

That's why the helm I grasp
is not the ship's helm.
It's the helm of the ocean.
It's the helm that steers the endless sea.

That's why I'm neither just a helmsman
nor even the helmsman of this craft.
I'm helmsman of the world,
a helmsman steering the wide world.

A young Japanese seaman,
today as usual I stand on the bridge.
I steer the Pacific with all my might.
I steer the world.

WINTER DREAMS*

Snow heaps up.
By morning the trails have disappeared.
Today's trails begin
over yesterday's.

Day by day
new trails get thinner and higher
till in February snow packs hard.
Paths appear where there were none.

Then sleds and children dash freely
over snow.

When spring comes
snow begins to melt.
Akebi vines and branch tips
stick out
from under straw boots.

Suddenly, as though startled from dreams,
people quickly find
they were walking the skies
of treetops and dales.

JAPAN'S CONSCIENCE*

This is the hamlet of Iwanezawa
in Dewa Province, the Gassan foothills.

Here, years begin and end in blizzards.

That morning at our little mountain school,
we held a ceremony for returning the Imperial portrait.
After the rite, I joined the single file of children
descending the mountain along the cliff–side path.

Fresh spring skies stretched uncommonly clear,
but icy mountain air blew up from the valley
to redden children's plump cheeks.
Legs in *monpé* trampled the snow with straw boots
that sought firm footing.
I bent branches along the way,
poked their ends into the snow,
and said to each,
> *Japan's sacred conscience passes.*
> *Keep out of its way awhile.*
Some branches sprang vigorously back.
I relentlessly broke them off
even as I thought of the green buds
they would have sprouted in spring.

The cry, *Obeisance!*
from one end of our file.
I caught a brief glimpse of our constable
on the steep path up the hill where the school stands.
Soon three or four people
hurried past our deep bows.
Lifting my eyes,
I looked off after them.
Wrapped securely in oilcloth, the Imperial portrait
descended the mountain on our principal's back.
In no time, the group disappeared
'round a bend in the path.

Everything happened so quickly.
Beyond doubt, however, I'd sensed another being
whose profoundly determined yet calm footsteps
joined those that had just passed by.
> When the nation suffers,
> even His Majesty goes down the mountain on foot.

Powdery snow fell silently
from pale green skies.

WILD CHERRIES

Snow begins melting
and paths sink lower by the day.
Cherry branches that once nearly brushed our foreheads
move higher and higher.
Gazing through those branch nets,
skies seem tinged with verdure.
Oh, soon it'll be spring.
When that radiant season comes,
apricots and plums bloom together
to make my heart leap.

One day, however,
an old mountain woman shared gloomy news:
"No cherry blossoms in the mountains this year," she said.
"Bullfinches came from the foothills
and pecked out every last bud."

SPRING NIGHT

At a small public school in the hills,
a youth out of college
and a teacher his age
climbed a cherry tree and talked
late into the spring night.

No one had the slightest idea that evening
if stars glittered or if the moon shone ...
or why the two had climbed the tree
and what they talked about
up there.

Maybe they'd climbed to their high perches after finding that,
however much they strolled the tiny schoolyard,
mere ground could no longer support
their thoughts and dreams.
Perhaps, as they leaned against forked branches
listening to the school clock strike one,
their sentiments registered powerfully
on starry skies.

In the drama of human life,
after all,
youth is a play within a play.

THEMES

Snow steals the sun
from children.
Snow steals places to play
from children.
Snow steals
colors and shapes of mountains and rocks, trees and grass
from children.
Snow steals bird songs
from children.

Just how do you suppose children survive
through each positively ashen and monotonous half a year,
with no sunlight, no sound, no color?

I have the children write themes in class.
Incessantly licking their stubby pencils,
every last child conscientiously records only that:
> *I wake up in the morning.*
> *I eat my meals.*
> *I go to bed at night.*

I feel as though powdery snow on mountains wrapped in wind
had swirled up from these pathetic blank pages
and fiercely flogged my brow.

MOUNTAIN SCHOOL

Every morning,
the children
dash over narrow snow paths.
They run along the steep lane below the grove
and gather from valleys, from foothills far and near,
at this shack of a school.

At dusk,
the children
retrace their steps
and vanish through swirling snow.

Little raccoons,
little foxes,
little rabbits and little squirrels,
little monkeys and boars and badgers,

little mountain goats and little wolves.
They push——they tumble,
they brawl——they bite——they scratch,
though in the classroom they're well behaved and still.

Well, one day
when the teacher in that mountain school
told them the Emperor's latest admonition,
little raccoons bowed their heads.
Little foxes bowed their heads.
Little rabbits and little squirrels bowed their heads.
Little boars, mountain goats, monkeys, badgers——
all the children bowed their heads.
Round teardrops even ran from the eyes
of one small wolf.

TRACKS

A clear morning.
We discover animal tracks.
The tracks cut across a sled path
and skitter to the hilltop
over snow's glare.

Four or five children on their way to school
stop and talk about the tracks.
    "Could be a fox."
    "Maybe a raccoon."
    "How about catching it?"
    "Let's track 'm down."
    "He's sure to be
    where the tracks end."

I told them,
    "The tracks likely disappear
    somewhere.
    There you'll find
    nothing."
The children looked around——
mountains on every side.
Every last child frowned.

POETS' FRIENDS

No friend
if he hasn't been defeated.
No ally
if he hasn't been deceived.

Reject those and the standards of those
who get ahead by elbowing others aside!

Restless legs——rooted to the spot.
Vagabond thirsts.
Humiliations you can't redress.

Those crestfallen glooms never identified
in midnight thoughts,
in wind–driven rain,
in the heart of the dark.

As allies, we poets have only
vague entreaties,
soundless sobs.

VISIONS OF FLOWERS*

Butterbur stalks
may already be smiling
through the soil.
Throngs of Amur Adonis buds
may already be swelling.
Perhaps soon–to–bloom *katakago* and *amefuri* sprouts,
quick to decorate the thawing hills,
have already begun to stir.
Still buried deep beneath the snow, however,
the eye cannot yet reach a one of them.
Nevertheless, we tramp over visions of flowers
on this soft–sunshiny early spring morning.
How buoyant my straw boots.
How filled with sparkle
my feelings!

MOUNTAIN CRONE*

Deep in the range, the *Tom–tom* bird
beats his drum——*tom–tom—tom–tom.*

There's the *Waa–waa* bird, too,
mimicking people with its *waa–waa*.
Both the *Tom–tom* bird and *Waa–waa* bird
cast tiers of shadows in cedar woods
that echo their songs.
Since cliffs rise sheer,
loneliness and sorrow fill the breast.

Ah, once a solitary pretty girl at the height of youth
worked alone on a field deep in the hills,
her hair ungroomed, no adornments.
Despite working hard at cutting brushwood
or picking mulberries, she never got ahead.
Her companions the *Tom–tom* bird, the *Waa–waa* bird,
she slaved day after day, morning to night.
Then one day she aged like a toad.
That's what the mountain crone said.

EVEN IN THE MOUNTAINOUS NORTH

It's June,
so even in our mountainous north country
plum trees shed white blossoms
and this refreshing season comes.

Walking the trail
is like being at home——not cold.
Sitting still in the house,
as refreshing as a rest in the grove.

Open the *shôji* doors
and breezes slip in from far–off hills——
everything melting cheerfully
into wind:
rustlings from nearby woods,
the drift of clouds,
cuckoo cries,
the glitter of freshly snow–free peaks.
Filling our lungs
with the landscape's expansive air,
hearts and bodies stretch mightily
like plants.

LIVING ALONE*

Walking half the day over snowy mountain trails,
I reach home at twilight.
Snow shadows chill even my mind.

Wearily I cross my legs by the *irori*,
get the wood smoking, warm my hands and feet,
hang a kettle on the spit, heat some water.

In those moments before my tea is ready,
I bend over to light a cigarette.
Suddenly I feel the urge to turn and talk to someone.
I say nothing when I realize I'm alone.

I guess it dropped from my clothing,
that lump of snow
melting now by the hearth.

HIGH VILLAGE*

I live in a village high on a mountaintop.
Sun rises each morning
from low, snow–decked hills
beyond the plain spread below
and shines from under my dream–hungry bed.
Like gasps, birds struggle one by one,
riding updrafts from the deep dell
toward the eaves of my lodge.
I look always at their backs,
never up at their breasts.

Since living in this high village,
day after day ... I've been watching
my future pale.

FATE (i)

Something that resembles a potato eye
tumbles from
the plowed–up earth.
In this region they call it a *hodo*.
When its roots ravel deep through soil,
something appears that endlessly intertwines,
like the end of a skinny yam.
This they call a *tokoro*. ·

Both the shape and the taste of the *hodo*
suggest a potato.
The *tokoro* tastes vaguely
like the sweet potato it favors.
What people here call *hodo* or *tokoro*, however,
they never plant in cultivated fields.
These always grow in rugged natural environments,
in uncultivated soil.

Farmers who carve stony fields from hillsides
chafe their brows today as well on the steep slope
as they brandish their picks the whole day through.
Occasionally, they strike their fate,
snatch it up, heave it.

CHORUS*

When teacher
plays the harmonium,
big and little birds
of scarlet,
blue,
or gold
flap their wings
from the keys.
They begin flying
round and round
over our heads.

High up in the classroom,
a broken pane of glass.
Before long, the birds
flee through it
into distant skies.

EARLY ON A MORNING IN SPRING

During the long winter,
snow so deep over mountain fields and paddies
we can no longer walk.

Rabbit tracks scatter
and vanish beyond the sky.
Winds rushing by
often sketch
then erase puzzling pictures

on pathless ridges
or on the valley floor.

Spring brings
mornings with crusted snow,
so we can walk wherever we want.

The instant birds set their minds to it,
they can flap through unknown time and space.
Like them,
we now can cut across fields
and head straight for our goal.
In less than half the time it takes on the path,
we can scamper early in the morning
through rose–tinted dreams
calling *Hi!* to friends.

Verdant classroom*

Climbing the slope,
we find deep in the oak grove
a classroom the seasons built.

A mosaic of dead leaves for flooring,
stacks of green leaves for siding.
Bent and braided branches frame both ceiling
and windows made from sky's clear panes.

Clouds glisten white beyond those panes.
Breezes sparkle through the room.

Children bring their notebooks and pencils,
duck under *akebi* vines,
trample over the *hitorishizuka,*
and gather here again today.

When they study arithmetic in this place,
their numbers become cuckoos or *uguisu,*
birds that turn into plus or minus signs
as they frolic in the rustling breeze.

Tranquil festival*

On a day when snow falls,
that hamlet on the valley floor
holds a tranquil festival. •

One hears
no drums,
sees no festive lanterns——
only the sounds of mortars
in homes.

Sons brandish massive pestles.
Daughters tear off pieces of *mochi*
and offer them
to the mountain spirit's little shrine.

Shouldering steep cliffs,
the spirit dwells
in heaped–up snow.
He dwells silently,
breathless
in twilight's pale blue.

MR. MOON*

When icicles hang from eaves
and people have no work in the fields,
a fellow nicknamed "Mr. Moon"
comes over the narrow snow path along the dale
to call.

"G' Evenin'."
"G' Evenin'."
He goes from hearth to hearth,
leisurely gossiping with people in every home.

Like his name,
Mr. Moon has a round and smiling face.
Like the moon,
he loves coming by at night.

AGES BACK IT SEEMS

Walking along the path
one evening during a snowfall,
I suddenly felt something
brush against my brow.

I looked up.

A cherry tree branch.
My! Could that much snow already
have heaped up?
Could snow already be piled
so deep?
Could the path so soon become this high?

I recall having glanced
at this very limb last spring.
Looking through its blossoms
into pale blue skies,
I recall that dazzling dream
as though it happened ages back.

WHITE PICTURES*

I asked the class to paint pictures
titled "Spring."
The pupils mixed their own colors,
but sat bewildered——nothing with color to paint.

Just   mountain after white mountain.
Just   undulating white fields.
Only   branch tips in sparse groves
piercing snow here and there
through faint India ink shadows.

I colored one child's sky a light cobalt.
Then, by mistake,
plop——a yellow blur
between still–damp branches.

I apologized at once for being careless,
but all rather enjoyed my mistake.
"Hey! A witch hazel's bloomed!" they said.
The children were thrilled.

NORTH COUNTRY

Whenever a roof–bleached train,
windows misted,
slid like an amazing chain of gloom
into the early winter station,
I thought,

——Oh, that much snow has fallen already in the North.

Now I live in the north country.
Once it's winter,
whenever—during the idle moments of a life
　　shut in by icicles and swirling snow—
I hear a far–off train whistle,
I think,
——The snow those trains hauled in then was from here.

I recall, as well,
the sun–starved eyes
of travelers who detrained on city platforms.
I wonder now if I, too,
have such eyes.

WITCH HAZELS*

Witch hazels blooming! they cried.
The children picked some for me
——light yellow and grainy flowers
difficult to identify.

Witch hazels blooming! they cried.
The children picked some for me
——flowers hardly flowers,
blooms that favor tiny droplets.

Walking through chilled twilight snow, the children cried out
from deep in sparse groves where mountain winds wail:
Witch hazels blooming! They picked some for me.

FOX*

They say no fox will dip its tail in water.
Even if you assume he cuts hurriedly across a stream
pursued by hunters or a bear,
people say he skillfully manipulates that thickly–furred tail
so no drop of water ever wets it.

I nevertheless once saw with my own eyes
a fox gingerly crossing some rapids.
The moment before touching the opposite shore
(what bad luck could have bewitched him?)

he dangled his tail in the stream.

He leapt up instantly as though attacked
and at full speed took cover in evening mist.
To my surprise, I momentarily caught sight of him
scampering off beyond the mist. He looked drenched with regret.
Oh, how he writhed with it.

THOSE PEOPLE*

In the bustling towns and cities of southern regions,
in those warmer places where I once lived,
I met and became friendly with
several people.

Using clumsy childish expressions,
those people addressed me in thick brogues strange to my ear.
If I asked them to repeat, they blushed like little boys
and became unresponsive, as though piqued.
Those people visited me unexpectedly——no goal in mind.
They sat endlessly still,
detached, apparently cheerless.

They were born in the north country,
so faint shimmers of snow
seemed always to trail them.

Yet, once in their native village,
I found in a single winter around their hearths
quite frank hearts and radiant lives,
faces and conversation as vibrant as vegetation.

Where do you suppose they are——those people?
I wish you'd return, all you wandering, lonely shadows!
I hear spring has come even in your North.
The glare of distant ranges dazzling,
both *katakago* and *amefuri* bloom now
in thawing fields and dales.

GROSBEAK*

Obanazawa,
Mizusawa,
Tsukiyamazawa——
all in the Dewa foothills of Michinoku.

Cutting through empty skies, over brightly cloudless reeds,
a bird sings its way
from hamlet to hamlet.
"What kind of bird is that?"
"A grosbeak.
Say, listen——you can hear it, can't you?
It sings,
Tsuki——*hoshi*——*hi*."

LOVELY NOTION*

Nothing is more strikingly lovely
than the notion
that stars shine in daytime skies
the way they sparkle at night.

Living on a mountain,
that idea somehow entrances me from time to time.
I then go deep into the hills
and peer intently through the surface of the pond.

Indeed,
I begin then to see glimmers of countless stars
coming from deep in the pond
where sun had silently set.

RAINY DAY

The janitor shakes the clapper bell
at school on a rainy day:
Clangalang ——clangalang.
The janitor rings the school bell.

Bell claps
clang urgently down the hallway.
Walls begin to sing.
Ceilings sing.

The huge gym floor, the beams,
the many windows
sing out:
Clangalang ——clangalang.
Everything starts to sing.

Even children at play
sing with the bell claps.

They sing:
> *Clangalang —clangalang.*
First graders sing.
Second graders sing.
Third and fourth graders,
and the bigger children, too, begin to sing:
> *Clangalang —clangalang.*
They gather quickly in their classrooms then.

When the last clap dies,
the whole school falls suddenly still.
Children
sit nonchalantly at their desks.

Teachers tread the corridor
through the hush.

SAILING DOLL*

Once when I took a cruise
on a training barque,
a female acquaintance
gave me a cute Western doll.

I spent fifty days on the high seas
living with that doll.
When I became bored and anxious to talk with someone,
I laid her out on my bunk
and left the cabin.

When the ship's bell under the crojik sail
tingalings six bells,
stewards bustle about serving our afternoon snack.

Returning to my quarters,
I find a dish of sweets and a teacup on the table.
The doll sits properly
in a chair facing mine.
(Whenever did she get out of bed?)

Putting her in my bag,
I safely set foot on land.
Whatever happened to her after that?

In defeat,
Japan's desertion of the seas
makes this yarn a relic.

BIRDS (ii)

Each time I wend through stands of cedar
down the steep path
to the valley's deep hamlet,
I hear vague voices calling me——
a single crow–like caw
or a surprising imitation of a turtle dove.
The voices come from houses scattered along cliff's edge,
from branch gaps filtering sunlight,
from far–off mountain pleats straddling streams.

I notice that
several mountain girls in my class
hide in the grass or behind trees ...
waiting eagerly for me to pass.

If I pretend not to notice their calls,
they deftly thread the thicket in pursuit.
If I stop and gaze in their direction,
they hold their breath and promptly hush.

If I dash about trying to find them, however,
they merge silently
into whispering water or rustling wind.

Oh, how these strange mountain lasses toy with me!
Far from the capital now,
I'm lonesome in this land of endless peaks.
Yet if on an autumn afternoon I stroll bored through the grove,
these phantom–like bird calls hug me.

BLUE CHALKBOARD

Even if we can't buy pencils,
we can write with our fingers, so it's okay.
Even if we don't have notebooks,
we can write on the sky, so it's okay.

Both math tables and words in our readers,
both sketches and essays——
we do everything in the air with our fingers.

Till the day we can buy
pencils, notebooks, and the like,
let's calmly face sky's slate
and do our studies with fingers of chalk. •

The sky's slate is roomy and fun to write on.
Even with every child in Japan writing,
we could never fill it up.

Day in and day out, clouds whitely
wipe it clean for us.

TWILIGHT CLOUDS

Because it's fall,
skies turn
clearer than clear.

Lumpy clouds line up
and march off
through high and faraway places.

They're like
still lifes,
like flocks of gentle sheep
disappearing beyond fields
that gleam in pink.

I hear somewhere a hymn
praising Christ.

Distant skies mirrored,
moreover,
even on water in the glass I hold.

As I drink from the glass,
twilight clouds march through my belly
in a hush.

WEIGHTY BAGGAGE

Look at the people packing every station,
waiting ever so long for the train,
their weighty, bulky baggage huddled on the platform.

They drearily blow cigarette smoke over their bags.
They talk vacantly to one another across their bags.
Obscured by their bags, they silently
    stuff their mouths with rice balls.
Lying on their bags, they sleep like stones. •

Perhaps remembering something, someone
    impulsively opens his suitcase,
then restlessly closes it.
Each piece of luggage blots up
    its owner's patience and concerns.
While the bags look increasingly bloated,
passengers' faces pale with strain and fatigue
that give them a bulky and dejected look.

Ah, yes, this luggage bears weightily——
even on the mind of one observing the scene.

Nobody knows when
each of these countless bags
will be hauled to where it should be.
Only when every one rests calmly in its proper place
will our Fatherland
echo with substantial sighs.
Stretching together, we'll pound each other's
    stiff shoulders then.

MOUNTAIN VILLAGE*

Atop this high mountain,
there's a village,
a post office,
even a store
selling things like clocks and spectacles.

On the playground
I hear children singing:
"*Dedepô*——doves cooing
deep in the cedar grove."

Mornings,
clouds come in by the window
and float through the house.
The old man who runs the spectacle shop
then hurriedly starts wiping
each pair of glasses clean.

PART III

POETRY PUBLISHED BETWEEN

1947 and 1948

昭和二十二年に発表された詩

MAGICAL COUNTRY*

Late each year,
bunches of grapes cover entire expanses of rock.
Here and there deep in the range,
akebi fruit hang heavy.
Hidden in thickets on steep ravines
and in remote beech woods, dusky even in daylight,
button mushroom coronas flare with rainbows.
Also *shimeji*——*maitake*——*yamadori*
and countless other mushrooms blanket the roots of trees.

Nature's cornucopia,
hidden far beyond sheer cliffs and rocky screens,
lies in a magical country no outsider has laid eyes on——
a place known only
to mountain family heads.

When autumn comes,
house heads secretly visit their family hunting grounds.
They stride through clouds, slip through mist,
fill their shoulder baskets,
and, under stars in the dead of night,
go back home.

No house head shares this confidential knowledge.
Only when the patriarch nears life's end
does he at last reveal the secret to his son.
His son, in turn, passes the secret to the grandson.
From generation to generation, so long as they live in these hills,
only the house head knows.

LIVING IN REMOTE MOUNTAINS

Trees flourish on the inclines of untraveled gorges.
Spring adorns them with artless flowers.

In fall they ripen tiny rounded fruit.
Their leaves redden as furious as fire
through those moments before winter.
Soon they're buried under snow.
The all–out performances,
and the painfully mute spirits
of those nameless, far–off mountain trees,
pervade my mind these days.

How abruptly sun sets
on a mountain trail!
As I walk, skies suddenly darken.
Shadows snuggling together from pleats in the inclines
envelop me, dissolve the hamlet,
shudder my spine with chills.
Ah, lonely dusk....
Imagining that I can still see,
my eyes blur dreamily
like a bird's.

MOTHER'S UMBRELLA*

Mother,
it's twenty days
since you passed on.
Autumn rains fall drearily
in this hillside hamlet.

To make a living,
I go out through the rain
under this tiny umbrella
you left as a memento.

Once you aged,
you never left the house
without this black–silk granny umbrella.
You brought it all the way to this lonely
    northern mountain country,
raising it on your journey to the next world.

This short–handled
Western bumbershoot
kept in its hand–crafted cover
brings to mind a girl's parasol. •

Holding it,
no rain falls on my head or shoulders.
I feel I'm still with you.

Besides, since days long past
when I was still a child and you were young,
till you became a grandmother passing your days serenely,
your devotion constantly warmed us.
Now, as though enveloped in the shadows of that love,
my heart warms pitifully
and throbs with indulgent memories.

Mother,
from under this tiny umbrella, I gaze now
at these icy passing showers that pelt the real world.
I gaze at fall foliage on faraway rain–blurred hills.

THOUGHTS ABOUT SNOW*

People in this mountain village complain
that they no sooner think of the snow,
so soon to come again this year,
than it already massively oppresses their minds.

Despite having spent only a single winter in these hills,
when I think back on those endlessly endless dusk–like days,
I keenly sense these people's groans.
Snowstorms rage from year's end well into the new year.
Unmelted, gray–ribboned snow relentlessly
bends tree trunks and leans like ponderous whale blubber
over the valley floor.

Harvesting comes late in these hills,
so chores become a blur of activity.
People haul in limbs felled deep in the range last spring,
cut reeds, disassemble the rice–drying racks,
enclose their homes with snow sheds,
        hang persimmons from their eaves,
stash walnuts, vegetables and such in storehouses,
buff their buckets, place weights
        on washed radishes and greens for pickling.
Having completed every preparation for the winter,
they at last sit carefree round their hearths.

Fresh wood chips burn there.

Winter winds roar from the peaks through dales.
Winds that do not yet bring snow
have already begun to scatter powder
over the people's chitchat, over their thoughts.

TSURUBE*

In the foothills of a much higher mountain,
a ridge beyond our hillside hamlet,
lies a community with the comely name
Tsurubé.
On starry nights they say you can see Yamagata's lights
blinking in the basin thirty–nine kilometers off.
They say Tendô's lights are visible, too.
Tsurubé has just over thirty households.
Blizzards blow more fiercely there than here.
Snow piles up more deeply there than here.
They've built a little branch school
where nine children's desks huddle numbly
in the center of the snow–dusted room.
A sturdy harmonium decorated with medieval carvings
squats ponderously near a window.
If a visitor whimsically presses a key,
the organ hums gently like a dream.
It hums in tremolo
like the song of one long inured to solitude.

IN A MOUNTAIN FIELD*

The valley between our mountain
and the one far off
is deep
and filled with lavender mists.

If you call out, however,
the sharply visible distant hills
appear close enough to call back.

Even the straw hats of children
working in burnt–over fields on the hill
glisten in the dazzling sun.

I can't explain why,
but since coming to these mountains

I've had the strange feeling
I'm at sea.

Singing the "Sailboat Song,"
we raise our hoes in unison.
We then send a semaphore message
from the field on this mountain
to the field on that far–off hill.
We signal,
"It's noon."

NEWS FROM THE MOUNTAIN*

Snow has begun piling up.
Not a single bird
left in the hills.
They won't be back
till spring.

Snow never lets up.
Dawn comes later now,
dusk earlier.
Before one knows it,
we've eaten the winter solstice squash.

Snow piles up.
Blizzards blowing through cliffs and dales
have buried even the tips of little trees.
Each day we walk
over treetops.

In our snowed–in hamlet,
brush gathered from deep in the range
crackles red in the hearths of every home.
Girls crack walnuts, read books
by the fire.

STRAW BOOTS

Straw boots line up
by the open hearth:
Father's boots.
Mother's boots.

Straw boots hang
over the hearth:
mine,

my little sister's.

Snow clings still
to boots by the hearth.
Water trickles slowly down.
Wisps of steam rise steadily.

Boots over the hearth
already thoroughly warmed,
dry and crispy.

Let's put new straw innersoles
into our dried boots
and wear them again
to school this morning.

Snow——deep,
but nearly as soft as cotton.
Feet inside my straw boots
toasty warm.

PRAIRIE

A friend from the ranging snowbound prairie,
extending north of the north country where I live,
told me of a curious custom they call "crow candle bake."
People hollow out holes in a snow–covered field,
place bait in the bottom of the hole,
and on the ground catch birds accustomed to the sky.
I've forgotten the derivation of the term,
whether from cooking the catch over candles
or baking it in a casserole and eating it as is.

The expression *waxchew*
describes what's insipid in life.
It moves me in a strange but intense way
to compare the unsavory candle,
        the hapless birds, and prairie snow
with the frantic and lonely flame–like yet focused lives
of northerners struggling against the wilderness.

Near the end of February, when blizzards at last blow out,
those vagabonds of the sky come from nowhere
to this high hamlet locked in on every side
by mountain on mountain, snowfall on snowfall.
Once perched high on cedar treetops to rest their wings,
they hack out determined coughs——

then fly straight to the valley floor.
By then winter's idleness nears its end.
Stored provisions now depleted in every home,
those so lonely hacks touch people to the quick.

BECKONING SPRING*

A letter from the south today
tells of cherry trees in bloom.
In this northern mountain village, however,
only a small patch of blue peers through clouds.
The frozen valley stream begins at last to flow.

Piled snow, still two meters deep,
packed hard over buried shrubbery.
Branch tips poke up sporadically through the white ...
tiny yellow lumps just emerging.
Children who find them sing out joyfully,
"Witch hazels blooming!"

Farmers everywhere stand up round their gloomy hearths
and stretch away winter's long seclusion.
They waste no time skipping out their cellar–like doors
to move about the bleak fields.

Working together, they dig up the snow.
First they make seed beds.
They then pile the dug–up loam on sided sleds,
haul load after load up hillsides,
and let them slide down to the valley floor.
Along the way, they scatter dirt over the fields
so snow will soak up sun's heat and melt.
Soon they'll bring in the heavy compost.

Oh, how north country winds chill!
The season looks unwilling to budge,
yet farmers beckon the distant spring
with unflagging will and brawn.

HUNTING BUTTON MUSHROOMS*

Clawing over crags,
cutting across ravines,
how many kilometers have I hiked by now?

I found them again this year
in the glooms of a deep mountain forest,

dripping at times with mist.
More than an armful on a beech stump
lush with button mushrooms
clumped tightly together——not a gap!

Just then,
actually I'm not sure of the time,
I saw the unspoiled vitality of countless haloes.
Their multicolored rainbows sparkle in faint sunlight
sifting through treetops.

How mystical!
Despite having grown up in these hills,
I fold my arms and simply ... gape.
Momentarily unfocused,
I involuntarily sit on a fallen tree trunk.
Thinking I'll have a smoke,
I reach for the cigarette case in my *obi*.

Song of the bird

Look at those birds
coming to the tree.
Raising or lowering their tails,
they flit from branch to branch.
They multiply like magic.
One bird becomes two, the two become three.

Catch a bird
and listen.
In your hand you can hear
sounds of its lovely breast.
There, you see, doesn't your palm report
its anxious beating?

If you open your hand,
the bird flies off in a trice.
It quickly spreads its rainbow wings.
Then you watch it dissolve
into the faraway glare of spring–time skies.

Ages*

Tsumura Nobuo said before he died,
"Though poets have youth and old age,
they know neither adolescence nor prime." •

These words verge on truth.
Actually, oh youth ... knocking restlessly on the gate to old age,
you've left a silver crown on my head.
Oh, those flute airs that drifted so far off!

FATE (ii)

To hone their skills,
sharpshooters on the otter boat
toss empty beer bottles from the deck.
They take aim and shoot the instant the bottles surface.
Spinning down through faint sunlight,
each bottle disappears into the sea——then bobs up in a flash,
like the sea otter's mournful face
poking up between waves to take a deep breath.

Supposedly the finesse thus gained
makes these sharpshooters so accurate they never miss.
The old man who told me this story had gone searching
        for the Father of his memories.
He spent some dozen youthful years roving the north seas.
Stranger fate than anything in fiction
had driven him to a half–life of rebelliousness.

DEVASTATION*

Flames enveloped the city.
As explosions became more distant,
the safety of his extensive collection
        of beloved English literature books
gnawed intensely on the mind of Professor 'D.'
Driven off by flames, collar and cuffs singed,
he had lost his home that night.
Now he rushed through smoldering fires
to his college.

Burned–down campus structures here and there.
Smoke still belching from rows of green trees.
As he stepped through the ruins
        and set foot in the shelter, however,
his heart vaulted at the glorious sight!
His ten–thousand volume library arrayed on the shelves,
as well–ordered as the day before....
Ecstatic, the professor reached

for a title.

At that moment, every last book crumbled silently
to ash.

WOLF PACK*

A wolf pack had been dogging the travelers.
When sun sank,
the wolves closed in around the campfire.

Travelers flung firewood to ward them off.
By morning, however,
the dogs had vanished one by one,
lost among their kind.
Beasts that look like dogs that look like wolves
little by little multiply.
They snarl, snap at, and shove one another——fangs bared.
Led and pulled by such beasts,
the sleigh continues dashing over the snowy tundra.

——Had the dogs been carried off and turned into wolves?
——Had the wolves been harnessed and become dogs?

Either way,
the thought agonizes me.

DOG WATCH*

On the barque I sail,
some call standing watch at sunset
"dusk watch."
Others call it
"dog watch."
For some reason, only on the dog watch
do they ring the eight bells in groups of four
with a pause between.
I don't know the origin of "dog watch."
Perhaps it's because dogs at this hour
assume man's role on land
and guard the home.

Well, there are no burglars at sea
so nobody keeps dogs on ships.

On the ocean, day fades to shadowy dusk.
Only waves' fangs froth.
Only wind howling through ropes
blasts the ear.

BALL

Our mothers got the money together
to buy a rubber ball for our school.
It's fun playing with it.
Even with a single ball,
we can play
with our classmates.

Spring comes…. We go out again today
to play with the ball on our snow–clear playground.
Lots of us run after it,
cheerfully bump into each other, tumble down.
The ball bounces nimbly,
spins round and round,
slips from the grasp of those who try to catch it,
zips off through our legs.
Sometimes it gets kicked,
zooms high into the sky,
and for a moment sticks to the blue….

The ball is free——alive.
Playing with it
makes the playground endless,
blue skies higher than high.
Our hearts bound joyfully
with the ball.

IN RICE PADDIES

Listen, you lads wielding hoes and looking down
into rice paddies under twilight's mist!
At high noon,
your arms
and shoulders,
your bellies, too,
smeared with mire.
Foreheads and cheeks as well
splattered with mud. •

Waists weightily numbed with mire,
nerves lavishly intertwined with mire,
fatigue reducing you to mire,
so like stirred–up mire
you burst into mirth.

Yes, under the blazing mountain sun
a cuckoo wings through deep–blue breezes.
Your laughter sparkles the paddies, too.
How cheerfully sound!

SUMMER DAY ON THE MOUNTAIN

Noon——I was talking with you
when a vivid rainbow suddenly arched up
and straddled the gorge before us.
It startled you. I sat silent,
momentarily entranced.
Soon something you happened to say
returned me pointedly to myself.

Dusk——I was talking with you
and in plain sight an updraft
shot skyward from field's edge like a Titan.
Both of us noticed it, stunned.
We momentarily looked up after it.
Once again the impetus of an unexpected word
dismissed it from our thoughts.

Yes——a summer day on the mountain
        when I met and talked with you.
Nature had displayed its grandeur,
entrancing us in a trice.
Such instants flashed away without a trace.
Each time, our dialogue revived hopes
for human life
or piques against it.

RAINBOWS

At a bend in the path along the rapids,
a spring nearly as brisk as a cascade
dribbles over a burly, jutting cliff.

By midwinter, mountain winds
freeze the dribble bit by bit.

Ice spears dangle.
Cones reach steadily from the ground.
They jut up a meter, three meters, five meters.
Finally their tips join and,
thickening,
become more than armfuls.
How splendid that stunning row of ice pillars!

On a day of solid blue skies,
those shafts soak up snowscapes
and furiously mirror glitters of light.
The traveler enters our neighboring hamlet
through rainbows.

SNOW PATCH

A bear stretched out near the peak,
a gigantic polar bear——one paw on a boulder's edge,
one wedged in a hollow.
He lay on his belly, hind legs stretched out in a "Y."

Suddenly he began to slide down the slope.
Slithering slowly,
he gradually gained speed.
He sent grit flying, flipped up pebbles, flattened shrubs,
then disintegrated the moment he crashed into crags.
Finally he fell from the cliff to the valley floor,
a powder ball.

A deafening rumble
assaulted the ear.

The bear's slide path
exposed the mountain's ruddy face.
They say spring has come.
Yet not a single blade of grass.

CHERRIES

Spring——tardy
in the cold north country.

But when it comes,
apricots, peaches, and cherries flower together.
White blossoms in apple trees as well.
In a twinkling ... summer. •

Here and there in cherry orchards,
wind jostling every cluster,
children climb
to pick their own fruit.

Yes, bittersweet cherries
glistening like cream!

Buried under deep snow
through the long winter,
green leaves riot now on fields and hills.
How cheerful these summers in the North.

Snow bugs*

Late one night,
a bug crawled toward me
along an edge of the open hearth.
Say, it's not the season for bugs, I thought.
I looked more carefully
and saw a gracefully slender insect,
somewhat like an ant with wings.

My landlord told me,
"We call them snow bugs.
They turn up now
just when we're weary of winter."

Toward dawn,
I heard an owl in a distant dell
hooting for spring.
That day the sleet began at noon.

When I climbed the trail up the incline,
indeed, bugs ... bugs——those snow bugs
waltzed sporadically,
their skinny legs rippling
here and there over wet snow.

Ah, where do those
wondrous waltzing bugs breed——
bugs that glow like sprites on heavy snow in the north country,
snow that massively, that relentlessly
shuts in one's life, one's thoughts...?

BALMY WEATHER

On the fourth day of an unusually long snap of balmy weather,
a photographer trudged up from some town in the foothills
and took pictures here and there in our hamlet.

Young people's reading clubs,
elementary school teachers on the eve of transfer, and,
aside from commemorative shots of those about to part,
he also photographed some groups
that for no reason simply invited kindred spirits to pose
in the schoolyard's snowy glare, at the saw mill, before the cliff.

Each time the photographer set his shutter
to capture the smiling faces of young boys and girls,
the early spring skies glittering behind them,
the tops of bright magnolias and cherry trees,
the lively chatter of birds hopping through wind
——all competed urgently
to enter the frame.

After siphoning off the mountain's balmy days,
the photographer packed his dry plates in their case.
At dusk, he solitarily descended the hill.

BUTTERFLY OR BIRD

Simply braiding leaves into their hair
casts green shadows over children's brows.
Then freckle–like verdure spots appear
on hands, on feet——everywhere.

When these children enter a mountain thicket,
they at once become invisible,
as though hidden by the hues of twigs and leaves.
Then they suddenly jump
from grass clumps along the path,
from behind trees.

This startles me.
It's almost as though
a butterfly had fluttered up before me in the woods
or I'd found nearby a little bird.

DEEP IN THE MOUNTAINS*

Snow melts in May,
even in this everywhere–chalky mountainous North,
buried deep through the winter under white.
Then tightly curled leaves and flower buds
in barren groves and in the soil
start all at once to stretch and move.
Flowers quickly bloom, then scatter,
and hills hurriedly don their verdure coats——
a positively awesome change.
Green grows lush under sunlight.
Sun sings raucously in the heart of the skies.
Honeybees fly through the fields like light dust.
Here and there, cuckoos sing to each another.
Uguisu warble keenly overhead.
Such lively summers in the North!

Along mountain streams rife with leafing butterburs,
this is when
ferns and bracken buds among marsh reeds
unroll under shadows by the cliff.

Mountain aralia stretch here and there,
high on the peak's barren crags.
Children climb steep boulders and cross swift rills.
However perilous, they bustle fearlessly about
hunting wild berries.

Deep in the mountains you find
that spring survives.
Something glints among trees near a hollow,
between hills where chilled winds breathe——
what do you suppose it is?
The children dash back breathlessly,
panting, "Yep, it's a bear——a bear's there.
A mighty polar bear lying there."
No bear
——only what's left of winter snow.

ON ADOLESCENCE

On any given day, one is unaware
when it's high noon.
Those at the height of adolescence

are similarly unaware that they are.

Chaste shyness——passion for beauty——a blaze of fame
——groping for the unknown——craving ideals....
Like fires on a prairie, countless fierce desires
    burn eagerly in youthful minds.
Exasperating, futile dreams
drive them day and night, trip them up,
cover them with scars and shame.

Adolescence——what an anguished time!
I think back on bitter days when that famished wolf
fed on my inner self and madly gnawed at me,
raging and howling incessantly.

Thus adolescence doesn't truly exist.
It's one's prime that dashes off moment by moment——
an illusion glittering like gold dust
only in the reminiscences of age.

The young person feeling haughtily elated
and jubilant over youthfulness
is the very adolescent
we might as well feed to the dogs.

FLOWERS AND A GOAT

A boy in my class wrote an essay,
"My Favorite Person——
    a Kid Goat."
The only child in his family,
he was born with golden eyes.
He lives friendless, therefore,
in a clump of three houses
deep in the dale.

The boy's grandfather
excels at grafting flowers.

After spring thaws,
the kid goat gorges itself on green grass.
The boy's grandfather walks through the hamlet
making peach blossoms bloom on plum trees
near the eaves of every home.

FAR MOUNTAINS——NEAR MOUNTAINS*

Both far mountains
and near mountains
turn color all at once,
like Kagura dancers who change into silk brocade gowns
in the shrine's dressing room.

Both far mountains
and near mountains
glow in yellows and scarlets,
like Kagura dancers
lined up on the shrine stage.

A shrike cries.
Akebi ripen.
Chestnuts crackle.

Somewhere far away,
the drums of the cascade boom;
we hear the rill's railing flute.

Both far mountains
and near mountains
array their sleeves   with a dazzle,
swirl their skirts   with a flash,
as they perform a serene dance
for Japan's joyfully ripening fall.

A YOUTH AND A HORSE

Reading a book,
a young man lies prone
on grass under a tree.
Five or so meters beyond,
an untethered horse
grazes.

I hear the horse munching
and chomping the grass.
The young man's face pales with excitement and hope
as he studies his book.

Watching them,
I become less and less sure

whether the horse reads the grass
or the young man eats the book.

Sometimes when breezes rustle branches,
glints the hue of golden gadflies
flicker between the young man and the horse.
The lad hurriedly brushes the hair from his brow.
The horse briskly flicks a hoof, swishes its tail.

Yes, even at this quiet moment,
I clearly sense youthfulness fluttering off
moment by moment
from those two dynamic beings——
and middle age winging
from me....

CLASS LOG*

Morning——
Before class begins, a girl raises her hand:
> *Teacher, the swallows are gone.*

I climb up near the window,
check the nest under the eaves.
Then, taking out my class log,
I add this postscript to yesterday's entry:
> September 28. Swallows leave.
> The mountain chills now.

SWALLOW (ii)*

Far to the south, a chain of high ranges.
When snow on the peaks glitters like crystal,
air above glows with a hint of indigo.
Mornings——children stand on the bluff before their homes
and gaze into the south.
They think that spring
will somehow visit them.

Fifty years back——another child stood on that bluff,
similarly gazing into the south.
A tiny dot appeared in that indiscernible space over the peak.
Suspended long in gray skies,
it suddenly accelerated toward the cliff.
By the time the dot registered on the child's retina,

it had transformed into a swallow flying all out,
an instant from the child's head.
The child cannot recall what happened next.
He covered his face, shrieked,
collapsed into the snow.

The swallow gouged the child's pupil,
leaving him one–eyed.
If you doubt me, come and see yourself.
He's an old man
still living in this snowy hamlet!

Rocks Roll Downstream

Listen!
Rocks roll down the gorge again today.
Gorogoro–gorogoro
——like a prodigious churning grinder.

The sounds gradually approach from upstream.
They pass before me stolidly, slowly.
Rocks collide with each other in the river,
bump——rebound——crash together
    ——tumble over one another.
Lightly grazing one——another slips by——dashes on.
At times deep, crushing noises convoy them.
Though sharp, the sounds decidedly neither echo to the clouds
nor peal through the hills.
They simply stab the ground with silently sorrowful gloom.
Taking their time,
the rocks pass by without pattern.
They move away, ever so ... ever so sluggishly.

Listen!
Droves of rocks roll downstream again today.
Thawed water propelling them,
they tumble through the valley stream.
They roll *gorogoro–gorogoro*
down the riverbed.

Flowercore

Every girl was smiling.
Not a one said,

"I like you," or, "I hate you."
They simply left me, one by one,
smiling … in silence.

Multi–petaled smiles
ever on my palm!
I pluck them now, one by one,
each to the flowercore.
Having lost their smiles,
fragrance alone survives.

RAINBOW

Each time I doffed my greasy school cap,
hurriedly bowing to greet someone,
sweat from unkempt hair dissolved into mist.
There a tiny rainbow arched.
The bow vanished in a flash.
Clearly my prospects were bleak.

Each time I met a teacher on the street
or ran into a girl I secretly adored,
I clumsily pulled off my cap.
Mist from my mangy hair then dissolved,
leaving a tiny rainbow to arch in that mist.
When the bow disappeared,
my prospects looked more bleak than I'd dreamt.

CONCERTINAS AND TRAINS*

My concertina had been singing
merrily, despite being tinged
with strains of grief.

Though pitch dark beyond the glass,
my train had been dashing floridly
through fields
in places unfamiliar to me.
Could that have been adolescence?
Could that have been my adolescence?

Layered on the tunes of my now mute concertina,
countlessly countless other concertinas play.
Trains arrive one after another
in search of an already irretrievable Time.

LONELY UNIVERSE*

Only starry skies dimly lit,
the ground so inky I can't tell where it is.
Singing frogs
roil up from the dark gloom.
I hear them, yes, I hear them,
their furious clamor uniform
since remote antiquity.

Earth spins stealthily toward dawn.
Night after night it leaves those clamors
        in the wake of its orbit——
one bundle of melodies after another
like serial nebulae.

Somewhere in the lonely universe,
frogs sing again today.
Hordes and hordes
of singing frogs.

FISH EYES*

Why are the eyes of a fish
round?

'Cause the fish
is amazed.

Why
is the fish amazed?

'Cause the eyes of the fish
are stuck
to either side of its head.

'Cause at any one time,
the fish always sees
different scenes.

That's why   it's amazed.
That's why   its eyes are round.

LUNAR CALENDAR*

After the solar calendar has its say,
the lunar calendar visits the Japanese countryside.
It's like night
following day.

"Second New Year" on the lunar calendar
visits this hilltop hamlet, too,
mid February's desolately heaped–up snows.

Tightly sealed houses
squat behind snowsheds.
Children bring sprigs of dogwood from the hills,
skewer dumplings on them, suspend folded cranes
to decorate sooty beams above the hearth.
Sprigs slender and red, round dumplings white,
plain paper cranes mirroring flames.
——So dreamily wistful!

Two young men
face a peach or a persimmon tree.
One raises an ax and addresses the tree:
——*Will you bear? Or won't you?*
    If not, down you come!
He then drives his ax into the trunk.
In pain, the flustered treetop screams,
    I'll bear for you.
    I'll bear for you.

Indeed, when fall comes
the tree bends deep with fruit.

SQUASH*

December 22 today.
Winter solstice,
the one day each year
when sun is farthest from Earth
and daylight briefest.

In Japan on this day
it's our custom to prepare the bath with floating citrons
and eat what we call
"winter solstice squash."

This year my family harvested
a heap of squash.
By the end of fall we'd eaten most of it.
For today, however, we saved the biggest
and what looked the tastiest.
It's a plant from warm Cambodia,
so we write "squash" using the Chinese graphs
    for "southern melon."
Squash.
Cambodia.
Chestnut squash.
I love squash.

IN A NEW AGE

Even in peace,
people ache.
Even with equality,
people grieve.

No limit to the anguish and affliction
of creatures on Earth.

But the glory of a new age will come
with tomorrow's sun.

Let's hope we'll live
in that new age.
We'll weep then from new aches,
suffer fresh griefs.

With a span of single–minded honesty,
we'll bridge these aches and griefs.

WHITE VALLEY

Soft spring snow
heaps on hard–packed winter snow.
Since the new mounds loosely on the old,
spring snow soon slips down the bluff——
soundlessly,
with demonic speed...
giving no one time to dodge.

Tragedy on a cloud–free morning.
Indeed, blizzards cease
and birds return to our hill.
The deep valley lies hushed.
Everything stark white, swelling grotesquely
like heaped–up cadavers:
overwhelming——the glare dazzling. ·

When I stare at them,
the piles appear to move a bit.
Then they truly do.
Silently and with surprising speed,
snow mounds swoop upon us.

EARLY SPRING (ii)

A sparkling forenoon.
Soft spring snows amass
over winter's crusted drifts,
new snow not sticking to the old.
Abruptly, the new snow begins sliding down the valley slope.
Soundlessly, serenely,
yet gleaming with infernal speed,
it scatters over the sheer precipice,
turns to smoke as in a painting,
plunges into the gorge below.

A baby squirrel looking up at sky
from an oak tree hollow on the canyon floor,
buried unseen.

GULL*

Pimples broke out on my face.
Imagining others would shun me,
I shunned them.

Inwardly full of fury,
yet   outwardly calm.
Wherever I went I went alone,
yes   entirely alone!

Hopes and dreams shredded.
Figuring I had nowhere to go but the desert or the sea,
I yearned for a photo of a handsome yacht
the way one yearns for a girl.

> *The gull must feel sad to sail aimlessly,*
> *untainted even by sea's indigo or sky's blue.*

I had hoped
to become that pure white gull
and wing through my eighteenth year.

Vaguely

While I had vaguely lost track of time,
little boys and girls I once loved
had already grown up.

Now young men and young women,
they stare at me
as though only belatedly aware that I exist.
Their expressions apparently ask:
"Are you still around, Mister?
Well, then, what do you dream of ... now?"

Lad

Arms and legs sprawling,
flopped down like a dog,
a lad stretches out asleep.

He'd worked eagerly and intensely,
thinking that in a world of mistrust
he alone would be open and trustful of others.
Now weary,
the lad rests.

Seeing him sleep
mists my eyes.

Sea Birds

Sea birds that flew through the storm
to the bluff on the point
lay scattered over the crags where they'd fallen,
an enormous number of carcasses.

One day I, too, will come to life's end
like that,
writing poem after poem about the fretful sea.
It's as though a beacon light existed
beyond the haze of Fate.

Ah——but why?

THOSE WHO STAND ON ICE AND SNOW*

I hear that plums bloom now in the south,
that peach buds also swell.
What of the violence in frigid winds
that blow through this northern land?
What of thick ice and heaped–up snow that deny movement,
hide hills, bury streams——bottle up our thought, our lives?

That's exactly why
we cannot idly stand by.
It's time to start the soil haul,
to dig through snow, strip the loam,
load it on sleds, haul it to flat places,
scatter it to winds.
Then blackness soaks up sun's heat,
quickly melting the snow on paddies and fields.

Those who stand on northern ice and snow
summon the distant spring
with sweat, with brawn, with strength of will.

MY FEELINGS AS WELL

Wind rises
in night's murk.

Like a colossal demon,
it violently seizes and shakes the house.

Then it dashes away,
creaking the roof.
Wind soon whistles far off
near the horizon.

——At that moment
the candle in my shut–up room
begins to flicker.
The flame quietly gives way,
collapses as though trampled.
Once prone, it fades,
then blooms again to flame.

Glowing ever more whitely hot,
its luster crests.

VALLEY TRAIL

An autumn day.
I make my way along the valley trail,
the mountain's deep thickets ... hushed.
Chestnuts drop from branch tips.
Beechnuts fall from branch tips.

Unexpected on such a steep incline,
I suddenly come upon a girl
as though in a buoyant picture.
She's breaking up brushwood, gathering chestnuts,
rustling cheerfully around.

She looks down, then quickly turns her head.
I glance at her and silently pass.
At that moment I somehow feel
like one of those furiously reddening trees
mirrored on the distant stream.

SPRING IN THE NORTH*

How wonderful
the savage sounds of water!
Rumblings roll from the gorge.
They summon snow from the peaks
and thunder down in torrents to flood the dale.

One by one tree branches spring up
from under snow's loosened grip.
Growing knots of hard buds,
the branches flail one's brow
like dauntless whips.
Soon, groves in the foothills
will take on faint green.
Among them, perhaps the wild magnolia's white flowers
will bloom first.

Early this morning when class began,
a girl raised her hand:
    Teacher, the swallows are here.

NEW BUDS

Each tree
still stark naked.
If, however, you look at treetops from afar,

they appear faintly, dimly green.
Queued up on the southern slope of the dale,
they lean together into sun
like little girls grown tall.
They chant their griefs into chill winds
that sled down snowy hills.

Climate

The roofs of every house slant sharply.
They'd been built on the slope of the dale.

The soles of the feet occupying those houses also inclined
——ever since father's time,
——since grandfather's time,
——since great–grandfather's time.

Child in a Dream

Last night I had a dream.
I dreamt I met a child.
The child dashed barefoot
from a queue of strangers.
He abruptly threw his arms round me.
Clutching my waist tightly,
he buried his dirty face in my chest.

"There, there," I said.
I held his head.
When I patted his streaked head,
batches of sand
poured from his hair.
They spilled endlessly,
as though his head were made of sand.

I'd been weeping
so I awoke in tears.
Well, this morning when I try to puzzle it out
I have no recollection of the child's face.
Wherever did he come from?
To whom could he possibly belong?

Pictures and Chinese Graphs

Day after day, little by little,
pencils and crayons shorten.
The shorter they become,
the smarter we get.

As pencils and crayons wear down,
our heads soon fill up with the pictures
and the Chinese graphs we want to put on paper.

The new Japan begins.
Smarter now, we'll make pictures and graphs
freely
on her blank–paper skies.

A Swallow Arrives*

Vast, vast skies.
One teensy–weensy swallow.

Blue, blue seas.
One faint black swallow.

Everywhere,
empty skies and the sea
melt together,
blue into blue.

One small dot   a swallow.
One faint dot   a lone swallow.

Compared to the endless skies and endless seas,
that dot seems as small as a millet grain
about to vanish.

Folded into the two wings attached to the dot
is courage
to strike through those endless skies,
to stride over those endless seas.
Half the globe reflected
in that dot's two eyes.

Wings beating hard,
a swallow arrows in from the south.
It reaches our North through blue
as pure as Time.

SEA FLAGS

June has come.
The sky——cobalt.
How sun
glitters!

I'll go to the beach
and gaze into the horizon.
I'll gaze at flitting gulls,
at white clouds that billow on the offing.

Whenever sea breezes blow my way,
something flaps
deep within me.

Ah, a mast!
A merchant flag tinged with peace
flutters amid my hopes.

When do you suppose
the world will take Japan back
and let her ply the seas again?

SUMMER BUTTERFLIES

Blossoms gone from cherry trees
now greenly lush with leaves
that leak sunlight
and rustle now or then.
Each of the many caterpillars
under those leaves
will become a butterfly
and dance off into gentle breezes.
Ah, in their wings——places that gleam,
that turn to shadow...
pretty as parasols.

Why do ugly caterpillars
suddenly become parasol–miming butterflies...?

SCENES BECOME CLOUDS

The puddle mirrored a cherry tree,
mirrored treetops with round buds.
It mirrored blue sky above the trees

and scudding ship–like clouds with sails spread.
It mirrored mustard fields under the clouds,
    butterflies, houses, telephone poles,
and smoke drifting from a chimney on the hill.
It mirrored more glistening puddles
farther off.

Drying in sun,
the puddles gradually shrank.
By afternoon, they'd disappeared without a trace.
Those friendly, dazzling scenes on the puddles
also turned to shimmers, each climbing skyward
to become sail–white clouds. So I suppose that
neither the cherry tree nor the fields,
    neither butterflies nor smoke,
nor even those sail–like clouds,
knew what had happened to them.

SPRING TO SUMMER*

Already spring on this mountain.
Uguisu warble everywhere in clumps of bamboo grass.
Yet here and there on the high range, in a valley beyond ours,
spots of unthawed snow.

Snow in assorted shapes:
A bear asleep in a mountain hollow.
A drake spreading its wings on the cliff.
Several rings floating near the peak,
like foam on waves.

Those patches sparkle endlessly
under bright sun.
They appear to shrink but never do.
On our mountain, every animal suddenly disappears
when the *uguisu* sings no more.

The bear has certainly rambled off carefree,
deep into snowier mountains to the north.
The drake, I suppose,
has already crossed the sea toward Siberia.
Those foam rings have climbed by now into the skies
and turned to cloud.

Eventually, azaleas on our mountain wilt.
Spring at last visits that higher hill.

POLAR BEAR

An enormous polar bear sprawls out
in the cliff's shadows
at the end of the gorge.

His back filthy,
bare spots here and there.
Deep within those dim openings,
the vague sounds of a stream.
A cabbage blooms
faintly white.

WHEN I WALK THROUGH FIELDS*

Faint, almost static clouds,
high, high fish–scale clouds——
yes, sky like water.

When I walk through the fields,
I find delicate autumn aromas
in grass, in sun.

A grasshopper soars high,
whirring, glinting,
adazzle.

Let's go pick
bellflowers.
Let's pluck
valerians.
Let's gather
eulalia plumes.

Tonight we view the moon.

HANDS

How beautiful
my hands!
They help me out, they work for me
readily,
cheerfully,
neither blemished by nor shrinking from
whatever task, whatever fate. •

Bringing both hands together,
I shade my eyes as I look into sun.
Then pink blood climbs like sunrise
through my fingers.
Or, when I soak my hands in clear water
in the washbowl,
my ten nails open like blooms.

WORKING GIRL*

After the drone of the belt stops
in that workshop at the foot of the slope,
the girl will pass my place again
on her way home.

Not weary from, not upset with
her daily labors,
her lively footsteps
regular as clock ticks.

Whenever she approaches,
even this head at my desk
bursts suddenly with energy.
It's as though my mind's spring had been re–wound.

Her footsteps pass.
Mixed with them,
the muffled clatter
of her aluminum lunch pail.

WINTER COMES*

Thin blue smoke rises
from beech roots.
Yellow flame sometimes flares
from oak trunks.
Resin oozes freely
from walnut branches.

Dry cedar needles
burn with a flash.
Their flames hold the roar of blizzards
that last year rocked the treetops.

Yes, winter comes.
Winter comes once more. •

Across the smoky open hearth,
an old man's dry cough.
Is that a whiff
of New Year's roasting *mochi*?

MORNINGS

Whenever Father opens his newspaper,
morning sun quickly floods
each column.

Fresh print reeks
in morning sun.
How pleasant the smell of newsprint.

I can't explain why,
but newsprint makes me hungry.
It's like the scent of jam,
the fragrance of bread.

TELEPHONE POLE

Whenever I put my ear to the telephone pole,
it was ringing.
It rang loudly——*konng*.

Whenever I stood away from the pole,
I no longer heard that sound.
Skies blue, I felt empty.

Whenever I put my ear again to it,
of course the pole was ringing.
It rang loudly——*konng*.

When I looked up, ear to the pole,
the sky was ringing, too.
It rang a clear——*konng*.

PAGE ONE

The first morning of the New Year comes,
the first sun of the year rises,
like turning to page one
in a just–bought notebook.

The dazzle of this year's snow
glances fiercely off my face,

sparkling like page one
in a fresh notebook.

I plod over snow to school
the way I write the beginning line
on that glittering first page
of my unmarked notebook.

I look back at my footprints
the way I stare at
the first line I wrote on page one
of my new notebook.

Yes, the first line on page one
of this fresh year
continues straighter than straight, track by track,
beyond the snowbound hills.

ⓞN THE WAY

Day near end.
Light surfaces again from the snow,
a bewitching dusk–like glow.

The light stabs my eyes.
I can no longer see the snow
nor the landscape around me.

I simply walk through an endless expanse of pearl–like glare.

Where am I headed?
I'm no longer on the snow.
I stride through life, bearing directly north.

Several chilled coughs
on life's path.

ⒹREAMING NORTH

Living in the North——now I yearn
directly for a deeper north.
Spending my days in snow——I've come
to think afresh of ice and snow.
Sitting in solitude——I've become
ever more absorbed in loneliness. ·

Oh, vagabond spirit
who's forgotten to go back home,
icicles have confined your thoughts!

Thus the dreams I see at sunup——vast snowy plains
traversing the rosy dawn near pale undulations,
a long string of migratory birds,
the growls of a shivering bear.

When those visions vanish, however,
the snowy plain turns instantly to ice.
Auroras glitter along the edges of the sky.

ON A MOUNTAIN PATH

A deep gorge snakes silently along, bend on bend,
paralleling the mountain's pleats.
Twilight mists seethe over one flank.

Now and then something rustles behind me
as I pass through.
At each sound I look back.
Is a bird there?   No bird.
An animal?   No animal, either.
Then at last I realize it's the sound of dirt
sloughing off the incline.

I notice gritty soil
slithering incessantly down the precipice,
bits at a time, just tiny bits.
What dislodges them?
Breezes that barely stir? Shudders from my footfalls?
Nothing in particular?

Rows of cedars shadow my goal.
Suddenly, as though he materialized out of air,
a child crosses in front of me.
As he idles along shouldering an empty bamboo basket,
infinite solitude closes in on him.
He looks so very small!

DREADFUL METHOD*

Rilke settled with a housekeeper
in Chateau de Muzot.... •

He raised roses
in the garden of that old chateau.
He disliked Muzot but genuinely craved
wind——isolation——light.

In solitude, he fervently made his person transparent.
Through his Self he focused on a single solitary image.
He wrote poetry using the dreadful method
of suspending, then kindling, life's flow.

The topography? The people?
I doubt he even tossed a handkerchief to them.

DEATH OF AN UNFORTUNATE

When he lived,
someone rubbed his troubled brow.
When he lived,
someone massaged his travel–weary feet.
Among those
who now heartlessly make sour faces,
oh, God in heaven,
do not fail to note
the only one among them
with a tender heart——
one who hopes to die with him.

SNOWY FIELD*

A child stands on the slope
holding a bamboo *wappa.*

He stares intently.
The fields thoroughly desolate,
everywhere only snow.
——The child knows, however,
what whiteness hides.

Soon, two meager dots take shape
in the distance.
Above each dot two slender objects move ...
then around them a faint circle,
as if shadow–sketched,
breaks the surface of the snow.

Taking aim,

the child hurls his *wappa*.
It wooshes through the air,
a swooping hawk.

Startled, the hare leaps up,
tumbles down the slope in flight,
becomes the child's catch.

Ｐeople of the North*

The roof sags,
so listen to how the doors creak now.
I suppose we'll have to clear the roof again of snow.

Oh, how snugly snow blankets
those terraced hillside fields, paddies, paths.
Snow dense as whale blubber
heaps high on slopes, on bluffs.
Snow——endless tons of snow.

More than simple scenery,
northern snows grind lives and spirits down——
a weighty reality, a state of mind.

Thus cedar roots grow lissome, stretching straight for sky ...
and so these people focus thought into scant words
with energy enough to raise a rock.

The essence of true honesty and cheer,
these folks are not in the least daunted
by counterfeit cavils.

Ｆlower Tree*

He hauls in fresh firewood through the back gate.
Bits of snow cling to the wood.
The house head breaks each piece off
and feeds it to the fire in the hearth.

Then
he says,
"That one's the barbinervis.
Here the flower tree.
This the magnolia."

I hear the barbinervis greens in the snow
earlier than witch hazels.

They say the flower tree abounds with leaves
    resembling the maple's.

Flashing instantly before my eyes
——groves in ravines that howl in wind;
——plump white flowers blooming between branches;
——early spring's pale blue skies.
A bird arrowing at a treetop
calls to mind
the title of a girl's collected verse:
Seat in a Flower Tree.

GIRLS

Deepening snow.
Snow masses over layered snow.
Morning. I run into four or five girls
on a narrow path through snow.

In hoods and capes,
the girls bustle by me single file.

I notice their cheeks glowing
like ripe apples.

I know
why their cheeks are round and red.
I recall that,
since they're north country girls,
their cheeks burn hot enough to melt the snow.

Suddenly behind me
a shrill of giggles.
Wind powders the shrill
with snow from limbs.

EVENING MIST

It wanders out of evening mists on the hill.
It tags along unnoticed by those on the path.
It flies around fleetingly then settles on a grass blade,
or flits into a tree again and rests under a leaf.
Each time it glares over its shoulder as it awaits a passerby,
then endlessly shadows him.

Once I, too, saw one.

It gleamed in speckles of gold and green,
an eerie phantom–like winged bug
smaller than a cricket.

At nightfall,
a villager trudging that long and desolate way,
struggled to the gate of his house, abruptly paled,
and died without a word.
No one knows why,
but people say that only one near death
can see the demon fly leave him and flee
free into the ink of night....

Foxfire*

A single glittering light
on the steep mountainside beyond the gorge....
The light busily reproduces itself,
forms a horizontal row, vanishes abruptly,
then becomes a vertical line.
That, too, evanesces in an instant.
Darkness returns.

This phenomenon they call
foxfire.
People talk about how the fox dashes
        through the heart of the hills,
bone splinters in its mouth.
They say, too, that wherever the fire appears
a fox will be behind you.

Even if true,
I wonder why it occurs.
Oh, those rustic cruciform blinks
that some hunted mountain beast kindles
——sorcery pregnant with pathos!

In Town

A girl who had gone down our mountain
just returned from the city
and said:
        "Snow in town
        has already melted.
        Everyone walks around

in clogs."

Being buried deep in snow,
I think of cheerful street corners
with peach and cherry trees bursting into bloom.
I think of red–thonged clogs
clip–clopping
over dried–out streets....

Spring Storm*

Why do winds in spring blow
so fierce?
Spring winds sling light and grit
against my brow.
They shred smoke and hurl it at me.
They break off twigs and send them flying.
They fling birds from branches.
Yesterday, a mountain girl off to be married
wrote this haiku on the road over the pass:
　　My hair ornaments shake loose.
　　　Oh, this spring storm.

Efforts

At times
the movements of my arms or cupped hands
appear peculiarly remote to me.
Mere efforts like
picking up a pen,
dipping it into the inkwell,
bringing it to paper....

Yes, my numbed late–night yearnings
at times mirror those movements as distant blurs.
It was the same when I viewed that crane
leisurely hoisting girders
or lowering them
through city skies.

Remembering Mother

How did Mother spend her time
those years before she died?

A silkworm quietly spinning thread——
what did my aged mother do in the presence of a son
who constantly harped on resentments
and thought only of himself?

Three years after she died,
I discovered the answer.
I now hold those crafts she left me:
restrained, sadly beautiful handiwork
for various occasions.

A diary registering disgust with an unfilial son
as she tried nevertheless to love him.
Many letter boxes and ink stone cases
　　decorated with figured paper.
Embroidery. Knitting. Dolls.
　　A quilt skillfully stitched with delicate patchwork.
Even a single, skirted pin cushion,
something a sweet little girl might try.

Making my way along a mountain path thick with snow,
near peaks where winds blow bleak,
I think of Mother——
of her lonely lot as an ordinary woman,
of her irrepressible, unspoken, persistent devotion....

EARS IN THE SKY

In a movie I'd seen,
I observed a heron suddenly fly up
from its nest high in a treetop.

Climbing a mountain,
I look up at venerable cedars and colossal pines
with the hope that something might be roosting there....

I find nothing,
just——wind blowing through the scene.
Though swaying unnoticed, those branches start to hum.

Then I feel that something in these empty skies
listens to those sounds.
I sense it's me.

BIRD CROSSING BLUE SKIES

Rapidly flapping its wings,
a gigantic
unfamiliar bird
cut through morning's blue.

Its beak flashed
as it skimmed the sun.
For an instant I thought I could see
its roundish face, its eyes.

Despite their lofty paths,
both the ubiquitous sun
and the distant flying bird
felt uncannily close to me.

CAROSSA AND RILKE*

In his *Roumanian Diary,*
Carossa wrote as follows
about a young girl suffering from consumption
in the aftermath of war's destruction:
    "The scant oxygen in her entire body
        gathered in those hugely opened eyes."
If at that moment
he had inadvertently approached her with the flame of love,
her eyes would have flashed away in an instant.
She would have gone to heaven.

They say Rilke's always limpidly blue eyes
profoundly absorbed imagery
without ever harboring even a hint of shadow.
What if we had sailed a boat on a lake of that hue?
Dread would quickly have driven us mad.

LIKE A LAMP

One loved me all her life.
One continues to love me.
My mother,
my wife.

Mother's love brightened me half a century,
then flickered out three years back.
Shadows gathered in a corner of my heart.

I shed tears in them.

My wife has loved me for twenty years
and never tires of loving me.

Doubtless she'll outlive me
and shine alone——
a lamp
in a mate–less room.

UNSPOKEN LOVE

When I pass over densely heaped–up snow
near the towering summit,
or under bowed trees bathing in sun,
I suddenly begin to reminisce.
I think of Mother no longer with us.
I think of my wife at home.

Or I think of modest, kindly acts
by women who came my way,
quickly passed, then vanished.

Memories of unspoken love
mellowing in Nature
hum at times in my mind——like wind....

CHILDREN'S SONG

Children play jump rope
in the yard of a house built on a cliff.
Two sing as they swing the rope
by the steep road descending to the dale.
Three take turns jumping into it.
 One teddy bear,
 two teddy bears,
 three teddy bears....
Moving into the rope, they become charming cubs.
 All three together now,
 turn about....
The cubs spin in mid–flight.
 Teddy bear, teddy bear,
 stick out an arm.
 Teddy bear, teddy bear,
 kick up a heel....
The cubs rehearse their stunts.

Padded *monpé* flap in the air.
Short bobbed hair bounces.
　Teddy bear, teddy bear,
　bye–bye now!
One trying to go through the rope
catches her foot in it.
The one who missed then swings the rope
and starts again to sing the song.
　One teddy bear,
　two teddy bears,

　. . . . .
　. . . . .

Suddenly a spring storm
blows from the summit into the dale.
Cedar tops wooshing,
the children remain visible.
Their song wanes.
Oh, little by little it gains distance——
only a memory now....

GREENFINCH*

Did my brief remarks dishearten you so much,
young friend?
In the letter I received this morning,
your cramped characters tediously record bewilderment,
thoughts going this way, going that,
self–confidence in disarray.
Your Self not yet mature,
this whole pathetic affair
as pitiful as a downed–in–flight bird
dragging itself along the ground.

At this moment, a greenfinch
flies above the head filled with these thoughts.
Settling atop an oak,
it immediately begins to shrill.
Unlucky for the finch, I have my air gun with me.
Actually, I came here to shoot a bird.

My shoulder swiftly pockets the butt.
I finger the trigger.
Oh! Reminded then of this morning's letter, I shoot the finch
whose silhouette shadows my thoughts.

SOOTED SKIES*

What's there
if you climb into those blue skies?

Nothing.

What's there
beyond those skies with nothing?

Nothing.

But, then, why have skies
with nothing?

Why, indeed?
Only God knows.

Where is God?
In the skies?
On some green star?

God's in a high place,
an unreachable site visible only to believers.

Will God come down from there?
Who does he come to?

God comes mainly to penitents,
to the brows of those who hunger for but steal no food,
to the backs of those who shiver but deprive no one of fire,
to the dreams of unrewarded children,
to the souls of those who share even a bread crumb.
Or, rather, he comes to the shoulders of any who,
even if they do not share the crumb, feel sorry they did not.

Well, then, he's sure to come to me.
If you believe....

And yet——oh,
cities filled with so much grime,
such sooted skies.
The soles of God's feet
defiled!

ABOUT LOVE

To be loved brings joy.
To love
brings greater joy.

Little girls!
Light a lamp of bright love
in your hearts.
Kindle the tiny world around you
with that glow.

Even if others are cold
and ignore you,
let your hearts
fill quietly with joy.
Be a lamp that continues to brighten the room
you've left.
——Imitate the moth that silently circles the lamp,
blazing the room ever brighter
with light reflected from walls and floor.

UNFAMILIAR LOCALE

I've come hundreds of kilometers sitting still,
wrapped in ruminations reaching into yesterday,
sound asleep——untroubled as paper.
I did not move by willing movement,
yet the train instantly carted me off.

What does distance mean?
I'm now in an unfamiliar locale,
but more often than not forget I am.

When I lean on the railing of a bridge
    that spans a finger of the lake
and look down into a school of transparent fish
    roving the water,
or when I stare into the clouds, the smoke,
    the hills mirrored there,
I'm instantly and wearily aware of what distance means.

BY A POND

Numerous whitebait
swim in clear water under the bridge.
They swim aimlessly,
each glittering with life.
They break the water like flashes of light.
Unfortunately, as transparent as glass chips,
they leave no shadow on the sandy bed
——quite like the trivial, rambling thoughts
incessantly coming and going through my mind.
Though piteous, bitter, painful,
and filled with life's quandaries,
they, too, leave no trace.

PART IV

POETRY PUBLISHED BETWEEN

1949 and 1956

IMPRESSION*

I slice open my thigh,
lay an ice bag on the incision,
lie all day on my back.

The slit stabs whenever I stir,
stabs more when I lie perfectly still.
Every last thought I think, eyes squeezed shut,
drenches me with agony.

Then, at last, dusk.
Look! Plaintive slits even in the clouds.

Finally, midnight. Sleepless.
When I open my bedside Bible,
blood dripping from Golgotha's shriek
twines like scarlet ivy
round my arms.

ALLEY HEAVEN

The child in bed with a high fever,
eyes that no longer see.

Inside, the house dims
like dusk.
Does his mother still jabber on?
Oh, no,
she's off to fetch the doctor.

Before he comes,
a strange woman enters the house
and folds her white wings.
Screened by the wings,
she applies something to the child's forehead
and suddenly vanishes. ·

213

The child opens his eyes.
Bright all around,
blooming flowers everywhere.
Ah, is this Heaven,
the Heaven of storybooks?
Water spouts up——
look, how high!

Just then someone shouts
from far–off Earth below:
    Whose brat is this,
    always forgetting to shut the tap?

ORIENTAL NOISE*

Once our talk turned to Chinese footwear. I mentioned the special characteristic of those shoes with ship–hull shapes and felt soles several layers thick. Unlike Japanese clogs and Western shoes, this aristocratic footwear makes no sound.

Cueing on what I'd said, the priest—who long ago had traveled throughout China—responded:

"That's why in the history of the Chinese city one never reads about footsteps. If you look down from a hotel balcony, those on the street pass ceaselessly by. Both men and women uniformly in light blue clothing and wearing those soft, noiseless shoes. In dusk's dimness, in light that soaks up one's sight, they walk as though melting into distance. Behind them, countless queues of shop signs and buildings whose roofs arc to points. It's as though these walkers are the flow of a gigantic, gentle river, or the movement of distant clouds. These passersby sound so close one might actually grasp the hum of their voices or see the sores their clothes have chafed. Then, you know, that utterly phenomenal and tantalizing sensation strikes you——Is China in truth an actual place? Is it an apparition? "

The priest's tale brought to mind the term "Oriental Noise" I once heard a sailor use. He meant those peculiar whispers of the Asian masses that glide across the harbor's silent waters ... sounds that endlessly and serenely enter the portholes of anchored ships.

DISTAFF STONE BUDDHA*

The head of the temple brought out several items to show me. A tea caddy dating from the end of the Ming dynasty. Seal stock decorated with a group of stylized lion heads. A large ink stone with as many as four concentric circles. A rubbing from the Six Dynasties. Finally, he hauled in a smooth chunk of stone the size of a large melon, placed it on the table, and said:

"This head is from a statue of Kannon carved into a grotto. I bought it from a Chinese who had broken it off. But take a look. See how on one side the lip is slightly distorted?"

I looked as he suggested. It indeed appeared that—if I focused on the groove between the bridge of the nose (quite close to the Greek style) and the upper lip—the shape of either side of the lower lip lacked proportion, though it was just a hair off.

"A failure of technique, you think?"

"Oh, no, this is one of a lined–up pair. Each outer side assumed a slightly relaxed attitude. The distortion in one side of the lip is, I'm sure, no doubt due to the artist's having made allowances for the tilt of the head."

Chinese mountains, their rocky sides desolately exposed, surface before my eye——pictures of their numerous carved grottos and the distaff stone Buddhas who had stood for centuries in their gloom ... steady embodiments of the subtleties of human physiology.

BLACK AND GOLD*

Once we'd cleared harbor, our ship killed her engine. Then every sail unfurled. Jostled by swells and the breathing sea, we set off through foam and glare——the first leg of our cruise.

Morning——so it seemed, but actually already near dusk. A light tap on my shoulder startled me. It was the Second Mate. He'd been on the afterbridge.

"Look," he said, raising an arm.

Peering toward the direction he pointed, I inadvertently swallowed in amazement. Directly west, some two knots away, a four–masted barque the very image of our own—the same shape, the same rigging as ours—sailed a parallel course, our bows aligned. The other ship also had every sail unfurled; catching the wind directly, each billowed full. Running headlong, she split the waves, wings extended like Pegasus.

The closer I looked, the more she appeared a perfect replica of our ship. The only difference was that, since sun was sinking behind her, Pegasus—wings, body, and all—had been painted perfectly black.

"Our sister ship. She left port ahead of us. Most likely she'll sail with us till dawn...."

Wind blew away the Second Mate's utterance——words I'd only vaguely caught, so I didn't immediately get their sense. I noted

only in that gigantic and lucid shadow how our own ship, moving
out toward sea, reflected the burning sunset. I recognized that
this parallel running indeed illustrated my own life. To imagine
that made me aware how impossible it would be for the silhouette
of this ship to watch itself. I gazed fervently into her black con-
tours, noting the flare–up of my passion for romantic thoughts.

The Second Mate, eyes pasted to his binoculars, spoke again as
though he'd read my feelings.

"They're as fascinated with our silhouette as we are with theirs.
Look at those young fellows crowding together on the poop deck,
in the forecastle."

Indeed, even with the naked eye I could see they were all look-
ing our way. They viewed our ship, however, immersed in the
glare of the sinking sun. In contrast to what we saw, I suppose
they saw a vessel glittering like gold.

Meanwhile, sun sank deep into water's arc on the horizon.
Even the glare from distant skies diminished. As it did, the ship's
black shape melted bit by bit into darkness. Together, I surmise,
with the glitter of ours.

Our ship and I sailed fully into solitude.

SEA WAS SOUSED*

Night after night I lay on my bunk, eyes wide open. When the
ceiling lights went off at nine, I lit my oil lamp. Under its dim
light, I buried myself in a book.

Nights aboard a sailing vessel are serene. No engine vibrations.
Sails billowing full under the trades, our ship rolled on like a
jumbo barrel——not a tremor. We moved ahead *goron* • *goron* ...
rolling to port, to starboard. With each roll I could hear the gaudy
slap of waves against the sides.

By then, heat near the equator oppressed. The simmer misted
our tightly–shut portholes and turned air below deck into an in-
tolerable steam bath.

One evening I opened wine brought from Japan and discovered
that every last bottle had soured. I decided to empty them all into
the sea——without even having tasted a one.

I forced open the wing nuts on the porthole. Then, reaching out,
I upended the bottles one by one.

Wine trickled out, gurgling faintly through the cool wind,
through the foam. After shaking out the last drop, I tossed each
bottle away.

I closed the porthole and returned to my bunk. No sooner had I
stretched out and shut my eyes than a poem came spontaneously
to mind——that well–known verse in which Valéry pours wine

into the sea....
    The intensity of sea's roar increased. Virtually in response to
the roar, our ship began heaving hard to starboard and to port.
    As the ship rolled, I felt great rapture. ——In having acted in
accordance with that witty French poem. ——In thinking that, as
Valéry said, "The sea was soused."

Night Journey

A body
between the rails and the coach.
The grating and grinding of bones
indicates the crush of someone's frame
where steel bites into steel.
Ah, wherever that massive hulk whirls and hurtles on,
unending human shrieks....
Weary–faced riders shut their eyes,
but do they truly fail to hear those cries?
Closing my eyes, I also pretend I'm deaf.

Flame*

Down the afterdeck's spiral staircase,
where the mizzenmast reaches straight up,
a small quivering oil lamp
with a bean–shaped flame——
night after night, the only light lit after taps.

Before daybreak at 0415,
the young lamp man off watch in steerage
descends the hatch under faintly flickering stars.
He never fails to blow out the flame.

One morning,
when as usual I was passing by,
the lamp man came along——pale,
shivering,
a fish just pulled from the brine,
spray and rain dripping everywhere from him,
bare feet trailing puddle prints....

The instant he neared the lamp,
its flame spontaneously died.

VERDANT SELF*

A family dispute
preoccupied Yasnaya Polyana,
so Rilke had to wait some time.
At last the Master appeared.
Carrying a cane and somewhat agitated,
the Count abruptly invited his guest outdoors.

Trees in the gardens glittered and trembled.
Flower fragrances swelled in the breeze.
The two strolled together
but only Tolstoy spoke,
stretching out rugged hands several times
as though tenderly to scoop in air.
Then, as the hands neared his nose,
he took a deep breath.
After that he resumed speaking——
impatiently, unceasingly,
the content possibly filled with contradictions....

In our modern age bereft of God and the external world,
Rilke's sap–like soul flowed intently still
toward his inner life.
Compared to him,
the white–bearded, hoary–headed Tolstoy brimmed with verve.
Jauntily pulsating at a high pitch,
he basked in his eternally verdant self.

BLESSED*

Rilke went to Russia
and soaked up the peals
of Easter's cheerfully serene and echoing bells....

Bells began to ring from emerald domes
sparkling in the Kremlin's dreamy mirage.
Once belfries on churches everywhere had joined in,
their knells boomed through Moscow's snow–cleared,
     evening springtime skies.
Jubilant, the people
melted into festivities.

Even Rilke's lonely mind brimmed over,
     moving gently away from itself.

Feeling blessed,
he was garrulous throughout his trip.

WIDE RIVER*

I moved into this small city and made friends with a priest. His temple stood in the center of town, so of course it burned to the ground during the war. The first rebuilt structure after hostilities ended was my friend's temple. To this day, several temples remain in ruins, yet the sanctuary and the priest's quarters of his temple alone had been rebuilt. They now emit the fragrance of fresh wood. Even the attached cemetery has been put into good order, the lots consolidated, every crypt strengthened with concrete.

One's first impression of this priest is that he appears to speak like a nincompoop and to idle away the hours. So I wondered where he harbored such resourcefulness, such competence. That's why one summer afternoon in the sanctuary I asked him, as he indulged in a cool rest, how he managed it. His response was, "I spent a long time in China. So the work didn't take long."

What possible connection exists between having been in China and rebuilding his temple? Well, it's a fact that he had wandered as a pilgrim across the Chinese mainland for some twenty years. Even now he feels an intense nostalgia for Chinese scenery and civilization. Since this priest never slandered anyone, he had probably mastered the etiquette of the Chinese gentleman.

The priest laced his conversation with opposites, intermingling the excessively boring and the extremely allusive. Two or three times I discovered in something he said clues to problems in my writing. I use his words to explain.

He said that the current of the Yangtze appears like nothing more than a grand and sluggish flow. But, casually looking down at his feet (this, too, part of the description), he claimed that the river rushed like an arrow. It rustled reeds along the shore as though a hundred million crabs crawled along the bank, ripping away the reddish soil. Its rapid current, moreover, amplified infinitely, he said, becoming a solid bundle of energy. Thus the river's entire landscape appeared slothfully heavy, prodigious ... motionless.

After telling me such things, he opened his mouth vacantly. His eyes then turned glassy——as though absorbed in marvelous memories.

SOLITUDE*

After her husband passed away, Hirô's widow constantly wrote letters. When her father–in–law suspiciously asked her to whom she was writing, she smiled cheerlessly but said nothing.... It was certain, however, that she had been sending her letters somewhere.

Her husband's younger brother, Tsukirô, tried hard but couldn't manage to get a peek at a single one of them. Then the next younger brother, Hoshirô, followed her one day when she left the house with a letter.

She walked to the bridge leading to the other side of the river across from town. Stopping midway, she leaned against the railing, casually took the letter from her kimono sleeve, and threw it into the river. A small ripple received it. Fluttering and bobbing leisurely on the water, it vanished into the spacious landscape of the River Min.

The next time, too, and the time after that as well——the same. Soon, Tsukirô's entire household let her alone.

Hirô's widow lived for many years in Foochow. All during that time she continued writing about what lay on her mind, continued casting her letters into the river ... into those extremities where the edges of the stream fanned out and vanished into the vastness of the skies——or rather into the private solitude she imagined certainly occupied the far away....

THINGS THAT BUD

A flying bug had hatched
from the tip of a withered branch.
Gleaming with hostility and solitude,
it soon began to buzz
through empty skies.

After that,
a bead–like object swelled up.
The object split,
teasing us with faint pink tints.
Does it intend to become a leaf?
Does it mean to be a bud?
Whatever ... this branch, too, was alive.

Spring——
oh, how sad I feel wherever spring performs,
for I then see nature
sprouting life.

INTO CHAOS

Why are skies so blue?
Do you know?
Is it because everything endless,
everything hard–to–grasp,
everything empty is blue?
No.   No.
It's because those billions of particles
floating everywhere in the atmosphere
become prisms diffracting sun's sparkle.
It's because the particles reflect only the color blue.
Once beyond the atmosphere,
the ether is no longer blue.
Imagine hanging from a balloon
or an umbrella;
once we push off from Earth, we rise endlessly up.
They say we would find that the sky gradually loses its azure
and blackens bit by bit.
Ah, the path to Heaven,
no end to its inky gloom.
The path to Heaven:
vast——colorless——odorless——echoless.
Oh, my, don't call that "Ascension"!
Would lemon drops tumbling through endless space
have either tops or bottoms?
Wouldn't they just radiate
     from this tiny mineral clump called Earth
and simply vanish into infinity?
Again, that word——*infinity*.
However can we imagine what it means?
An endlessly moving, unbroken space–time continuum
expands very much like ripple after ripple after ripple.
Doesn't merely entertaining such a thought
shatter our comprehension?
That frigid, inky, fearful path to the firmament!
The aimless, despairing desolation of Time!
Yes, and yet we somehow realize that
somewhere soon
—certainly on this globe, in human society—
we'll experience that desolation
in works of literature, music, and the like.
In poetry and painting, in sculpture and fiction,
the superb beauty and art of past and present
call for rueful flights into chaos....

Sparks*

During a torrential downpour,
odors of soaked rain gear thickened the air.
Heading somewhere, the young Akutagawa Ryûnosuke
happens to look up——high over his head.
Doesn't that trolley wire flash?
Doesn't it radiate purple sparks?
Near the end of his life,
he registered that moment's gripping impression:
    "When I take stock
    there's not much I want in life
    except only——just those purple sparks."

Many a poet has written
about the beauty of sparks.
But he—Akutagawa—was likely the first
who candidly expressed a craving for them.

Ah, to reduce one's longings
to those pyrotechnics on a trolley wire,
to pyrotechnics glittering as splendidly as his talents ...
simply because he so intensely craved them!
What had deranged the gifted Akutagawa?
Even to me that's clear.

"X"

Egyptians mothered geometry.
Arabs solved quadratic equations.
Spherical trigonometry and astronomy, too,
from the people of the Koran.
Before that, magnetic compasses had been directing
Saracen camels and sails.
    Aladdin's lamp.
    Aladdin's lamp.
    Aladdin's lamp.
Poet! Keep chanting those words
of Sinbad the sailor
lest these desert metaphysics
vanish mist–like from the palm
and gradually turn to colorless flame.
Those desert folk originated
even the alcohol sustaining the flame.

CALLING MOTHER*

Mother,
you've aged.
Whenever I look at you, you seem to have shrunk,
your head so white.
Yet on this rare holiday,
when I'm home with you,
you are young indeed
and I remain your child.
Distant memories spring to life.
——That swing on the rain–drenched persimmon tree.
——My toy car flipped into the sandbox.

Faraway days become the present.
Those days, for no apparent reason, I called,
    Mommy!
    Mommy!
——flying at your apron from the back door, from the *engawa*.
Now, puffing a cigarette, face in the paper,
this forty–year–old child still ceaselessly calls you.
Unmindful of age, he calls in his heart:
    Mommy!
    Mommy!

ANIMAL OFFSPRING

Animal offspring,
all adorable.
But animal progeny
uniformly exude a sad scent——
the cheerless odor
of their natal place.
It's the scent of each animal's hill or field,
of its primordial past.

ZONE OF COLLAPSE

When you enter the eye of a typhoon, wind–beaten waves die down, driven rain abates, swallows flutter vacantly through breaks in ultramarine clouds. On rare occasions, even butterflies flit aimlessly about. It's precisely like the zone of collapse surprisingly created at the core of the anguish that some endure.

Those human beings, unrelated to the swirling atmosphere around them, continue to cruise the seas of daily life. Eventually, out of extreme exhaustion, I imagine, they may surrender to the waves——from a lack of resistance and a lackadaisical attitude.

Once, slightly north of Luzon, we crossed through just such a low–pressure area. A dragonfly—having slipped through the pale sunlight—sat motionless on the compass glass, apparently resting its wings.

BUBBLES*

This happened in the East China Sea. One morning, eerie bubbles beset my ship——an absolutely amazing sea of foam that covered everything. North to south, east to west, as far as eye could see: dirty, gray–laced bubbles frothed the surface of the sea.

Every single seaman said this was his first such experience. Whether on deck or in their cabins, the men debated the nature of the bubbles. One enterprising fellow even managed to lower the gangway to the water and scoop some up with his hand. In the end, the crew arrived at the opinion, "Maybe they're roe."

"Rot!" an officer said, putting them down. "I figure it's rather some effluent the yellow continent disgorged!"

In any event, as though to confound us a second time, the mysterious bubbles covered the ocean nearly a day——I mean our ship sailed through bubbles for almost the entire day.

Somehow they started to thin out, however, when sun sank in the west.

I stood in the stern. The bubbles retreated to the southeast. They moved off toward the far reaches of the Pacific, as though they were floating leisurely, or, in fact, as though they might rapidly disappear.

For the third time, their absurdity confounded me.

SHANGHAI*

Late at night a traveler staying over at the "H" Temple Annex on the corner of Chafu and Wuchang Roads heard curious noises. It sounded as though rickshaws and cars passing the Annex constantly splashed through water. "Gee, it hasn't even rained," he thought. He peered out through blinds in the corridor. Sure enough, stars sparkled clean throughout the night sky. His suspicions cleared the next morning. Not rain but river water had puddled the street.

The mists of Lu Shan and Ch'ien–t'ang's tidal bore——
Sights worth viewing again and again.

Once a year, tides in Chekiang Province suddenly burgeon. On

that day, a tidal bore surges up through cracks in the stone
pavement of the severely potholed Wuchang Road. The night in
question was the day of that eagre.

Shanghai is built on a delta, after all, and means "on the sea."

THAT MUCH

After all,
human beings are animals, you know.
Notice
the deeply longing eyes
of girls staring at boys,
the wild breathing
of a young fellow after a girl.

We're not even likely to preserve the peace
short of shedding blood,
how much less can we preserve love
without ransoming our lives?

Those of us in scholarship, in poetry,
live continually with ideas and dreams of the future.
We nevertheless—indeed—have yet to understand
that much ...
at least that much!

THINGS THAT FLUTTER

At times air smells absolutely pure.
No odors of either sooty smoke
or dust,
much less of streets or crowds.

I feel drearily flat when I sense those smells
in the peeled–off gloves, overcoat, or whatever
of my wife back from an errand,
of boys or girls dressed in their best.

Whatever has fluttered in the wind
—flags, telephone lines, and such,
or even the wings of a shot–down bird—
has a similarly powerful scent.

TREE VOICE*

Was it a Chagall painting?
Once I saw the following scene:

A solitary girl on a high treetop.
She's holding up a lamp.
Though standing, she doesn't touch the branches.
Wrapped in the lushness of the tree,
her hair simply streams as though swimming in space.

What metaphor does this painting suggest?
I can't explain.
Curiously, however, the picture truly inspires me.

Immediately before sinking into sleep,
I often think of trees seen during the day.
Then, I soon hear
someone calling me
from beyond the silent secrets of branches
that steal deep into the starry dark.
At such times, I also become vaguely aware that dreams,
so well prepared to soar,
have already lit their lamps.

SNAKES

Some children in our mountain village ate snakes,
garter snakes a meter or more long.
First the children chopped off the snake's head with a hatchet.
They prepared the body before your eyes with great skill,
stripping the skin, removing the entrails.

In no time the snake
was merely a dangling string of bloody white meat.
Of course it was dead——it had to be dead.
The children insisted, however, that it was alive.
They then carried it to the base of the bluff to wash.
What happens when icy mountain water touches it?
The string contracts and quivers violently.

The sensibilities!
Oh, how charged with murk.

CROW FLOCK

I often pick the last car
when I ride a train
and take a seat facing the rear.
There I can enjoy watching the rails
rush lickety–split away from me.
The present squeezes moment by moment into the past
and at length folds into loss.

On a dashing interurban,
I sometimes stand up front.
There I see vague, far–off forms take shape.
Future moves incessantly into present,
and new futures unravel from the cores of unfamiliar skeins.
That experience enthralls me, too.

Yes, but why?
Crows occasionally flock
on crossties, atop signal towers.
Though the birds tend not to surrender their space,
they fly up ponderously in the nick of time,
then soon settle down again.

Visible ahead.
Visible to the rear.
Deep in thought, they sit motionless between the rails ...
no, they sit among the dreary hours of life.

MY WINSOME WIFE*

Fugitive memories suddenly come to life:
thoughts of distress ...
of shame ... of indignation.
Long–past incidents
gnaw at my mind as though the past is positively the present.
I stand up then, unwittingly break into a sweat,
    and again carry on
as though I'm defiant.

My wife eyes those gestures and monologues
suspiciously.
At other times she mishears
and replies with striking animation. •

Miserable me.
My pitiful wife.
My pitiful
but winsome wife.

SEA'S EYES

Each time our ship heavily heels,
my life instantly dives below the billows.
My porthole turns deep blue
and sea's cold eyes peer in.

As in days long past, when I watched fish
through the aquarium's thick glass,
sea now stares at me——a fish in that small cabin.
The sea stares at this hapless fish who,
having fled it on land,
cannot avoid unrest at sea.

NEWS FROM THE CAPE*

Over the last two or three days,
sea has been intensely transparent,
sky pure blue.

Turning up my heels,
I dive each day
deep into the sea.
Marvelous! Marvelous!
Before I know it, I'm in the sky.
Through my diving goggles,
I see the sun between a cleft in the rocks.

Holding my spear high,
I rush toward the light.
Then somewhere a harp
starts its serene song,
and a file of fish circles the sky
as in an ancient Egyptian mural.

Reaching out gingerly,
I pry sea mussels and abalone
from behind the sun.

AROMA

When I sniff a rose,
    its balmy aroma
revitalizes my agonies.

As the scent of certain medicines
brings sickness to mind,
I invariably sense my pains
in a flower's fragrance.
I wonder why?
Oh, baffling!
Nature's most glorious symbol
spellbinds an insect with aromas
that in man alone stir up such agonies....

PICNIC*

In my knapsack:
rice rolled in laver,
chestnuts,
caramels——see,
even two boiled eggs!

I already drank
half my canteen.
Listen! Splashing sounds
like the *slosh–slosh* of minnows.

Let's go along
that glowing path through the fields,
everyone singing briskly.
Hey! A locust flies up
from someone's cap——look!
Glittering brightly,
it lands on a eulalia plume.

Two minds*

A poet has said:
"Through a telescope, moon's face looks pitted.
But that doesn't in the least
diminish her beauty for us."

That's precisely how it is.
Why?

Well, hardly mystifying.
We are, after all, human beings
and two minds exist in each of us.
We have a mind wanting to know reality as it is
and a mind wishing to fashion beauty——
the mind of science, the mind of art.
Both minds properly apprehend reality.

This evening, my dog stretches out beside me.
He sees the moonlight as well as I.
What can he make of it?
I somehow feel
for him.

⒣ANDS AND BREAD*

Fresh–baked,
browned,
warm bread
straight from the oven;
plump——supple as rubber.

Break a loaf in half
and steam rises like dawn mist.
Morning sun
tumbles rosy
from the steam.

Near dawn,
a distended glove–like hand
gets a loaf of bread
from the corner store.
The hand walks along patting the bread occasionally,
as though to caress it.
At each pat,
the loaf echoes the sound——*bread ... bread.*
Absolutely no exaggeration.
The loaf echoes the sound——*bread ... bread.*

A loaf will indeed sustain life for a single day.
It sounds clearly more cheerful
than a briefcase stuffed with bills.

⒩IGHT TREES*

Before falling asleep at night,
it's delightful to think of trees——
of enigmatic tree shapes
breathing high into the starry dark of open skies....

I recall every possible tree seen during the day.

Coiling like a van Gogh cypress,
a *hinoki* I noted somewhere along a fence.
That giant aspera in the park——a tolerable imitation
    of a Chagall canvas.
Every tree charged with sunlight, with rustlings
that layer the lively chatter of birds
over arabesques of branches and leaves....

At that moment, I suddenly become aware
that tree songs and tree glares surely vanish.
They mysteriously turn into silent ebony shadows
marshaled in my imagination....

My consciousness
melts gradually into sleep.
I lose my me.
Another self materializes
in that space.

Green lantern ready,
I make no sound opening the shutters.
Just like that I soar into night skies,
my long *yukata* fluttering in space.

I'm in the midnight sky.
Without a wing flap, I move from one tree clump to another,
treading gently over treetops.
Illuminating gaps in branches so mystic and curious to me,
I swim off under the glitter of stars....

Stars*

In his prose poem *"Les Etoiles,"*
the poet Alphonse Daudet
borrows a shepherd's expression
to convey the Alps' nighttime hush.
He says each star in the sky breathes.
He can hear even the vegetation grow.

The northern mountain village
where I lived until two or three years back
    was precisely such a place.
There, earth turns absolutely black
the instant night falls.
Mountain flumes roar deep in the throat of the dark.

From the opposite direction,
light as fierce as flame crackles from the stars.

My place sat on a bluff,
high on a hillside overlooking the plain.
Stars sparkled everywhere.
I could scan them below eye level
on three sectors of the horizon.
When I thrust out a hand,
my palm took up the same space as the stars.
If I stretched out a leg,
I could stomp on them.
Life was simply a matter
of getting up or sleeping amid millions of stars.

When winter snows melted,
mountainsides suddenly burst with patches of green.
Night reeked lustily then
with grass and trees and stars,
with vegetation, with minerals....

Mars——Venus——Sirius——the Polestar——
the Big Dipper——Scorpio——Cygnus ...
whichever I watched,
I felt that nothing inched nearer into intimacy than those stars.
Nor did anything feel as increasingly remote.
Midnight. Shutting eyes weighty with watching,
I drifted pleasantly into sleep.
I slept perfectly sound
in my mountain abode——dreamless
till bird twitters in the forest
cheerily signaled dawn....

HANDICAPS LIKE THESE

Adolescence grows its hair too long.
Adolescence is grimy.
Adolescence constantly stammers.
The hobnails of adolescence peek from its soles
    (painful hobnails of regret).
There's no bottom to the pockets of adolescence.
The arms of adolescence blaze.
More than that——
    Adolescence ...
    adolescence ...

adolescence....

Afflicted with handicaps like these,
adolescence remains oblivious to adolescence.

DAY OF THE STORM

On the day of the storm
——I saw wind and rain blowing fiercely
through branch gaps in the trees.

——I saw soaked masses of green
pounded, pushed away;
I saw them reel, fall, dragged down,
spring up, bend back.

In the ceaseless jostling that monopolized my view,
I saw again
the endless shapes of resignation and enmity
in a grief–disheveled mind....

ATOMIC BALM

Rather than sticks of TNT
to blow up half the Earth,
why not drams of incense
to scent the world's windows, fields, and oceans ...
our thought,
our freedom of expression?

Can't someone formulate
such a balm?

Create an international committee
charged with making a single precious vial of it!
That will be a dazzling dawn——man's supreme glory.
Let its mists
fall from lavender skies.
Let them saturate streaming pink handkerchiefs.

FIREPLACE*

Our house had a fireplace when I was a small boy.
I loved watching its flames.
Once his guests had left, Father bustled from the room,

and I slipped in silently through the partly–open door.
I then gazed intently
at those silently fading coals
——through vapor climbing from left–over black tea,
——through scraps of smoke rising from ashtrays.

Whenever winter nears,
I still long for a fireplace in my living room.
Moving from one rented place to another,
our walls all drab, cracked, and soiled——
ruined rain–tracked walls where crickets chant.
In my whimsy, I sketch on each such wall,
    so like the brow of a beggarly and cruel stepmother,
those brightly burning flames....

WITHIN THE SUN*

    "When I die, I'll live again within the sun."
I know a young tubercular patient with that conviction.
Whenever crimson blood courses through his throat,
he says he's that much nearer the sun.
    "Ah, and yet
    sun has crowded altogether too close.
    Searing, tormenting——it consumes everything.
    I never knew being born in those flames
    would be such agony,"
he cried.

What imperishable life.
What an awesomely passionate view.
I've never heard
such a wholesome thought.
How, in what way,
had he acquired that certainty?
Wasted to a shell, he lies on his sanitarium bed,
powerless to move.
His life nevertheless hurtles through space,
roaring like a rocket.
Moment by moment he closes in on the sun.
A single speck, he'll plunge into its flame
and in an instant be re–born.
The sky will be slightly hotter, slightly brighter.
Ah, how beautiful his re–birth!
No need to lay a crucifix on his corpse.
Don't you find "going to Heaven" too tinged with twilight,

smacking of sorcery performed by a star and an angel?
I curse every unclean spirit,
protest the ambiguities of every conceivable creed.
In this man there will be no death, no gloom, no chill.
He'll be eternal.
Transformed into the imperishable energy of matter,
his life will radiate toward the planets.

How destitute was his childhood?
What did he love? Whom did he hate?
What hardships had he endured?
None of that matters now.
I wonder if the life in him has already left our globe.
If it has....

Morning.
I look into sunlight pouring over all.
I look into sun's heat,
I gaze at its glare on grass, on trees, on birds, on man's work,
on sunflowers stretching insatiably to absorb it.
Drying sweat makes me an intimate participant.
I can feel him there within the sun.
I love the him in me.

WORLD

I'm sick inside.
Doctor, put your stethoscope
to my feverish skin.
What——you don't recognize
the syndrome of the anguished?

Surgeon, take your scalpel,
make an incision here.
Mass is under way inside.
Look, look——hymn–singing voices
trickle out.

AWAKENING*

Everyone has tried at least once
to visualize the world of death.
No one alive
can speak with authority about

that unknown, apprehensive realm.

For all that....
Death, they say, resembles perfect sleep,
free from dreams, free from sensation
——the absolute repose of consciousness.
Sleep may be the perfect counterfeit of death.

... If true, it means
we trek to death's domain each night.
This causes no anxiety
because we know we'll be back
at dawn.

Nothing's more truly refreshing than adequate sleep.
We wake the next morning
a mere stride from the previous night.
Replenishment of life,
an instant transformation from the jaws of fatigue!

Already   I'm in the light of a new sun.
Already   I'm among cheerful, greening aromas.
Uguisu warblings echo over the globe!
The world born again in this moment
with the beating of my heart....

Ah, what if death
is such a moment of sleep...?
What if it leads to instant *awakening*...?

FREE FLIGHT*

No doubt the yen for flight
still survives in people's hearts ...
not to fly in an airplane
or use the thrust of an engine,
but to fly alone through the blue.

A recent newsreel featured an experiment.
A German attached bird–like wings to himself,
moved them with his arms,
and from a hillside tried frantically to ride the wind.
His experiment failed, of course.
Unable to give up his dream, he had a crane lift him into space
where he leisurely flapped his arms.
That partially satisfied his yen for flight. •

Oh, ever since primitive times
humans have so envied birds their soaring through the blue!
Till men become birds,
they have no way to realize their want to fly.
The newsreel pictured onlookers laughing
at the man's single–minded drollery.
The theater audience laughed as well.
... For some reason, I could not.

Why?
If you want to know,
it's because we sometimes realize free flight in night dreams.
No, not *sometimes*——for even this night
I may soar effortlessly into space.
I may fly softly through the blue,
more nimbly, more free than any bird.

MOON AND SATURN*

PART I

At twilight late in spring,
I visited a private observatory
on the shore of a suburban lake.

My host had responded to my request to view the heavens.
He showed me into his study
for the brief wait till nightfall.
There 'K' explained to me in detail
his moon charts, his planetary maps, and the like.
For my part, I told him
about the poet Miyazawa Kenji's great interest in science.
Soon 'K' invited me outside.

The observation platform stood behind his home.
A 6.5 inch reflecting telescope on an equatorial mount
aimed its inky shadow into night skies.
Star glints emitted an animated green.
Among their glinting,
a thin lemon–slice moon hung high in western skies.
The telescope rotated nimbly
as 'K' operated the wheel.
Once fixed on the moon, it stopped
like an anti–aircraft gun tracking its target ...
    then, before I knew it,
a tiny light flashed at the base of the platform.

The motorized pendulum started its *clack–clack–clack*.
Simultaneously, something inside me as well
began ticking busier than those clacks.

Frankly,
I found everything as small and charming as a model;
not a soul nearby to watch....
Still, at that pitch–dark moment
ecstatic throbs began to quiver my entire frame.
I shivered with the illusion that 'K' and I alone
stood at a point on Earth's glittering surface.
We were nearer those heavenly bodies
        than anyone on the globe.

        PART II
Though the telescope aimed at the night sky,
I did not look up into the heavens
        to see the stars and the moon.
I looked obliquely toward my feet
at the heavenly bodies in the lens.
I looked through a narrow branch–like tube
attached at a right angle to the end of that thick barrel.
It was very much like peering into a microscope.

The telescope had only 150x magnifying power,
so stars and moon appeared small.
Moon's surface was nevertheless marvelously distinct.
Both its jagged hills and countless crater–like pits,
as well as shadows called mares,
were individually distinguishable in sharp relief.
Saturn wore its rings lengthwise,
slightly red,
all lovely.
The depths of the universe that encompassed
        those two heavenly bodies
appeared all the more uncommonly dazzling.
Ever so close to that dazzle, I imagined at my fingertips a Time
tens of thousands of years in the future.

I looked away from the bodies in the lens and, with naked eye,
stared again at the moon, at Saturn.
For an instant, I sensed that the space and time
        stretching before me
again went rushing back, rocketing into the far–off future,
deserting me in the painful present....

HERONS

Only on the lake's sunset surface,
a dull white sparkle.
Whatever could it be——
birds settling down?
The instant that thought came to mind,
the birds scattered like an eruption.

Oh! They're herons——herons!——
a flock of herons flapping off.
A host of white fans suddenly flicked open.
They appeared to sweep away sky's afterglow.
Abruptly veering, turning to flame,
they disappeared.

I couldn't believe my eyes.
Uneasy, I watched with greater intensity.
... Might they momentarily change the vector
    of their furious flight
and flash again into view?
Even so, how strange!
Nothing had changed.
Nothing else occurred.

What had I hallucinated?
Had I seen herons or an apparition?

Whatever I saw ...
my train quickly left the shore.
Sun set abruptly in the window of my coach.

ON THIS PLANET*

I saw my first comet—Halley's—
when I was eleven or twelve.
They say it nears Earth
every sixty or so years.

I've forgotten precisely
from which quarter of the heavens it approached.
I remember only that it brightened a corner of the sky
like a misty beam of dim light,
its tail (bushy as a horse's) not directly attached.
Rumor held that several days after passing,
its tail would brush the Earth.

Enveloped in a gas cloud,
we'd become sleepy and die.
Yes, everyone on Earth would die!
These absurdities—the murmurs, the anxieties—
touched even a mere child like myself.
I realized we live not only in a family, in a nation, in a world,
but also on that isolated heavenly body, Earth....

Well, the dreaded day came.
Perhaps the comet's tail
had covered Earth for a few hours.
Luckily, however, nothing happened.
I felt relieved.
It was exactly as I'd figured.
The next day I cleanly dismissed my dread.

Then this year, near spring,
that long–dismissed panic returned.
Radios and newspapers abruptly announced
that an absolutely new planet
hurtled at dazzling speed toward Earth.
Such velocity offered the strong chance
of collision in a fortnight.

The certain feeling that this could not be true
soothed my anxieties. On the other hand,
its being "an absolutely new planet" bothered me.
A rendezvous appointed by the boundless universe
over a cycle of light years ...
what if that ill–fated moment had come?

More than one radio and newspaper reported the new planet
already visible to the naked eye.
At dusk, I stood on our *engawa.*
Umé bloomed white in that corner of Earth called Japan.
Two or three stars already blinked
from bright skies visible through treetops.
Near those glittering evening stars,
I imagined the planet spinning earthward bit by bit——
my imagination, a stunning poem.
Somewhere within it, however, emerged
the forlorn and dreary tang of physical laws.

Before anxiety overcame me,
the news media confessed their fault.

It wasn't an unknown planet.
Absolutely no chance of impact.
Once again I felt relieved.
Ever since, however,
the thought has been crossing and re–crossing my mind:
We live on planet Earth.
In my imagination, I sense our planet's curvature
the way a girl balancing on a ball senses its curve.
Cherishing that sensation,
I sleep.

WITH BUT A FEW WORDS

It should be possible to snare a poem
with but a few words——
just a few simple words,
no more than children have in hand,
merely by weaving them inventively together.

I'd rejoice if I could write a poem
that profoundly explores daily life,
traces the streams of feeling, the flow of thoughts,
swims life's transparent depths
——those shadows of man's unique mind,
shadows that one scoops up like little fish
… figures that burst fresh with life,
flipping in words' net,
often about to slip through the mesh.

Moved to tears
by the gamble,
how beyond dreams
if I could convey this experience in a natural way.
I think always: that's the poem I'd love to write.

LONER

Whenever I'm alone,
my eyes become more attuned to truth,
my ears more sensitive to candor.

Enlivened then
by unaffected sentiments and words,
my mind gradually surges and warms. •

My courage intensifies
like a grand symphony orchestra
prodigal with energies
that not even a hundred thousand could command.

Should my shadow fall desolate,
I'll no longer be alone,
for countless allies support me.

How lucky the loner!
Destitute or deserted, I much prefer my solitude.
I hope to share the mind
of those who outstrip distance.

MIDNIGHT MIRROR

Midnight mirror.
That hushed glass
reflects but one corner of the room.
Nobody looks into it. Yet someone's eyes—no,
no, the eyes of the entire world—focus on
and stare with excitement into that glass.

At that moment, a young girl abruptly appears.
She slips off her clothes before the mirror.
——Wondrous shivers tingle her spine.
Entranced by the pallid light,
she gazes intently at her naked reflection.

Taking a step forward,
the cold glass before her,
she kisses her other Self.
One second. Two seconds. Three seconds.
The girl stands motionless,
——Then she abruptly steps back——turns——
snatches her pajamas from the wall——vanishes.

After that, not a stir.
Hushed again,
the glass mirrors the curtains.
An empty room and, yes, the eyes of the whole world merging,
stare without a blink into that glass.
The mirror stands at the focus of those eyes.
Its lipstick smudge alone lingers
flower–like till dawn.

Poem of idleness*

Hopeless,
I've lost the will to act.
No longer caring for people, I lie on the grass
and gaze into sky....

Then, what misery!
Sun burns even at such moments.
Corona ablaze,
it scatters bundles of blinding heat
through the infinite universe.

Sea of okhotsk*

A friend told me,
"I'd really like to show you the Sea of Okhotsk."
He said, "Until you've seen it,
you lack authority to write about the North!"
He even remarked, "The very colors of the sea
    merit amazement.
They swell massively, deep with melancholy ... no,
no, they're beyond words."
I asked him, "Would you say they're like the back of a fur seal?"
Closing his eyes he said, "Right. ... But not quite."

A letter came from my friend.
I went to Hokkaidô and took the trip with him.
We rode from Sapporo to Asahikawa.
    From Asahikawa a stop at Kitami.
    From Kitami we headed for Kushiro.
Finally Abashiri——I saw waves from the coach window.
The Sea of Okhotsk.

Yes, the Sea of Okhotsk.
Quite an ordinary body of water.
The offing bright, cattle roaming the strand.
"Is this Okhotsk?" I asked.
"Yep," he acknowledged. "This is it."
He said no more.
When the train stopped he stood up.
"Shall we go pick sweetbriers ... or something?"

MAN WHO ENCOUNTERED A BEAR*

Something blackly black slid
with a rumble down the slope,
poised on haunches, front paws raised....
A bear! The moment I realized it,
he tumbled sideways into the cover of some bamboo bushes.
——I'd no sooner thought he was gone than I saw him again,
scurrying away from me
up the mountain trail.
Setting out again,
I resolved not to look back.
Though I moved deliberately,
I told myself I needn't make such a point of walking so slow.
I took a cigarette from my pocket,
finally found a match and lit up.
Half a kilometer down the mountain, I met a woodcutter.
He badgered me about my pale face.
"A bear!" I told him.
"Scary?" After thinking it over, I replied,
"It certainly was uncanny."

Indeed, no deception there.
Quite an eerie sensation.
When the beast looked at me with those eyes,
innocent yet burning brightly deep within,
I immediately sensed reality fade.
No, no, not exactly——I sensed rather that Time
from an entirely distinct dimension
had crossed the Time where I existed,
    in which I continue to exist:
an unknown Time breathing and pulsing wildly like wind.
Unexpectedly—and positively unanticipated—
I stood at the spot where they merged.

Instantly the mountain stream stood still.
In response to the hush,
forest, grass, earth, and rocks briefly echoed the shriek.
Even now they resound through my mind.

LIVES OF TREES

Among the seasons that visit trees, I like winter best. Because I
sense a tree's greatest beauty in its bareness.

Winter trees are not dead. Nor do they sleep. Their morbid outward appearance gives the impression of demise, but in preparation for spring tree lives burn like fire.

They're like silent people——not those who withdraw and become uncommunicative, but those so consumed by vivid dreams and ambitions that chatting does not interest them. Barren trees bring to mind such intensity.

On the roadside near the knoll, leafless trees stand hushed under cloudy skies. If only their trunks had apertures that we could wiggle through! If we could infiltrate their xylem, its whirling bustle and hum would astonish us.

WHERE SKY IS NO MORE*

Severe dizziness besets me.
I sense my body leave the bed.
I'm about to float unsteadily into space,
drawn—still on my back—out the window.
I feel I'm on the verge of vanishing for good,
the burnt–out hulk of a rocket engine
that gravity forsook.
(Oh, do you suppose I'm a goner?)
Doctor! Quick, an injection, please.
Good wife! Shut the curtains.
Lash down my arms and legs.
Through the window, I see an angel hovering
in the inhospitable regions of outer space where sky is no more.
Despite life's bitterness,
roses still bloom on Earth.
I remain attached to it.

BIRD

It climbs to the stratosphere and,
the instant it decides a direction,
wings toward the South Pole.
Ignorant of compass error,
no instruments to go awry,
it slices headlong through the blue.

A life of straight lines,
instinct transcending thought.

Well, what is it?
"A bird! It's a bird."

——Even as you respond,
your eyes already resemble the bird's.
See! Shadows transporting sunset
fade like the eyes of the bird.

. . . .

CRANE (iii)*

A crane soars
over the blue sea.

A sooted and frayed umbrella
singing sadly.

That so long–cherished
bubble reputation
turns to shadow and slips away,
mirrored black
on creases in the brine.

SEA COLORINGS——ON AN AUSTRALIAN FREIGHTER*

– 1 –

Again and again sea filched my colored pencils.
Again and again it also snatched away my pen and ink.
Worse, it pilfered even my words....
Faced by these setbacks, I despaired.
Despairing, I cast myself into the brine.
Waves near where I drowned
creased into deep shadows——
so perfect that their flickering foam took on the glitter of clouds
as day after day sea enriched its brightness and its blue.

– 2 –

The cook threw meat scraps from the fantail.
Gulls swooped down the moment they saw the scraps
and pecked at the falling meat.
In the instant before scraps touched brine,
        the birds scattered in every direction.
Each day when the cook disposed of his scraps
gulls in flight contested them.
Blood reddened their beaks, their eyes, their wings.
How long will they heel our ship?

– 3 –

When herds of cattle cram our decks,
the stench of oil and tar clears.

Then aromas from Down Under winter fields blanket the ship.
When sun (risen from brine) strides over the mast
　　and sinks back into sea,
dandelions bloom on sailors' caps.

THAT FELLOW WITHIN*

The old days were wonderful.
I craved only
what I craved.

Life is different now.
That fellow within,
who wears a face like mine but is not me,
covets everything.

He's divested the sea of women,
wrestled saké from the skies,
stripped verdant potentials
from future time.

Oh, I take all his parts,
crunch them and dump them together.
Chomping and gulping,
I bolt them down.

Good riddance!
That fellow in me is not me.
A monstrosity,
I can't let him go on living here.

TREE IN ME

I don't know when it began, but a tree has taken root in me.
It grows through my growth.
Spreading branches from my maturing limbs,
its leaves thicken into shapes of grief.

I no longer go out,
no longer speak with anyone.
Not with Mother, not even with friends....
I'm turning into the tree in me.
No, no——I already am that tree.

I stand quietly, far beyond the fields.
Whenever I greet morning sun

or look off after sunset–fired clouds,
my silence glitters,
my solitary Self sings.

MY WOMAN THE SEA*

How do I care for her?
As much as the volume of her heaving breasts,
as fiercely as the tempestuous passions
of those breasts,
of storms that rock even 100,000–ton tankers.

If she asks why I care so for her,
I couldn't possibly offer anything like a reason.
She ignores my stammers,
turns at once into a swirling flock of waterfowl,
or into a rainbowed school of flying fish
winging off the globe
toward Uranus or Neptune.

The mere thought of a world without her——
desolation worse than death!
For me she's a venerable, dear wife … and more.
She's my woman, the sea,
still singing youthful songs.

HOSTAGE SEA——ON OCEAN DAY*

Fettered by a line of steel chains,
she's been dragged toward the offing
year after year, meter by meter.
Eyes moist with the hue of seaweed
stare intently at the horizon off Japan.

A sea that in our youth breathed,
once so very full of life,
violated now,
heartlessly polluted.
Her breasts, her entire body——paralyzed by poisons!

This morning, Ocean Day visits the port again.
Beyond scattered banners and soaring gulls,
the bright wake of a waterway
that won't come back.

SEA BEAST*

Ocean glitters under sunset.
Oh, that gigantic fish who eyed me for an instant,
leaping high with a *whoosh* through flying foam!

A year since then, and thousands of knots.
I'm sure that fellow even at this moment
swims some globe–girdling current.
Now or then he thinks of me....
In the same way, his face floats into my mind from time to time
as I swim the congested waves of life on land.

You wonder why? Actually, in a dream last night
he unexpectedly came by to greet me.
He wiggled his fins silently,
a grizzled and haggard expression on his face.
Then he promptly plunged into that endlessly expanding sea,
deep in the depths of my consciousness.

PART V

POETRY PUBLISHED BETWEEN
1957 and 1974

A. FROM 1957 THROUGH 1967

昭和三十二年から昭和四十二年の間に発表された詩

LOVERS' WHISPERS——DARK NIGHT:

OVER THE GLOW OF A BOMBED CITY
Burning in the distance,
the city bloodied clouds on the horizon.

Suddenly, like an echo, a cheerful, tender voice:
  "Oh ... that's wonderful!"
Only that——lost in gloom.

More than twenty years since then.
Who whispered those words?
That family had three girls,
now wives and mothers....

CORAL SEA*

Massive waves surge against the bow,
turning up endless furrows.
Gleams that differ from yesterday's,
shadows that differ from those the day before that,
frolic over
every emerald pulse.

From those gleams,
from those shadows,
something dances up nimbly, quickly.
Objects stream by now and again in the wind
to graze funnels and portholes.
Are they sea gulls?
Flying fish?
No, no——they're leaves,
cheerless withered leaves
scattering over autumn sea.

VISION

Up from the seabed
an anchor spitting brine.
No——not an anchor,
a woman
dangling from the end of the chain,
an absolutely naked woman
smeared with mud, trussed up in seaweed.
Look——How pitiful!
Isn't she frozen blue and spent?
And yet, she's winched up
relentlessly,
dried in sea breezes, arms and legs folded,
fixed with a clang inside the anchor ring ...
no, no——fixed in the men's minds ...
a frozen vision
borne to sea.

AUTUMN DREAMS

Evening insects hum.
Whenever I hear their voices,
my body appears outside the window:
it's lying on grass.

Evening rain falls.
Whenever I savor its scent,
my mind materializes beyond the door:
it's resting on the ground.

Both insect voices and the scent of rain
saturate my spine, steep my head.
Asleep at last,
I dream cheerless dreams the night long.
I see my house dilapidate,
rot, collapse.
        My wife?
        The children?

Dawn.
My cries waken me.
Rain stops.
Winds blow.

Poetry*

I waken at midnight.
Loathing the glow of electric bulbs,
I light a taper.

I prefer a candle,
for in it I hope to kindle my Self.
Beyond its flickering point,
I hope to refashion that Self.

I haven't stirred yet,
but I can clearly see
the flame gnawing into night.
The more it eats away the dark,
the more plainly my agonies light up.
I also see dust particles swarm the halo
where flames consume them.
The more dust specks the flame devours,
the more purged this midnight hour.

At last——
a moment of ecstatic calm.
I stand and pass through the flame.
As the candle fades,
I become a butterfly at sunup ... transformed
into a chilled, an absolutely solitary butterfly
at this dawning of a winter day.

Afterimage of a Picketline

Ranks of demonstrating young people,
arms meshed
like gears.

Line after line after line of them,
swaying sharply to the right, to the left.
They chant something softly,
sweat beading their necks.

My TV screen then suddenly fades.
Only faraway clouds persist.
Yes, a perfect picture of fall.

MINATO WARD, NAGOYA——MEMO
ON THE ISE BAY TYPHOON*

Mackerel bob up from the kitchen,
enter the alleyway through a window;
    revived, they swim down the street.
Threading slanted utility poles,
they head energetically for the estuary, for the sea.
From deep riled–up eddying waters,
    women,
    children,
    old people—
souls exchanged instantly with fish—surface here and there.
Now towed off on rafts,
they pass again under twilight eaves
that hold their breath.
Tomorrow, cremation under sunny skies.

SNOWY MOUNTAIN*

Morning in the north country.
Supposedly its spring, yet snow still heaped cold, still deep.
From the far side of a mountain I'd never seen,
two tight–lipped young men come to meet me.
I go with them to their hamlet.

At the foothills, they have me remove my straw boots.
I hang them on a nearby branch,
slip into snowshoes they provide,
then climb the steep mountain side.

On the way up I trip three times,
twice nearly slipping into crevices in the snow,
but the lads' strong arms instantly prevent my fall.
Finally at journey's end, I spend the night;
then I shuffle back through still heavy snow.

Reprise: Mute lads escort me.
Reprise: I slip the snowshoes off under that tree,
take my straw boots from the branch, and then....

YOUNG SAILOR*

Stern already frothing,
the capstan winches a heavy hawser.
    ——The lad

jumps on the hawser's writhing tip,
tries to bend it.
Instead, the hawser bends his entire frame.
Barely sixteen or seventeen, wouldn't you say?
What was I thinking at that age?
I dare say a boy like this has tender dreams.
And yet, that deck–cap chin strap hugging frantic cheeks,
the tang of the sea, of the tar, of smoke,
the flutter of departure flags on the mast——
enough to make him seem a man of the world.

Our ship leaves the quay without good–byes
for the offing where winds wail....

DREAM

Despite torrential rains,
the eerie radiance under that tiny umbrella persists.
Why hasn't a single raindrop
even touched the girl?
Like an autumn flower,
she's dry from the inside out,
a bloom flourishing on wet pavement.
I suppose she's been waiting some time for a cab.
        Hey, Taxi! Hurry it up
        before this girl gets wet.

——Fretting about such things,
I wonder if I might melt away, pelted by rain.
I can no longer think of anything else.

OUR NATIONAL ANTHEM*

I can't quite grasp the sense
of the phrase,
"A thousand, no eight thousand ages."
My heart quivers and warms, however,
at the suddenly resounding drum beat
near the word *pebbles*.

Callousness and solitude crowd together in me
and simply sing, drunk as the sea,
of a moment sliced from our past.

Someone stoops surreptitiously

to retrieve a handkerchief
where surf roars rise ... fall.

LINE FROM THE NORTH*

Washed–ashore driftwood.
A herd of horses hunting heads down for grass.
I wonder what fodder they'll find there.
This a picture postcard of Okhotsk Strand.
Near a horizon folding summer into distance,
the one–line scribble:
Sometimes sea devours horses.

ON THIS FOSSIL*

What star is that?
It glares green in night skies.

That's a nova.
We once called it Earth.
The day it was "observed," it became a star
spinning off in orbit.

This evening I note these planets with my naked eye:
Mars——Jupiter——Venus——Saturn
——and the Moon.
They're joined now by another, all six twinkling.

Well, then, what of the place we live?
It's this future castoff, this spot of shadow,
this static fossil
where two behemoths chomp into each other
silently spurting blood.

SAILING THROUGH AUTUMN*

Morning....
As I shave in the cool breeze,
a shell–shaped island trailing two or three
smoke puffs
floats through the fathoms of my mirror.

I go to the salon.
Everyone wears a jacket

except one crewman in a sport shirt.
"Autumn before you know it," he says with a sneeze.
"In a couple of days
we'll be into winter."

Sky and clouds sing in the distance.
In time with their airs,
the Coral Sea spends another day
pitching,
rolling.

FUTURE

Throughout the night,
the sculptor chipping the stone to shape me
never rests the hands that govern chisel and mallet.

When morning sun
warms my naked marble, however,
he brings his cheek close to my rose–colored head,
then listens raptly:

——To the solitary woman who sings
inside that me still lacking either eyes or nose.
——To a solitary woman I do not know....

GRAY BEAR

Rising leisurely
and glancing our way,
his little black eyes
melt into absentmindedness.

Tongue drooping
from the side of something like a smile,
his expression ... so human.

The soul of this one, however,
quite murky,
spellbound at times by the illusion
of mauling us under the midnight sun.

Then an abrupt *Crack!*
Had he slapped at a gadfly?
... Vast shadows shut out the aurora,
shake the skies.

EERIE TREES——TO POET FRIENDS
WHO DIED YOUNG*
Tachihara Michizô hid himself in them.
Nakahara Chûya ran off into them.
Tsumura Nobuo disappeared into them.
——All into those trees standing along the way.
Not a one came out.

Before I knew it, I found myself alone.
I'd been walking ... I'd been walking.

——In those days,
our paths were green, our skies at song.
Ranked silently on either flank of the road, however,
those eerie, shadowless trees.

I see it now.
They're the trees of Death.

ILLUSION IN THE REEF*

The chalky coral grove
floats transparently to the surface,
a sunken image
deep within a poem.
A single baby shark undulates through coral tips,
sunlight streaming everywhere.
No, that's a boot, an airman's boot
——beginning already to dissolve
like a shadow, like kelp.

HORIZON*

Not a single galleon at anchor,
and yet an antique boat rows toward me.
Dangling pigtails, cutlasses at their sides,
the men on board disappear over dune–like silhouettes.

Once again ...
a single mermaid spewed
from the endless petitions
of sea's hundreds of protests,
of waves' thousands of sighs.

She leaps onto the beach, glances up at empty skies,
then at once rides off on a receding wave.

Ah, that horizon folding up the far–off future.
But now only cheerless phantoms of the past
dash from there ... at me.

MALLARDS

When mallards flew up together from the lake, I decided to fo-
cus on one specific bird in the flock. The mallards, however, in-
stantaneously began to swirl furiously overhead. Because the bird
I'd chosen merged with a horde of look–alikes, I lost track of it.

Doubtless he's still in that crowd, yet I could no longer differen-
tiate him from the others.

Dizzied—my mind wandering aimlessly—I recalled several
people I had met and associated with briefly. After a while, how-
ever, our correspondence ceased and I even forgot their names.
They're now countless strangers. Among the uncountable com-
pany of those I've met, I nevertheless recall people I imagined had
prevailed through life by kindling an individual existence. And so
it comes as a surprise to realize that in their thoughts I, too, am
clearly one such faceless person.

Unexpectedly, the mallards fluttered again to the lake's sur-
face——as though to brush off the sky. I'm certain they'll soon
take flight. Next time, I'll fix my gaze on a single one of them.

TREE-LINED PATH——MOURNING *SHIKI**

When did we
begin strolling this path
together?
Whatever do they symbolize ...
those hushed rows of trees
pursuing me like phantoms?
Those eerie tree tiers
waiting just ahead?
One by one friends disappeared
into trunk–cast shadows.
As though blotted out, they never re–appeared.
Nakahara Chûya   never came out.
Tachihara Michizô   never came out.
Tsumura Nobuo   never came out.
Though I called to them, they never again emerged.

I wanted to put a stop to those eerie capers.
How distressing——that eternal game of hide–and–seek.
The skies in those days
were still young.
Branches above our heads intermeshed with fresh buds,
rustlings wrapped in bird song.
Exhilarated by our redolence and our glitter,
we'd been strolling——enthralled hearts linked.
Then, somewhat later,
Hagiwara Sakutarô faded away.
Murô Saisei disappeared.
Suddenly, even you——
even Miyoshi Tatsuji vanished.
All, every one lost in those trees....

The path endless.
Trees loom in deathly silent rows,
incrementally intermeshing their branches
     as though to lure me on.
I walk solitary beneath them,
entirely alone——nowhere to hide.
No turning off this isolated path,
this lengthy lane of lyric trees
synonymous with Death.

IN THE CORRIDOR OF OMAEZAKI LIGHTHOUSE*

Soon, I guess, the lamp will begin its rotation.
They say that every twenty seconds
Omaezaki's million–plus candlepower lamp
sweeps some forty knots of offing.

From near the beam's reach,
from waves far on the horizon where light stubbornly lingers,
griefs bearing the silhouette of a younger me
unexpectedly drift my way.
I feel certain I once was there.
Yes, I'm sure they bear the silhouette
of a younger me.

BIRDS (iii)

——Birds flock together
before dawn

and pass from night's dark side
over high mountain ridges
into a dawn about to bask in sun.

The flock instantaneously scatters into space,
into light striking the ridge line.
Then, as though plummeting,
they flutter down the gentle slope of relief.

They've now become separate birds
in the forest, in the field, in a nest, in the thicket.
Each pecks on a treetop or hops along the shoreline of a stream.
Each calls for its mate
in solitary joy ...

till suddenly an impulse
drives it toward an adjacent ridge.

Deer*

Lattices on homes in Nara (called "Nara grills")
are stoutly built, they say,
since deer come by and crack them.
It's accidental, for the deer only chafe their antlers on the bars.
Late at night when the town sleeps,
horned deer stealthily roam the city's back streets.
Symbolic meanings permeate this imaginary scene.

Entering the park
you see two deer, apparently stags, facing off.
Heads lowered intensely, they make no move.

They're not in pain.
They simply burst with the spirit of combat, eyes up,
each scrutinizing its rival's mood.
That step forward signals
the clash of horns.

Standing transfixed like stationary trees,
they nimbly attack, then disengage.
This occurs on the third day of de–horning
when the stags lack the antlers for a fray.

Two and a half months later——
I hardly imagine the antlers have yet grown back.
Today, the first of the year,
sun casts classic silhouettes over withered grass....

Early Spring Sea

Trillions of plankton
no doubt cause the hues
that make the distant offing blush.

Suddenly, a mermaid's face
emerges from green waves.

Looking from a wave top, she rushes at me.
Hair streaming wavily,
she then races pell–mell toward the beach.

Finally ...
she vanishes
the instant she touches sand.

Mermaid and I

A mermaid approaches
over the emerald surface of the sea.

She climbs
or slides the waves.
She stares at me with transparent eyes
and from far off begins to chant.
I hear her sing on wind, "I long to be with men."

Each time I hear it, I resolutely grip the helm,
then think scornfully,
    You're a fish.
    What comes of embracing a fish?

Suddenly the mermaid's expression changes and she shrieks,
——*You miserable old man*!
Scattering foam, she dives headlong into sea.

Sky now at noon and yet ...
ah, stars dot the sky.

Visiting Matsue*

Warrior mansions stand unchanged
on one side of that road along the moat.

(In those days, I'm not sure *koto* strains soothed the scene.)

On a stone pillar standing serenely by the gate,
where dusk's glow peeks in, the inscription:
HISTORICAL SITE——KOIZUMI YAKUMO'S FORMER RESIDENCE.
Ah, that little boy of five decades back
comes dashing into this traveler's mind.

Those days I knew nothing of the poet's solitude.
Daily I walked through this place on my way to school.
I strolled innocently half way round the castle,
tossing stones at dabchicks on the water....

FACE WITH ANTS*

Ants crawl over eyelids.
Then that nearby hollow suddenly gathers shadows,
as though engraved.

Ants lick the inner corners of the eyes.
From there they move straight down the cheek.
——While I watch,
that nearby hollow deepens, seemingly scooped out.

Ants circle that mole by the mouth,
then scurry into breathless nostrils.
They won't show themselves again.
They may never reappear.

Oh,   the shame of gawking so.
Oh,   the shame of being so gawked at.

ROOM WITH BIRD*

Whenever its master calls, the bird flies straight to his arm.
If his wife laughs, it comes directly to her finger.
Each time it picks up bread crumbs, apple pulp, whatever,
from their palms or the tips of their tongues.
Sometimes the bird rests its wings
     on my shoulders or on my head.
I don't mind, so it pecks at the mole on my neck.

Each time the bird moves about,
the hues of far–off skies flare and unfold from its wings.

Bit by bit those hues fill the room.
The couple's talk, not to mention mine,
    the dining table——everything quite divine by now.

One daybreak
this momentary bliss will appear in my dreams,
tinged, however, with bittersweet shade....

Tenth floor bar in the 'q' hotel*

Panorama beyond the glassed–in lobby,
a spectacle of lights and stars sparkling this spring night.
Though this fantasy challenges me,
my mind no longer stretches its wings.

Had it been the me of a decade back,
I suppose I would promptly have
    booted myself off this lofty structure
and started flapping in the air.

Whenever did I change?——And why?
In the soaring stance that is Poet, my future stands vacant,
something reflected on shut eyes.
It's now simply a space–time continuum indifferent to me.

I'm an old bird——motionless on its perch,
highball fizzing vacuously in one claw.

Heartrent ...

I tossed a pebble into the tree.
It bounced off a branch with a swish.
I heard a voice in the twilight treetop,
a tree voice screaming shrilly,
    That hurt!

When I tossed a pebble into the tree,
it glanced off a branch.
Faster than a leaf could fall,
birds flew up from dusk's lushness.
Bird after bird
after bird
twittered off.

How my heart quavered as I watched.
I looked off after them, heartrent....

DISSOLVED

At a fork deep in the forest,
a massive python
suddenly began curling itself around me.

Ever so slowly it formed loop after loop after loop,
coiling round me
like a silent machine.
I soon found myself encased by snake.
Then it squeezed mightily.

I thought, How endless my sense of unease,
    how desperate my struggle!
(No, truth is it probably took but a brief moment.)
After the terror, weighty lassitude.

My whole body hopelessly pulverized,
I at last no longer felt the slightest agony.
The snake swallowed me headfirst into its murky innards.

Bloated as a barrel,
the python lay on the grass awhile.
Little by little it then constricted itself.
Potent gastric juices began dissolving me.
Not only my flesh but my clothing, too, and everything on me:
the memo pad in my pocket, several pages of manuscript,
as well as every grief, every pique,
    every love not yet forged into words.
The viscera of this abominable reptile soaked up
even my minuscule interest in the world,
transformed it insensibly into heartless flesh and blood,
one part mounded into droppings on the soil.

To be formless in this domain of cognition
means that I exist everywhere.
That's why I see and hear everything in heaven and on earth.
Each time breezes quiver the leaves in a tree,
I hear the voices of friends searching for me.
Soon even those sounds cease.

What's become of the snake that swallowed me?
Having intermingled with the countless numbers of his ilk
    who inhabit this jungle,
I can no longer recognize him.
Wherever you go, they're in the grass or under flowers.

They catch wild beasts, seize birds,
occasionally swallow children or hapless old folks.
By now, they've become gigantic pythons
slithering over the ground.

From the ground they slink into tree limbs, over swamp water,
    through river's flow ...
bellies clinging always to soil.
Like dirt, never free
from its stench.

DROPPING ANCHOR IN AMOY HARBOR*

When I awoke,
the ship had already dropped anchor.

Decks still damp after morning breezes washed them down.
Every sail secured on the yards.

Straddling the bowsprit,
a young seaman sang something.
He sang drolly as he lashed the jib.

Glittering green trees flutter.
Is that Ku–lang Hsü Island?

Let me check with the binoculars.
I invert the lens.

Under upturned eaves in the Chinese section,
a woman who leans against her balcony looks this way——
as though gazing at tiny, faraway memories.

Looking at me this morning, at our ship
that has staggered 4,000 spray–drenched knots ...
like viewing phantoms of a bygone day.

MORTIFIED FIGURE*

Reaching from beyond the cosmos,
dusk's silhouette is neither Earth's contour crossing the moon
nor moon's profile veiling the sun.
One day that shadow will surely edge toward me as well.
When it shrouds my eyes and ears, when it clogs my breath,

I'll leave this Self behind,
attended by a flea.

That Self with long fingernails the hue of rotted leaves——
who would lift its white face cover again
and peer at that mortified figure on display ...
    a figure no longer my Self?

An enfeebled elephant quits his herd,
    stumbles through the jungle,
works his way upstream, cuts through a waterfall
deep into an unexplored grotto, to abandon himself.

Far beyond the horizon, black smoke rises.
Crouching low, their rifles at port,
    soldiers step over a face–down man.
Outstretched palms meet like fly legs.
He's not praising his God, Allah.
He's a mute, immovable carving engraved on burning sands.
His mortified figure now
exposed to every eye.

FISHING IN THE STREAM

After I dropped my line
and concentrated intently
on the bob,
I wasn't aware of my boat drifting off.

Carried downstream with sweetfish
in a whirlpool that swirled round an abyss,
I drifted from the hills to the river through town,
and off to the widening estuary.
Then, at last, to the sea.

I suppose I'd drifted this way a number of times
from summer into fall:
now water's heart,
now a fish's heart,
now a vagabond's heart.
Here now——never to return.

Autumn Rose

The weather report predicted clear skies.

According to the TV weather map,
this morning the Japanese archipelago
lies entirely
under a high–pressure ridge.

In the core of its core,
my tiny yard ...
a yellow rose
blooming on the lawn.

Vivid to behold,
chiseled into unwavering air,
an autumn rose
glimmers.

昭和四十三年から昭和四十九年の間に発表された詩

Such scenes ...

Railroad tracks
customarily run near estuaries.

There the river widens
and its bed forms sandbars.
Its flow pinched, splitting into several forks,
the river relinquishes its shape.

As the train crosses the trestle,
my eyes instinctively look downstream.
Land breezes melt into sea breezes.
Fresh water mixes with tidewater.
Skies over land merge with skies over sea
where they redden expansively.

Here, any flying creature
already a sea bird.
Whatever exists disappears,
then transforms into something new.
I love such scenes.

River (ii)

The old man lived his whole life on the river.

He stood in the rapid rush of the gorge.
He squatted on the shoreline off a back street.
He moored his boat in that reed clump under the bridge.

Always gazing at the water,
eyes fixed on his float,
motionless against the flow
though actually swept along by it.

Both his thoughts and his life
swept downstream with clouds and wind and tree shadows,

swept toward the river mouth, toward the sea——
destined for that timeless time beyond all things.

One day the old man no longer appeared.
A boy now drops his line at the spot
where the man once fished.

BIRDS (iv)

Unexpectedly, absolutely unexpectedly,
a flock of mallards flew up from the lake.
No sign that anything had threatened them.

I wondered why. Might it have been because
a certain apprehension fermenting in each of them
had simultaneously intensified?

Spiraling, they swirled furiously into sky.
Rainbows unveiled in water drops left behind.
Promptly orienting, all flapped off in the same direction.

They flew beyond sight.
Have they fluttered down somewhere
    well beyond the surface of the lake?
Or soared past the snowy range?

Curiously, however, almost before I'm aware of it
the mallards return.
They'll paddle nonchalant over the water
till a lull in the air again magnifies their skittishness.

WATERFOWL

He remains motionless
in the pointless clamor of the screened enclosure.
He's almost a part of the concrete crag
as he squats in that corner by the cool waterspout.

This shabby, inconspicuous, smallish waterfowl,
a phenomenal vitality of flight compressed in his pose!
At times—no, periodically—
he puffs his feathers up as though irate.
Once unruffled,
he leans forward, at the ready. •

He then stretches his wings.
He spreads those phantom–like wings
farther and farther, endlessly farther.
Ah——that instant dazzles me.

The bird does not fly, however.
He folds his wings back up, closes his eyes,
stands motionless again ... as though asleep.

To Mikago

The future shapeless, difficult to discern.

In early spring,
barren branch tips brighten faintly at sky's far edge.
The new day departs
and the present closes in on me.

Mikago——beautiful girl!
Go your way, picking flowers as your name suggests.
Continue fulfilling yourself with blossoms.
Even should you sink into sorrow and misfortune,
seek a single bloom of joy
to grace your inner self.

Here and there in the fields——wildflowers, briars,
window–box flowers for each day,
blossoms on life's path.

Captain 'S'——An Album of My Cruise*

Captain 'S' was an extremely cranky fellow.
He often spoke English glibly to foreign traders visiting the ship.
In the wardroom, however, he acted
      extremely brusque to junior officers.
He always kept the door to his inner self tightly sealed.
If unexpectedly he happened to open it,
      some dreadfully tangible phrase flew out
with force enough to floor you.

Every time we left or entered port, a pilot came aboard.
The captain then directly left the bridge
      and disappeared into his quarters.
Perhaps having someone else command his ship

affected his pride as Master.
When he was navigation officer on a transport,
    a bomb blast blew him overboard.
He pooh–poohed his long and wretched
    prisoner–of–war experience in the Tropics.
To the well–meaning, he nodded silently
    or sometimes turned coldly away.
Even single deeds of kindness he offered matter–of–factly.
In a yacht harbor in Manila, Captain 'S'
used all his brawn to reel in a heavy hawser for me.
It was but a surprisingly menial act of courtesy,
though to this day I have forgotten
    neither his astonishing steely strength and will power
wrung from that lean middle–aged frame,
nor the lightning–quick wrath
    that could instantly flash across his face....
If you crossed him, his covert whip would one day lash the air.
Fear of that alienated his crew.

I strolled the boat deck every morning——actually,
I surreptitiously checked the bridge from the blind side.
Once I ascertained he wasn't there,
I hurriedly climbed the steel ladder to the chart room
and copied out the previous day's navigation log.

Even after ninety days, I never became friendly with Captain 'S';
still, I had faith in him at least in foul weather.
I figured that on the high seas
    I could certainly entrust my fate to such a fellow.
Yet his masthead flag was surprisingly tattered and troubled.
In front of others, he displayed no fondness for alcohol.
He even sternly cautioned the chief steward
    about the dwindling beer supply.
In fact, rumor had it that he was a heavy drinker,
that late at night in his cabin he freely tippled wine.
More, I once personally witnessed proof of it.
The captain's cabin lay on the starboard side several levels above
    the upper deck, directly under the bridge.
Next lay the chief radioman's quarters,
    immediately beyond the wireless room.
Especially thick carpeting cushioned the passageway
where sailors other than cabin boys rarely set foot.
Late one night I couldn't sleep, so I figured I'd visit the radioman.
About to climb the steps, the captain's door opened with a thud;
startled, I pulled up.

In that instant I saw him stagger out like a shadow.
Obviously dead drunk. I didn't imagine he could have stood alone.
Despite being accustomed to the sea,
    despite the steadiness of the ship,
he groped toward the head. Two paces, three paces,
shoulders heaving, stopping and starting,
    muttering sobs or hums,
hugging the bulkhead like a lizard.
The monster whale he pursued chomped a leg
    off the Pequod's Captain Ahab.
But our Captain 'S'——what ocean brute gnawed at his heart?

I'm looking now at a picture in my album,
a photo snapped on the sly in Sydney Park, close to Brown Pier.
The sun on that morning twelve years back
    cast vivid shadows across the sun dial.
Near the dial, stone steps behind him,
    the Captain walks toward me.
For the first time, I notice,
from behind his unusually guileless shoulders,
a bird about to overtake him.

BIRD TALK*

Birds chatter ceaselessly in the trees.
Is that clamor moments before sleep
the sound of wing flaps contending for a roost?

Absorbed in bird talk, I sit on a bench.
I forget it's not human conversation,
forget I'm on the other side of the globe.

The park overlooks Brown Pier
where my ship has lit its mooring lights.

HUNTERS AND I*

        – 1 –
We cut through thickets on the slope,
away from paths that people use.

In the inky dark,
tree–shaded lush grass high enough to hide in.
Look,
bent grass tips,

the snapped–off ends of little twigs.

This is an *utsu,*
a trail that only animals use.
    No, no——the secret path I take
    when something baffles me.

It isn't the only *utsu.*
A network links hills
and mountain streams.
Near the heights where we'd climbed trailing one fellow,
we found the lair of a beast polishing his tusks,
    the cliff his canopy,
ferns strewn over a bed covered with cedar greens.
    Or is the beast my Self?

Oh! The far–off yelps of contending hounds
signal it's time
to release the safety catches on our rifles.

    – 2 –
I heard that one survived some years
with my round
deep in his thigh,
and that these hunters had brought him down
two hills from here.
That happened yesterday.
    I, too——plugged with a round of frustration....

It's no longer necessary to continue tracking
the boar I shot today.
I figure that near midnight
he'll surely come down to the mountain stream.

Moon was up.
Sure enough ...
emerging like a half–shadow from a clump of weeds,
he tottered as he neared water's edge.
Slurping sounds
made me think he was drinking.

No sooner had he raised his head
to let out a flute–like sigh
than he tumbled in a heap to the ground.

    – 3 –
We used to haul the boar down from the mountain,
slit its belly, and roast its entrails on the fire.

Our whole party shared them.

Oh, yes, before eating
we took a slice of his liver and stuck it to a tree in the copse.
I pierce my liver with a pen point.
Then everyone offered prayer.
Not a man among us had the slightest idea
which god we bowed our heads to....

> You died so nice for us today——*right!*
> Do it again tomorrow——*right!*

Only echoes from the mountain stream responded.
Merging with them, the wind——*my mind*——
groaned past like moans
through vacant skies above the far–off ridge.

Stream——TALE OF AN OLD HUNTER*

A stag broke through the foliage
and pranced along the opposite shore,
obliquely upstream.

About to step into the water,
he turned gracefully
and headed downstream.
He dashed over the riverbank all out.

What speed!
Under his vaults,
the river instantly reversed its flow.

On this shore hunters,
rifles lined up,
simultaneously opened fire.
Not a hit.

Then he came directly in front of me.
I brought him down with my trusty single–shooter....

As it soaked up the fallen stag's antlers,
the river again began
flowing toward its mouth.

Sea Near Chichijima*

On that cruise already a decade back,
we left Sydney's winter, sailed direct
for Japan, entered port in September.

Only two weeks of days and nights,
yet sea expressed all four seasons.
Most unforgettable, her autumn mien.

Eyelash–shadows penetrated waves.
Bell echoes rang from the ocean floor
(not from Dehmel's narrative poem).

Near Chichijima, as I recall,
a lone swallow returning south
plummeted to the boat deck and rested.

I worked up a sweat trying to catch it.
It flew off always in the nick of time.
The Captain chuckled on the bridge.

Plovers——At the Dunes on Nakatajima <II>*

Plovers visit the beach
at dusk, at dawn.

Hidden in twilight,
they crisscross in flight, crying *piririiiii*
as they stitch the spray of raging waves.

At sunrise,
they vanish into skies over the dunes.

At nightfall,
they retrace their course upstream from the estuary.

Some people talk as though they've seen the birds.
Some imply they haven't.

All say they've heard them, however,
and claim, "Those are surely white plover cries."

House at the Foot of the Mountain

I spread bread crumbs
over a white rock in our yard
for the elegant mountain birds

who come to drink from a hollow in the rock.

Yet not a bird came yesterday or today.
The crumbs simply disappeared.
"Sparrows eat them at dawn, you know."
My wife's smile offended me.
Say, you sparrow masses,
chaotically legion—packed with vitality—
I'm not spreading this feed for you!

"But the mountain birds are related to those sparrows!
    So are we."
My wife smiled again.
    Is that why you say, "Give some to the sparrows, too"?
    I, a sparrow, to my sparrow clan!

In the grove behind our house, a pheasant cried ... twice.

POND'S EDGE*

Twisting its head under a folded wing, a white swan sits plant-ed on the shore like an oval jewel——not the pose of a sleeping bird but of one intently hiding its face out of indignation and shame.

In the noontime sun, a marble Adonis stands with vacant eye sockets gaping——blank eyes not blind but off searching for sight.

Soon the swan unfolds and flaps its wings, then stretches its neck and begins swimming proudly over the pond. The pupils, however, will never return to Adonis' eye sockets.

People admire the swan's elegance and applaud. Before the marble face they pull up, momentarily sink into feelings that fall short of words ... then hurry off.

DREAMS I SEE IN THE SEA*

Wanting money to buy a calf,
I went to sea out of middle school.
In twelve years I worked my way up from apprentice deck hand.
Finally I became an able–bodied seaman.
Now I'm the quartermaster.
Mornings and evenings I take the helm, check our bearing,
and at times lapse into those precious dreams I had so long ago.
The expansive sea turns to pasture,
ruddy clouds to milch cows.

EVEN NOW

Poetry–writing girls cross my path.——On some days I talk with several of them. But our relationship lasts only a matter of months, at most several years.

Sooner or later these girls find a love nest, become wives and mothers, then promptly stop writing verse. They scatter and disappear into the thickets of life. That's a woman's joy.

Some nevertheless continue to meet with me. They're housewives or nursing mothers. But that shadow cast over the face comes from being neither wife nor mother. That demeanor has already been transformed into the demeanor of a bird pecking at insensitive space. Two or three such fowl constantly flutter into the barren branches in my yard. Their twitter lonely.

TREES AND BIRDS

When the ground began shaking violently, I dashed out the door. Trying to keep swaying utility poles and rock fences out of view, I then looked up into woods on hills that closed in densely behind our house. I wanted to see the expressions of the trees and birds.

But wind nonchalantly quivered the treetops. There was no confusion in the continued calls of the bamboo pheasant.

Once during a solar eclipse, however, I noted that they'd paled!

ABALONE*

Plunging impulsively in the buff
at an acute angle——direct for the seabed
with neither air tank nor flippers ...
there she is, an intrepid Itoman–style abalone harvester!

Born in the Gotô Islands floating in the ocean west of Kyushu,
'N–ko' dives deep into the choppy Genkai Sea
to help her father reel in squid lines.
After six years in a Hakata shop,
she returned to the Islands and again became a diver.

Early this spring, she unexpectedly appeared
in my hospital room——
more large fresh abalone than hands could hold
crammed into her travel bag,
one strap torn.

At that moment, I lay flat scrutinizing

the Roentgen photograph the hospital head was explaining to me.
The X–ray traced in my chest cavity
the very old and darkly–sedimented sea of my youth.
The remains of that longed–for barque,
already scuttled by now,
had transformed into rusted keel and ribs.

    Look! It's cloudy there.
    Certain confirmation of your old disease.

Instantly, blood that raised no cry
responded to his words.

    No, no!——Surely that's the shadow
       of my attachment to the sea,
    now a barnacle bonded firmly to my ribs.
    Doctor, can't you see
    the swimming silhouette of 'N–ko'——metal pry in hand,
    an underwater butterfly threading sinuously
    and flashing through the grove of my ribs?

HAIR

Supple, pliant hair
dangles halfway to her lids.

    Long ago,
    Mother tenderly combed my hair.
    Father's immense, firm hand
    sometimes whimsically stroked it.

How many years since then?
She apparently waits for somebody's hand,
    her hair color and its sheen enriched.
Yet only wind annoyingly teases it.

The girl looks away from her book.
She gazes vaguely through her bangs
——into distance where, from beyond a destiny
    that mists in time,
a young man with neither eyes nor nose approaches.

She stands impetuously,
grabs her racket, rushes from the room.

Aesthetics of the Sea*

Container ship——perfect image of a centipede's belly.
Tanker——bridge and vents tacked to the stern.
Each a ridiculously hulking barge.

When we talk of merchantmen,
I want a jauntily tilted funnel rising from a chalkstone boat deck
——even if it's only a mock–up.
All those neat–looking vessels ... wherever have they gone?

Only surviving four–masted barques or sea–going yachts
express some dash on the waves of these "economic seas"
that shipping firms have managed to create.

We could nevertheless do without
bikini–clad nudes in photos of the yachts.

Sea's a woman, ships are shes.
——If so, men should sail them.
Indeed, the realm for males to navigate reaches far beyond
the sea's *esprit* of tranquil blue.

Moon passage*

— ✳ —

From near the end of last year into this spring, I spent nearly
four and a half months on a hospital bed. Probably because I was
so long confined, I developed the habit of waking well before sun-
up. Still abed, I greeted dawn on my back.

At that hour near month's end, I could see through my windows
a half–chipped moon spread across my southern wall——a moon
in its last quarter. Emitting glints like just–burnished brass
against deep mauve skies, the moon passed obliquely from east to
west across the windows.

The scene reminded me of an Akazome Emon waka:
> *Lying awake late into the night,*
> *I watched the moon till it waned.*

For this mid–Heian court lady, the moon was no doubt a phan-
tom remoteness external to the real world. Its distance from earth
probably also rivaled the immeasurable depths of her sighs.

— ✳ —

Today, in the latter half of the 20th Century, Apollo spacecraft
have already circled the moon. They swept over it several times.

The craft returned to Earth twice after leaving footprints on lunar dust. Praising this victory of science as the glory of the century, many on the globe responded with applause. It's as though the moon, having already bounded from every mind, had now become a reality in cosmic space. But the distance: 390,000 kilometers! The astonishing velocity of the spaceship escaping Earth's orbit forces association with the "Cloud Trapeze" in the *Hsi–yu–chi*. By contrast, such speed, such distance, made the moon even more remote than I had sensed it was.

— ✳ —

It happened, I believe, after the second moon landing. Some scholars and professors appeared on a television round–table discussion of the event. The head of a polar expedition, a man with noticeably tanned and dauntless features, joined them. For whatever reason, he gave only minimal responses to the moderator's questions——awkwardly and self–consciously. But he referred to the satellite as "My dear moon, my dear moon." This gave the agreeable impression that here was a true scientist, one who lived his profession.

— ✳ —

Among Miyazawa Kenji's poems is one entitled, "Emperor Moon." I remember the content roughly as follows: Viewed through a reflecting telescope, the face of the moon appears pitted. The moment Kenji looks away from the eyepiece, however, the moon certainly creates a feeling of awe. It's as though it were the "Emperor Moon" reigning high in the skies. Kenji was both poet and scientist. That poem etched itself deeply on my mind.

— ✳ —

As dawn swept night away, moon gradually lost its glow and crowded into a corner on the western side of my windows. In the end, even that moon paled and became quite faint: a soup–bowl fragment about to vanish into sky's abyss. In my heart, I always said "Sayonara!" to such a moon. I figured that, like its silhouette, my life, too, would soon return to space.

At that moment a raucous shout assailed me: "Hey, Dummy! Get a move on——wash your face." Day's sun rose from the ridge of eastern hills.

POST OFFICE PENNANT

Urged by a deadline,
how often, on how many occasions, had I rushed off,
a finished manuscript marked SPECIAL DELIVERY in my pocket?

Each time I move——oh, those bantam post offices
nestled among rows of city houses
    or by the bridge in a mountain hamlet.

How many late replies—
to that friend in Munich, the young man in Australia,
    the professor in Toronto—
have I dropped into that red box by the entrance?

My correspondence——always a refrain
    of anxiety and reassurance,
an endless path that I figure
will continue till life ends.

That instant feeling of relief when I push open the door and leave!
Stirring to my whistle like a butterfly,
oh, that hair ribbon over the clerk's smile.
It flutters only in my mind,
singularly linking far–off distances with nearer feelings
——that post office pennant.

REEF AND WAVES

An isolated reef
approached leisurely from the distance,
passed directly abeam our ship,
then as leisurely vanished.

In the midst of the sea,
its slightly–protruding face
allowed a sea bird to rest on a tapering tip....

Constantly washing the reef,
waves at times sent spray high.
Each time, the bird reeled and flapped its wings,
then re–folded them and settled again on the reef.

Observing the process, I realized that
the cycles between oncoming waves and rising spray
were less than seconds apart.
That scene,
pictured vividly like Technicolor animation,

lingered a while in my mind——
blanked then by the glare of tropical skies and tropical waters.

Confronting each frame of that animation,
I somehow sank into unfounded apprehensions,
into useless—yes, useless—apprehensions....
. . . .
I guess by now the bird has flown off.
But, since I no longer watch,
I wonder if those waves continue washing the reef?
With nobody observing, does that spray
still rise with identical regularity?
——If so, how dreary the laws of Nature
to one as full of life as I.

My JOURNEYS (i)*

Hokkaidô, Tôhoku's six prefectures, Kanazawa
    and Noto in Hokuriku——
every journey to the North
in response to requests for talks.
From destination to destination, a succession of rides
    in trains or cars or what–have–you.
Though in each case doubtless well–meant,
my hosts dragged me about in every spare moment
    to see the sights or whatever.

Each experience a schedule that others had planned.
——As in "The Panther,"
that Rilke poem about a beast circling its cage,
the natural features of each area I visited,
    and the faces and words of those I met,
were all countless steel bars that endlessly abraded my eyes.

Every meaning, shape, and color
    melted together behind those bars.
Harboring the void in which I have lost my Self,
I go back home, worn to a shade.

My JOURNEYS (ii)*

South from Abashiri....
Cattle loafed contentedly near lapping waves.
All along I thought they ate grass in pastures!
Could I parody that brief Kitagawa Fuyuhiko poem,

> *A horse bellying the naval base*
with   *Cattle bellying Okhotsk … ?*

From Hiroo round Cape Erimo toward Samani.
At dawn——dragged from dreams by a dreadful ruckus.
Only as I start down the stairs
do I notice crows skittering incessantly
over the staircase skylight.

I walk from inn to station along the strand.
Waves lap gently, yet it's a desolate scene
　　　　——fabulous crags jut up,
　　　　——crows that ought to be white gulls flit about in flocks.
Where what should be does not exist,
exists what should not be....
I board the train with these thoughts, head for Tomakomai.

SHADOWS (ii)

Twilight. Whenever the lights come on,
dim shadows concealed in the corridor,
　　　or in the corners of the room,
flee one by one into open air.

When evening comes,
lights glow ever more brightly,
and those displaced shadows
paint out everything around the house.
As a child, it frightened me dreadfully
to watch through our glass doors and see that happen.

At that crook in the fence, where roots in the thicket
　　　　　were visible during the day,
I sensed someone holding his breath
and looking my way——determined.

Sooner or later, I figured he'd appear as an eerie hulk,
dash into my room,
and with a shout stomp over the floor.
Then he'd shatter my lamp, kick over the furniture,
blade glinting——oh, he lopped off my head!
Crying tumultuously, I clung fast to Mommy.
. . . .
I had such dreams.

GOLDEN CUB*

I need neither precious stones nor a marble statue.
I want only a lion cub glowing with glints of gold
and romping over noon–time, wave–washed African bluffs.
Those cubs have vanished now from the plaintive, dozing eyes
of that old fisher in Hemingway's novel.
Ah, those innocent lion cubs, a single one will do....

My wife grew old without bearing me a child.
I feel no sense of loss
because I've been thinking,
how fitting if a lion would spring from her womb:
a male——king of the distant savanna.
Legs bursting with sinewy aggressiveness,
    his mane inspiring awe.
Though latent with potential,
never yielding those spots on his soft coat.
Rolling like a ball, he'll begin to frisk at my feet.
At times, showing his tiny fangs and claws,
he'll growl and nip at my neck or scratch the back of my hand.
——In no time he'll be taking buffalo or wapiti.
I want such a lion cub glowing with the luster of gold,
a cub the image of what he was at birth.

Secretly, I hope to nourish
his innocence, his ferocity, his warmth,
so long as I have life.

SNARES*

There are men, there are women,
attracting each other, being attracted.
They wander near sites lush with grass,
exchange love poems, write and enjoy verse,
    stories——whatever.
Once you accidentally saunter into a thicket,
you aggravate your agonies, your grudges, your tears.
In the end, you kill your partner and snuff out your life.

Listen to their cries of grief, to their screams!
Doesn't every conceivable ploy
exist in snares set up by God
(whom I've not yet had the pleasure of meeting)?

Let's move ahead, eyes alert.
It's best to step lightheartedly over snares.

If by chance your foot gets caught in one,
you're not to shout and thrash fecklessly about.
I'd rather you imitate the courage
    and determination of the hyena.
It escapes by chewing off its paw.
True love starts there.

MY JOURNEYS (iii)*

Summers in Shiretoko——short and cold.
Yet going there in summer is a summer trip.
Sixteen years ago my summer voyage
crossed the equator and became a winter cruise.

Coral Sea waves——emeralds——glints of autumn.
I changed into winter clothes at Brisbane.
August 1st, we arrived in Sydney.

Brown Pier nestled among city streets.
Botanical gardens on a bluff to the right
    just outside the customs gate.
"I'm sorry," said the agent's representative.
"It's got its seasons confused...."
An *umé* labeled JAPAN blossomed anemically
among brilliantly colored plants.

In that single bloom——the far–off, skimpy,
defeat–distorted features of my fatherland.

STROLLING THE DUNES——AT NAKATAJIMA <I>*

As I think of you,
you are far off, your shadow small.
Soaked up by the volume of the backdrop,
my voice cannot reach you.

You   retreating.
I   pursuing.
Second by second, however,
the unobstructed space between us somehow swells.

What's the essence of the drab resignation,
of these stunning silences,
these gigantic, irresistible heaps? •

Wind blows.
Sands stir.
Waves lap the shore.

Only sea unfolds its songs into headings through the blue
I do not choose to take....

Far FROM HUMAN EYES*

Far from human eyes,
deep in the hills,
those trees live in solitude——
trees that spring adorns with blossoms of life,
trees that autumn blazes with scarlet flame,
have now become ... my Self.

Return TO THE MOUNTAIN VILLAGE*

We turned off the highway and began our climb into the hills.
Hunched up nearby and buried in vegetation,
    the Stony Mountain Witch
drenched my back with her chilly voice as I passed by.
    Go back.
    The hamlet ahead is no place for you!   .

Cedar tops swished along the way
round curve after curve on the road through the gorge.
I lived there more than three desolate years,
summers short, winters long——shut in by blizzards ...
wood chips blazing in the hearth,
    the hearts of these north country people warming me.

Today, twenty–four years later, we dash up this hill by car.
What was that stone figure grumbling about ...
    or was she grumbling?
That thatched–roof house now boasts showy roofing and walls.

The youngsters of those long–past days,
    every one a mother or a father.
Under late autumn's azure skies, they brush aside
    the mists of memory
and beaming ... crowd around me.

Unveiling Ceremony in the Hills*

The road to that village deep in the hills where I lived
    when I evacuated Tokyo
    bends again and again along the gorge.
Unceasing winds sang lonely in cedar tops.
In those days, one descended six kilometers
    to the end of the branch line
    that branched off a branch line of the railway.
——An ordeal to descend, to ascend.

Twenty–five years later, the road so improved
that we drive up this evening
in a single sweep.
How splendidly the cedars have matured!
A single star peeks through the stand of trees, stabs my eyes——
a ruby glint I hadn't seen in town.
Then the north country's autumn chill suddenly numbs me.

Near the entrance to the village, our headlights
    light up tiny shadows
that leap from lush branches——then vanish.
A goblins' brood? Bamboo pheasant chicks out of their nests?
No, mountain children come to greet me,
youngsters I had taught in that tiny classroom.
No, no, not so——merely illusions that sentiment conceived.
Those children of long ago by now are fine adults
whose fond faces will gather here tomorrow.

When we reached my lodgings in the dead of night,
    a rainstorm had blown in.
Well, I am in the mountains!
And yet, the storm will certainly clear when dawn breaks.
After all, they're unveiling the poetry stele that the village people
set up for me by the playground at school.

WHITE MAGNOLIAS ON MY MIND*

Their flowers bloom more unspoiled each year,
last year's purer than those of the year before,
this year's purer than last.
On a leisurely side street, a blaze of blossoms had kindled
the glowing treetop——something the owner
      of that paltry little yard
and the tree itself had awaited with such hope.
Perhaps similar blossoms also inconspicuously ignite copses
here or there on the slopes of unknown, distant gorges.
They would be wild magnolias or *kobushi.*
Daybreak in early spring.
In skies——moon and stars covertly kiss.
From soil——the scent of flaring buds rises high.
At that moment, as white magnolias flower
far more lovely, more sadly by the year,
my life drains gradually away ...
soon to make such sights past sight.

SUPPLEMENTARY

NOTES

Poem titles with a raised asterisk (＊), together with a handful of individual Japanese words italicized in the poems, appear below in ABC order (excluding articles). Entries like "barque" or "knot" explain terms that appear frequently. Much data I culled from notes in the *Maruyama Kaoru Zenshū* [*Works*]. For most nautical matters, I rely on Gershom Bradford, *The Mariner's Dictionary* (New York: Weathervane Books, 1952).

Substantial information derives from interviews or correspondence with the following: The poet and his widow Miyoko in Toyohashi. Ms. Watanabe Hanako and Mrs. Katakura Fujiyo in Iwanezawa. Mr. Haraguchi Saburô (first in Toyohashi and later in Seattle); by checking and supplying countless details, he greatly improved the reliability and completeness of the notes. I also recognize help that Mr. Inoue of Yamagata offered. Of course, I remain responsible for the way all provided information appears.

Specialists know or can readily uncover most information presented here. Students and lovers of poetry—indeed, any who do not handle Japanese with ease—may find it somewhat more difficult and time–consuming. These notes intend to provide such readers with data that may at times satisfy curiosity or clarify an image or symbol.

The slanted arrow (➹) indicates new, relevant but different aspects of—or purely gratuitous information about—the item. The pointing finger (☞) suggests an associated note (in SMALL CAPS) or a poem (in quotation marks; page number keyed to the text) that may cast light on the issue.

❋ ❋ ❋

ABALONE—These gastropod mollusks [*awabi*] resemble ears, so some call them "sea ears" or "ear shells." *Awabi* have commercial and culinary value. Iridescent mother–of–pearl lining provides stock to make buttons; the large muscular foot that clings tenaciously to rocks on the ocean floor is edible. ➹ Itoman, known for excellent divers, lies on the west coast of Okinawa, ca. 10 miles south of Naha. ➹ The Gotô Islands lie west of Sasebo off the Kyushu coast. The Genkai Sea is west of Saga, a province in northwest Kyushu. ➹ 'N–ko' is Nishimura Masuko (Maruyama "disguises" names by taking the next letter of the alphabet). ➹ Hakata, a metropolis in northern Kyushu, lies ca. 550 rail miles from Toyohashi. ➹ "Metal pry" renders *fuguse*, a tool used to pry shellfish from rocks. ➹ On the butterfly's symbolism, ☞ POETRY and TRACES OF A BUTTERFLY. ➹ Some years earlier, Ms. Nishimura had written to ask Maruyama for comments on her free verse about the sea.

ABOVE OUR VILLAGE—Iwanezawa lies 400 meters above sea level; ☞ HIGH VILLAGE.

AEROPLANE—The title *eropurein* is in ☞ KATAKANA. Flying machines enthralled Maruyama as a boy; ☞ STARRY SKIES.

AESTHETICS OF THE SEA—Boat deck is for lifeboat storage. ☞ BARQUE.

AGES—As a student at Keiô University in Tokyo, Tsumura Nobuo (1909–1944) became a fan; a 10–year age gap didn't prevent friendship. ♣ Maruyama found him "somewhat spoiled [he came from a well–to–do family] but a nice fellow." Tsumura published much poetry in *Shiki [Four Seasons]*. He succumbed to Addison's disease. ♣ Flute airs imply the art of poetry. For centuries, this instrument has stood for verse (or the spirit of poetry), its player for the poet. The French poet Guillaume Apollinaire (1880–1918) wrote, "…it is myself / Who am the flute I play upon. / A whip to punish other men." ♣ Flutes symbolize the explosive imagination that, in direct opposition to science, would maximize ambiguity and free association. ♣ In Greek mythology, Euterpe, the Muse of lyric poetry, carries a flute; Erato, the Muse of erotic poetry, usually carries a lyre.

ANCHOR—Either rum or grog (watered rum) has been the beverage of British seamen since the mid–18th century.

APPLES—Spar deck is the upper deck of a vessel that has a flush or continuous deck. ♣ At that latitude, 6 knots is nearly 8 m.p.h.; ☞ KNOT.

AT SEA—☞ SWALLOWS. The 4 brightest stars in the Southern Cross (Crux) constellation form a Latin cross (the vertical ca. 2x as long as the horizontal axis). The brightest star at the end of the long axis points south. Crux may be seen year round; May marks its highest point in southern skies.

AWAKENING—A subtitle indicates "For recitation." ☞ UGUISU, the bush warbler.

BACK IN PORT—☞ KNOT (Maruyama writes "sea mile"); this amounts to ca. 4500 land miles. ♣ Nautical terms are English because Japan modeled its navy and merchant marine on British counterparts. ♣ For pitch, ☞ SONS OF THE WINDJAMMER. ♣ Ayamé, very popular in the late 1920s, is an inexpensive pipe tobacco for the traditional *kiseru*. The *kiseru's* small metal bowl holds only enough for several puffs before requiring a refill; the stems are usually long (up to a yard, which provides a sweet, cool smoke), but the short (5" or 6") variety is more portable. ♣ The persona could hear the pack torn open, the tobacco tamped into the bowl, and the match being struck. ♣ Smoking in bed was taboo.

BARQUE—Barques (or barks) are navy and merchant marine ships that train future officers. Barques have either 3 or 4 masts; optional diesel motors serve primarily to navigate in and out of port. At least 2 of the masts have rectangular ("square–rigged") sails. ♣ On a 3–masted barque, the mizzenmast lies nearest the stern; on a 4–masted barque like Maruyama sailed, it is separated from the stern by the jiggermast. ♣ Each mast (☞ MEMORIES OF MASTS) on a full–rigged sailing vessel has a royal sail, the 2nd highest sail immediately under the skysail.

BAR SONG I • II—For the import of "wings of poetry," ☞ TENTH FLOOR BAR IN THE 'Q' HOTEL. ✦ Maruyama once thought that alcohol induces the dream state he believed favorable to the creation of poetry. Japan's leading modern poet, Hagiwara Sakutarô (who frequently drank with Maruyama and spent many waking moments inebriated; ☞ TREE–LINED PATH—MOURNING *SHIKI*) doubted a person in a drug–induced state could write poetry of value. He may have convinced Maruyama to change his mind. ✦ The I and II marking the bar poems, and similar numbers attached to poems that deal with Nakatajima ("Strolling the Dunes" and "Plovers"), are the only numbers the poet inserted in the collections.

BECKONING SPRING—☞ WITCH HAZELS [*mansaku no hana*]. ✦ The doors are "cellar like" because one must climb up to the road through heaped snow.

BECOMING WOLF—Wolf in Japanese [*ôkami*] similarly connotes paying unwanted sexual attention. ✦ Maruyama writes "Jon" in ☞ KATAKANA; it could as well be "John." Japanese in those days (1929) liked to give their dogs foreign names. ✦ On dogs becoming wolves, and vice versa, ☞ "Wolf Pack" (1947, page 170).

BELL SONG—Japanese generally regard bell sounds as refreshing and cooling; folklore accords bells the power to expel demons. ✦ Kunié loved the small, round, tinkling bells that children attach to footgear or sashes [*obi*], women to such items as scissors and pets. ✦ Maruyama's sister–in–law so loved these small bells that even as an adult she wore them on her person. Re Kunié's bells, ☞ "Her Remains" (page 89) and "Night Bells" (page 90).

BELOVED TOMB—"Broken shoulder blades" implies cremated remains, which are never pure ashes. The small interred box contains larger bones as well. ✦ Grave marker refers to the tall temporary wood strip marking a new grave.

BIRD TALK—The gardens face Sydney's harbor; ☞ "My Journeys" (iii) (page 288).

BIRDS (i)—The forecastle (fo'c'sul) is a raised deck in the bow. In merchant ships, it houses the crew. ✦ The jibsail is one of several triangular jibs set on stays that extend from the foremast to the bowsprit——a heavy spar projecting from the bow over the water. ✦ Sailors on guard or watch are not to converse with passersby.

BLACK AND GOLD—☞ KNOT; here ca. 2.25 miles. ☞ BARQUE ✦ Pegasus carries the thunderbolt of Zeus. Gordo–Medusa, daughter of marine deities, gave birth to Pegasus as she died. Poseidon, god of the sea and navigation, fathered Pegasus. ✦ The poop deck is at the stern, above the main deck and behind the rearmost mast; ☞ YOUNG MEN SHOULDER THE SAIL. ✦ The forecastle is in the bow; ☞ BIRDS (i).

BLESSED—Rainer Maria Rilke (1875–1926) loved to travel; he visited Russia twice between 1899 and 1900. Rilke died of blood poisoning contracted after being pricked by a thorn on roses he was tending. ✦ His work and poetic theories had a profound effect on many Japanese writers, especially those associated with *Shiki* [*Four Seasons*]. On Rilke, ☞ DREADFUL METHOD, MY JOURNEYS (i), and PANTHER.

BREEZES FROM LAND—FROM SEA—Ku–lang Hsü Island, in Amoy (Xiamen or Hsia–men) Harbor, was Amoy's foreign settlement under China's treaty port system. It was a high–level residential area when Maruyama visited. ☀ On Amoy, ☞ DROPPING ANCHOR IN AMOY HARBOR.

BUBBLES—Fantail, a ship's most aft • rear part, refers especially to the stern overhang.

BULLETS' PATH—The largest coastal or battleship gun is ca. 40 cm. (16"). A note (*Works* I:521) claims this is a siege (or defense) mortar, which by 1929 could be slightly anachronistic. ☀ The machine gun came into its own after 1914 when most mortars were portable infantry models.

CALLING MOTHER—The poet wrote this in 1949 at the request of the magazine *Haha* [(my) *Mother*]. The editor knew he had published verse about his mother; best known among these was ☞ "Mother's Umbrella" (1947, page 162).

CALMER THAN THE FLOWER—Mrs. Maruyama says the poet describes this experience accurately. They held the wake for neighbors till midnight; family members sat by the bier till dawn. Japanese do not embalm, so cremation takes place soon after.

CAMELLIA—Not long after blooming, the entire camellia drops precipitously——petals and all. This flower consequently symbolizes a sudden and unexpected demise, an appropriate image for the death of a young person. ☀ For Maruyama's image of cranes, ☞ CRANE. ☀ *Otomé* [virgin, maiden] camellia [*tsubaki*], a relative of the snow camellia, is a popular species of this plant generally planted in yards or as a hedge. Maruyama had one in his yard. The showy white or pink flowers contain 35 or so petals; some bloom in fall, but the peak for most is between March and April.

CAPSTAN—This thick round post—one of which stands on the forecastle (☞ BIRDS [i]), others near the masts—has slots just below the top called "pigeonholes." Seamen insert into these slots sturdy wooden bars that they push in unison. Turning the capstan in this way heaves in the anchor or (as in this poem) hoists the yards to raise the sails. The pawl's ratchet action prevents the halyard from slipping.

CAPTAIN 'S'—AN ALBUM OF MY CRUISE—'S' (Sano Toshinori) captained the Yamashita Maru, the freighter on which Maruyama sailed to Australia (1955.07.07 to 1955.09.15). ☀ To circumvent his government's ban against private travel overseas, the poet served pro forma as purser. ☀ One expects the Captain's cabin to have its own head (toilet), which Maruyama describes in ☞ KATAKANA as *rabatorî • rûmu* [lavatory room]. ☀ Reference to Herman Melville's 1851 masterpiece, *Moby Dick*, suggests the universal appeal of the novel, known to Maruyama in Japanese translation. ☀ The bird image in the final lines may refer to a maritime superstition: a man's soul taking the form of a bird indicates he is doing penance for his sins.

CAROSSA AND RILKE—Hans Carossa (1878–1956) was a German poet, novelist, and physician who opposed nihilism by asserting "a Goethian faith in life." He hoped to harmonize his poetic vision of life with the scientific data of medical science. ☀ Carossa's *Rumänisches Tagebuch* (1924) describes conditions after World War I. In

1929, A. N. Scott translated it into English as *Roumanian Diary*, one volume of an autobiographical sequence. ✦ On Rilke, ☞ BLESSED, DREADFUL METHOD, MY JOURNEYS (i), and PANTHER.

CATCHING BONITO—Like tuna, bonito are swift–swimming members of the mackerel family that feed in schools. Their sleek, seemingly scaleless skin has an iridescent sheen; powerful, oily muscles increase their food value. ✦ At this latitude, 8 knots is 9–10 m.p.h.; ☞ KNOT. ✦ The ship heads from the northernmost Mariana Islands toward the northern tip of Luzon; it had already covered 66% of the distance. ✦ The bowsprit projects over water beyond the bow.

CHEERFUL BOOK—Suruga, an ancient province [*kuni*] now part of Shizuoka Prefecture, abuts Suruga Bay. Maruyama passed there whenever he traveled between Toyohashi and Tokyo. ✦ This view of Mt. Fuji is probably from the southwest.

CHERRY BLOSSOMS—These scatter several days after blooming, so they've long symbolized evanescence. Well before the age of the warrior, fragile cherry blossoms described the ephemerality of beauty——apt symbols of Kunié's untimely death.

CHORUS—*Shôka* means a singing lesson or a practice in the classroom, connotations not found in "chorus." Maruyama had another teacher handle the music lessons.

CITY AWAKENS—Like several other pieces in *Day by Day* (1936), this anti–military poem makes subtle comments on the times. The government discouraged any view even remotely critical of its policies or their effects. ✦ "Neither chirrups nor wing beats" implies the absence not only of birds but of the freedom they symbolize.

CLASS LOG—☞ SPRING IN THE NORTH for the observation of this little girl (Itô Mitsuru) that the swallows had arrived; ☞ SWALLOW.

CONCERTINAS AND TRAINS—"Concertinas" renders *tefûkin* [accordion]. This figure relates to the expandable hood [*horo*] connecting railway coaches. Maruyama felt the accordion suggested too large an image and insisted I use "concertina."

CORAL SEA—An arm of the Pacific Ocean bounded by New Guinea (Papua), Australia (Queensland), the Great Barrier Reef, and New Caledonia. ✦ The 2–day Battle of the Coral Sea (1942.05.07–.08) checked the southward expansion of Japanese forces during World War II.

CRANE (i) • (ii) • (iii)—As a pudgy boy, Maruyama admired the slim stuffed crane [*tsuru*] in his grandfather's entryway. Cranes in zoos he thought ugly. These birds regularly roamed the grounds of the family mansion in Seoul. Maruyama thought its flight (seen only in photographs or on television) exquisite. ✦ Japanese regard the monogamous crane—a symbol of fidelity and longevity—an auspicious bird. It generally lays 2 eggs and stays with its young for nearly a full year. ✦ The government designates the large Japanese crane (almost 5' high; its 20–22 lbs. complicate takeoff) a "special national monument." The crane refuge in Hokkaidô's Kushiro Marshlands hosts some 320 birds, nearly 10x as many as existed in 1952.

CROW—The sinister and ominous crow serves in Japan as the messenger of death.

CRUISE DUTY CHART—The *hoshi* of Hoshide [literally, Starout] means star, the *tsuki* of Tsukihara [literally, Moonmoor] means moon. The *katsura*—mistaken for the smaller Judas tree or the redbud bush—boasts legendary associations with the moon. Since ancient times, East Asians have imagined the *katsura*'s shadow on the lunar surface. ♣ A Chinese legend tells of a man on the moon who tries constantly to chop the *katsura* down; like Sisyphus, he never manages to get the job done. ♣ The *katsura* is a deciduous tree (some grow 90' tall) with red flowers and dark–purple or brownish fruit. *Katsura* wood resists rot so is sometimes used for ship's timbers. ♣ "Compass bridge" refers to the stern bridge that houses the primary compass when the ☞ BARQUE is under sail. The "well deck," on the main deck between the forward mast and forecastle (☞ BIRDS [i]), houses pumps.

DAWN—"Tube lamp" registers *kantera*, from the Dutch *kandelaar*. A hand–held lantern, it stores oil in a tin–plated cylinder and uses a cotton string as a wick. ♣ Elsewhere (☞ REMINISCENCES OF LAMPS) I render *kantera* "lantern."

DAYBREAK—The gingko [*ichô*, the maidenhair] is a stately deciduous tree imported from China. Tolerant of low temperatures and little water, it grows to 90'. Japanese once regarded it as sacred and so planted it near many shrines and temples.

DEEP IN THE CASTLE—In the original, the retainer does not draft "prudent counsel" but prepares *kangen no kusuri* [admonitory medicine]. Notice the proverb, "*Ryôyaku wa kuchi ni nigashi*" [Good medicine is bitter to the taste]——that is, good advice is hard to take. Professor Iida Gakuji provided these clarifying details. ♣ Alas, the retainer's lord was (again?) sporting in the garden. ♣ An armrest makes it easier to sit on ☞ TATAMI for long periods of time. ♣ "Mock hill" refers to the miniature rise built in a Japanese garden to imitate a mountain.

DEEP IN THE MOUNTAINS—The cuckoo [*hototogisu*; or *kakkô* after its call] arrives in Japan between mid–April and mid–May; it leaves in mid–August. This long–tailed, thin bird (slightly smaller than a dove) thus announces the end of winter. ♣ I use ☞ UGUISU rather than "bush warbler" simply because I prefer the sound; ☞ SPRING TO SUMMER. ♣ Butterburs [*fuki*, bog rhubarb; ☞ VISIONS OF FLOWERS] appear in early spring and poke up through thawing snow; they are universally seen as harbingers of spring. ♣ Bracken or brake [*warabi*; Latin name, *Pteridium aquilinum*] is a fern with yard–long triangular fronds. They grow wild and in a garden become invasive weeds; their fronds will poison livestock. ♣ "Unroll" refers to the way the plants develop. To the Japanese, the frond ends that unfold resemble a baby's fists; to Westerners, they resemble fiddleheads. ♣ "Mountain aralia" renders *yamaudo* (Latin name, *Aralia cordata*), a prickly shrub that grows about 6' high and sprouts tender buds in the snow. I derive the name aralia [*yatsude*, literally, "8 hands"; Latin name, *Araliaceae* or *Fastia japonica*] from the Latin. Dictionaries describe the *yatsude* as an evergreen shrub with shiny leaves but offer no English term.

DEER—Tame deer roam Nara's park. ♣ Lattices resemble wooden bars; owners install them over the windows of homes built virtually flush with the street.

DESTITUTE FRIEND—Ironically, pears symbolize generosity; despite poor soil, they produce ample fruit. ♣ In the West, their heart shape (Japanese pears look more like apples) also suggests affection. ☞ KOTO.

DEVASTATION—Professor 'D' refers to Doi Kôchi (1886–1979), a 1910 graduate in English literature of Tokyo University. Doi chaired the English Department at Tôhoku Daigaku, the national university in Sendai and scene of this poem. ♣ Doi, who unsuccessfully crusaded for "Basic Japanese" (cf., C. K. Ogden's *Basic English*), regarded Japanese literature a branch of world literature. Maruyama met him when he visited Sendai to talk on modern Japanese poetry. ♣ Sendai (now ca. 600,000), capital of Miyagi Prefecture, began as a castle town in 1602. It lies about 200 miles north by northeast of Tokyo (45 minutes by air) and contains many gorgeous groves (some style it the "sylvan city").

DISTAFF STONE BUDDHA—Ming emperors reigned from 1368–1644. ♣ "Seal stock" are plugs of stone, ivory, metal, wood, or shell on which the owner's name is carved to make a chop (official seal). "Stylized lions" [*shishi*], the imaginary beasts that guard temples, frequently decorate chops; ☞ RHINOCEROS AND LION. ♣ The ink stone provides a place to mix ink (with an ink stick and water) for the calligraphy brush. Concentric circles or "eyes" in the stone increase its value but render mixing difficult. ♣ The Six Dynasties date from 220–581 A.D. ♣ Rubbings, valued since ancient times, are copies made of graphs carved on wood or stone. ♣ Kannon is the Buddhist goddess of mercy (and source of the name for Canon products).

The priest was Fujii Sôsen (1896–1971), born March 4, the birth date of Maruyama's wife Miyoko. Fujii's Jôdô (Pure Land) temple, the Jôenji, was then in Hanazonochô; the restaurant Rakuraku and a parking lot now occupy the spot. Relocated to the north side of Toyohashi, the Jôenji's chief priest is now Fujii's oldest son. ♣ An active tanka poet and follower of Bokusui (☞ GULL), Fujii published several collections of verse. The first, a 110-page work, appeared in 1919 when he was studying for the priesthood at Ôtani University in Kyoto. ♣ Fujii also authored haiku, essays, and research on Buddhism. ♣ Most of the articles Maruyama describes were going–away presents when Fujii left China. I am grateful to Mr. Haraguchi for tracking down this information.

DOG WATCH—These watches (rendered in ☞ KATAKANA, no Japanese term exists) split the normal 4–8 P.M. (1600–2000 hrs.) watch into 2 short stints of from 4–6 and 6–8. This split staggers the rotation and thus prevents sailors from constantly standing the same watch. ♣ The origin of "dog watch," though unclear, could connect with the sense of dog as "unappealing." ♣ Aboard ship, dogs are metal fittings used to close hatches, manhole covers, and bulkhead doors.

DOG WATCHING HORIZON—The shepherd's purse [*penpengusa* or *nazuna*] is an annual crucifer related to the mustard family. The plant blooms cross–like white flowers, star–shaped leaves, and produces deltoid seeds that resemble the plectrum Japanese use for the *samisen* [banjo]; *penpen* refers to the plucking sound. ♣ This plant can root anywhere, even on a rotting railing; many regard it a weed and a nuisance.

DREADFUL DREAM—Japanese compare cirrocumulus clouds with fish scales; ☞ WHEN I WALK THROUGH FIELDS.

DREADFUL METHOD—On Rilke, ☞ BLESSED, MY JOURNEYS (i), and PANTHER. ♣ One scholar describes Chateau de Muzot in Switzerland as "a small stone tower of Muzot." While there, Rilke produced 2 major works, both published in 1923: *Sonnets to Orpheus* and the *Duino Elegies.*

DREAMS I SEE IN THE SEA—In that milieu, "out of middle school" (a 5–year course) means the persona was about 17. ♣ In the army, a quartermaster dispenses supplies. A marine quartermaster, however, serves as assistant navigator, helmsman, or signalman in charge of navigation equipment.

DROPPING ANCHOR IN AMOY HARBOR—Amoy (Xiamen • Hsia–men) lies at the mouth of the Kiulung • Chiu–lung River in Fukien (directly west of Taiwan). ♣ Bowsprit——a sturdy spar projecting over water from the bow. ♣ The jib is a triangular sail spread forward of the foremast. ♣ For Ku–lang Hsü Island, ☞ BREEZES FROM LAND—FROM SEA. ☞ KNOT; 4000 knots come to ca. 4500 land miles.

DUSK—Similar water imagery appears in ☞ "Water's Spirit" (page 76).

EARLY SPRING (i)—"Tree nymph" registers *ki no kami* [tree god]; for god • *kami,* ☞ GOD WHO WEPT. ♣ Maruyama refers to this *kami* as "she" [*kanojo*].

EERIE TREES—TO POET FRIENDS—N.B. ☞ "Tree–Lined Path—Mourning *Shiki*" (page 261). ♣ The order is by age at death. Tachihara Michizô (1914–1939) died at 25 from tuberculosis. In 1934 he entered Tokyo Imperial University to study architecture; the next year he joined the editorial staff of *Shiki* [*Four Seasons*] and worked with Maruyama. ♣ Poetry lovers appreciate Tachihara's poems for their poignant expression of private feelings and their most delicate (some say saccharine) tone. ♣ Nakahara Chûya (1907–1937), a favorite Maruyama drinking partner, died of acute meningitis at 30; ☞ POET'S WORDS. ♣ Tsumura Nobuo (1909–1944), a close younger friend, died of Addison's disease at 35; ☞ AGES.

ELEGY—Both men and women put the left side of the kimono over the right. When dressing a corpse, however, Japanese reverse this order——right side over the left, as with women's blouses, etc. in the West. ♣ "Prayer beads" renders *juzu*, the Buddhist rosary. ♣ Here I arbitrarily convert *kami* into the capitalized God, which is no doubt how the poet's Christian wife Miyoko expressed her grief.

ENGAWA—This 3'–4' wide wood–floored hallway runs along the sunny side of traditional Japanese homes. Sliding glass doors—covered at night with *amado* [rain doors, i.e., sliding shutters]—separate the *engawa* from the yard. One enters the family's living space from the *engawa* through sliding ☞ SHÔJI doors.

FACE WITH ANTS—A news photo of an American soldier killed in Vietnam inspired this poem. Note that the poet, too, has a facial mole near his mouth. ♣ On Maruyama's aversion to the viewing of corpses, especially his own, ☞ MORTIFIED FIGURE.

FAR FROM HUMAN EYES—Written for the poetry stele erected on the grounds of the elementary school in Iwanezawa (dedicated 1972.10.08). ♣ The poet gave this work no title, so I use the 1st line. ☞ "Return to the Mountain Village" (page 289) and "Unveiling Ceremony in the Hills" (page 290).

FAR MOUNTAINS—NEAR MOUNTAINS—Kagura [literally, "sacred music"] dances are masked mimes performed in damask silk gowns. They originated at the dawn of Japanese history when dancers performed before the cave of the mythical sun goddess, Amaterasu–ômikami, in hopes of luring her out of hiding. Kagura dances consequently relate to Shinto, the indigenous "religion." ✦ The shrike or butcher bird [*mozu*; literally, "bird of a hundred tongues"] is a predatory songbird. The designation "butcher" derives from the way the *mozu* impales on twigs or thorns the small birds, mammals, and large insects it catches; it then tears them apart with the hooked tip of its notched beak. ✦ For *akebi*, ☞ MAGICAL COUNTRY.

FATHER—He didn't hate his father, Maruyama told me, but resented him deeply. His resentment stemmed from Shigetoshi's preoccupation with work; he felt his children got in the way. Not only did he seldom pay much attention to Kaoru, he never ate with the family but dined separately with his wife (not uncommon among professionals in that milieu). ✦ In Shigetoshi's last years, a kidney disorder and diabetes made him indeed a bit "crazy" and extremely difficult to get along with.

FIREPLACE—In Maruyama's youth, a Western–style *hekiro* [wall–hearth] could be found only in a stately mansion. ✦ Having a fireplace inevitably suggested an aristocratic and non–Japanese setting——both of which suited Maruyama perfectly. He claimed to dislike Japanese cuisine and life on straw mats (☞ TATAMI), much preferring Western food (omelets were one of his favorites) and furniture.

FISH EYES—This work appeared in a publication for 1st graders. Maruyama was regularly asked to submit such verse. When he wrote works for children, he invariably asked his wife, Miyoko, if she understood what he had written.

FIVE MINUTES TILL SUNSET—Uracas (Urakasu) Island (or Farallon de Pajaros) is the northernmost isle in the Marianas (the Ladrone or Thieves' Islands); they lie ca. 1200 miles south of Yokohama or 500 miles north of Guam. ✦ Balintang Channel, separating Balintang and Babuyan Islands, lies 100 miles north of Luzon. This 50–mile wide channel connects the South China Sea and the Philippine Sea. ✦ Mariners use the canvas windsail to channel fresh air into the holds or below–deck cabins.

FLAME—On a 4–masted ☞ BARQUE such as the Kaiô Maru [Neptune] that Maruyama sailed, mizzenmast refers to the 3rd mast from the bow; it stands before the jiggermast, located farthest aft. ☞ MEMORIES OF MASTS. ✦ On old vessels like barques, steerage refers to the junior officers' quarters.

FLOWER TREE—A regional term for the "flower maple" [*hanakaede*; Latin name, *Acer rubrum*], this tree grows to a height of 60'. People used to boil its bark or leaves as a folk remedy for eye ailments. ✦ Barbinervis (derived from the Latin) registers *sarunameshi* [literally, "monkey tanning"], the local designation for a *ryôbu* (Latin name, *Clethra barbinervis*). Its smooth bark would keep even a monkey from climbing this tall deciduous tree. ✦ Magnolia renders *kobushi* (Latin name, *Magnolia kobus*), Maruyama's favorite tree (☞ "White Magnolias on My Mind," page 291);

this may be the variety that some nurserymen in southern California designate the kobus. Mr. Inoue Yûji provided part of this information. ♣ In 1977, Yayoi Shobô published *Seat in a Flower Tree* by Yamamoto Okiko (real name Tsuneda Chieko, born 1924); she was 24 when Maruyama saw this collection shortly after the war.

FOUNTAIN (ii)—Hibiya Park, which opened in 1903, features largely formal Western–style arrangements with some Japanese elements; it faces the south side of the moat around the Imperial Palace in central Tokyo.

FOX—Iwanezawa people find it unlikely that Maruyama ever saw a fox. By the end of the Pacific War, foxes no longer inhabited the area.

FOXFIRE—Dictionaries call foxfire "a phosphorescent glow, especially that produced by certain fungi found on rotting wood." ♣ Japanese folk stories sometimes depict foxes as magical animals able to transform themselves into humans or possess people's souls. ♣ In the history of Japanese æsthetics, moreover, anything ephemeral (like foxfire) has connoted sadness or pathos.

FRAGMENTS—The mortar is a 16" coastal defense gun. The scene here is the same one Maruyama describes in ☞ GUN EMPLACEMENT.

FREE FLIGHT—Subtitled "For Recitation." ♣ The dream–like, surrealistic scene that the final stanza depicts resonates with the Chagall painting Maruyama describes in ☞ "Tree Voice" (page 226).

FUNERAL OF THE CRANE—For Maruyama's image of this bird, ☞ CRANE.

GLIMPSES OF THE CIRCUS—As a youth, Maruyama had observed circus scenes similar to what he describes here. He said, however, that a tent "patched together from scraps of sail" derives entirely from his imagination.

GOD—Renders *kami*; for this vague term, ☞ GOD WHO WEPT, immediately below. ♣ In interviews, Maruyama insisted that the referent for this *kami* be masculine, so "goddess" would not do. In short, he does not refer here to Amaterasu–ômikami, Japan's sacred Sun Goddess.

GOD WHO WEPT—God [*kami*] defies precise translation. *Kami* can refer to dead spirits or to the living great——including military heroes. *Kami* describes the subjective re-action of veneration or wonder to such things as greatness, the numinous, or what-ever inspires awe, whether a person, a rock, or a tree. ♣ The single Japanese word *kami* covers a large number of English terms for "gods" or spirits. These include: Ariel, dryad, fairie, faun, fay, lares, Mab, naiad, Nereid, nymph, oread, penates, pixy, satyr, and sylph. ♣ Japanese military involvement on the continent began in the summer of 1937. Because this poem dates from the following December, Maruyama describes one of the earliest casualties of Japan's entanglement in China.

GOLDEN CUB—Hemingway's *The Old Man and the Sea* (1952) describes a man who fished the Gulf Stream in vain for almost 3 months before landing an 18' marlin.

After days of struggle and suffering, he finally brings back into port what little the sharks had left. The novel ends with the old fisher "dreaming about lions." ✦ As a psychological image, lions represent the potential perils of the unconscious mind and the latent passions that "devour" the careless. In myths, the young lion corresponds to the rising sun (doubly related by the word "golden," that also suggests fertility and ultimate wisdom) and epitomizes sun's power. ✦ Maruyama gave the original— which appeared with ☞ "Snares" (page 287)—the subtitle, "*Poésie paradoxale* 1."

GREENFINCH—Only an exceptional marksman could easily hit this bird (used symbolically; the poet had no air gun), for a greenfinch is smaller than a sparrow. Finches are seed–eating songbirds. Greenfinches [*hiwa*, identical with *mahiwa*] are related to the siskin and the green linnet.

GROSBEAK—Obanazawa could mean "Tailbloom Tarn." ✦ Dewa is the archaic name referring to all of present–day Yamagata and most of Akita Prefectures. Michinoku (another reading of the graphs for the ancient region called Mutsu) includes the area in northern Honshû now occupied by Aomori, Fukushima, Iwate, and Miyagi Prefectures. ✦ The grosbeak (its beak thick and conical) is a small, colorfully feathered seed–eating bird of the finch family. Its Japanese name is *sankôchô* [literally, "3–light bird"]: the moon [*tsuki*], the stars [*hoshi*], and the sun [*hi*]. This appellation derives from what Japanese hear as the grosbeak's song: *tsuki–hoshi–hi.*

GULL—The poem Maruyama cites in 2 lines—a tanka by Wakayama Bokusui (1885– 1928)—reads as follows: *Shiratori wa kanashikarazu ya sora no ao / umi no ao ni mo somazu tadayou.* My interpretation aims to fit Maruyama's context. ✦ In the 1st edition of *That Far–Off Self,* I read the title the Chinese way as *hakuchô* [swan] instead of the Japanese way as *shiratori* [white bird, doubtless a seagull]; consequently, I both mistranslated and mis–titled this work. Mr. Haraguchi called this error to my attention. ✦ Bokusui published his first tanka collection in 1908 while a student at Waseda University. He remains best known among poetry lovers for his early work; scholars value him especially for his unique experiments with tanka content.

GUN EMPLACEMENT—This defense mortar captured during the 1905 Russo–Japanese War memorialized the attack on Port Arthur under General Nogi Maresuke (1849– 1912); it stood on Kudan Hill, immediately to the north of the Palace grounds. ✦ Maruyama told me that the mortar and its mount, both in deplorable disrepair, reminded him that in those days he felt as "buried" by the world as the gun.

HANDS AND BREAD—The sound echo works in Japanese, where the word for bread is *pan*, which does sound like a tap or pat.

HELM—This functions as the tiller or steering wheel. Tars wheel the helm (attached to the rudder) to guide the ship. For the helm's symbolic significance, ☞ page 54. ☞ BARQUE. ✦ On masts, ☞ MEMORIES OF MASTS. ✦ Also ☞ "Helmsman of the World" (page 139) for a later adaptation of "Helm."

HELMSMAN OF THE WORLD—Doubtless derived from ☞ HELM, this poem originally appeared in *Strong Japan* [*Tsuyoi Nippon*] (1944). ✦ What he regarded the nationalistic tenor of certain works moved Maruyama after the war to reject this collection of verse for children. It seems quite bizarre to me that, "unjust" war or not, many writers could not allow themselves to admit love for or pride in their country. ♣ Notice the symbolic significance of the helm or tiller, page 54.

HIGH VILLAGE—For another description of this setting, ☞ "Stars" (page 232). ♣ Maruyama said in interviews that this poem resulted from his realization that the kindness of the people of the North enticed him to become ensconced forever in Iwanezawa. He feared that remaining there—pleasant as it was for him personally— would be tantamount to burial as a poet. ♣ The last line of the poem uses the word "fate" [*unmei*]. The poet permitted me to change this to "future," which he agreed renders his intention. The word "future," however, lacks an important connotation in *unmei*. Maruyama felt, partly because of the firebombing of Tokyo, that he had incomplete control over what was happening to him. ♣ A marker in the yard of the school where the poet taught makes clear the metaphoric dimensions of this poem— —and all works describing the "high" altitude of where he lived in the North. The sign laconically states: "Elevation 400 meters [i.e., ca. 1200']."

HIRAGANA—The cursive syllabary. In Maruyama's day, children learned *hiragana* only in the 2nd or 3rd (now the 1st) grade after having mastered ☞ KATAKANA (block letters). Most American schools similarly switch from printing block letters to cursive writing (penmanship) after at least the 1st grade.

HORIZON—The last lines state a theme echoed "In the Corridor of Omaezaki Lighthouse" (page 262), published more than a year later.

HOSTAGE SEA—ON OCEAN DAY—Celebrated July 20. ♣ Aside from his justified stand against pollution, the poet told me the Pacific felt "empty" to him because virtually the entire Japanese fleet—including most of her merchant marine—had been sent to the bottom during World War II.

HUNTERS AND I—Originally "*Hantâ no Hanashi*" [Tale of a Hunter], this work appeared in *Shiki* [*Four Seasons*] (1968.10) prefaced by the now separate poem "*Nagare*" [Stream—Tale of an Old Hunter] (page 277). ♣ The hunter image matches the poet's stance in search of his far–off Self. This work thus indirectly reveals Maruyama's æsthetic. ♣ The wild boar [*inoshishi*] symbolizes courage, tenacity, and fierce perversity. It is extremely difficult to kill this animal, a potential danger because boars rarely fear attacking the hunter. ♣ This peril resonates with the poet's commitment to confront the psyche, a similarly risky enterprise.

HUNTING BUTTON MUSHROOMS—This designates *nameko*, which belong to the *matsutake* genus and grow during winter on rotted trees. They are commercially produced and canned. ♣ The *obi* [sash] reveals that the persona wears a kimono; wearers stash items in the garment's long sleeves or in the *obi* because a kimono has no pockets.

ILLUSION IN THE REEF—Maruyama had heard stories of pilots shot down in World War II, but told me he never witnessed the scene this poem depicts.

IMPRESSION—Golgotha [skull in Aramaic and Hebrew] refers to Calvary (from *cal-*

varia, Latin for skull). Calvary, just outside Jerusalem's walls, served as the Roman execution ground. There they crucified Christ. ⚓ "Golgotha's shriek" refers to the words, "My God, my God, why has thou forsaken me?" (Matt. 27:46, Mark 15:34). ⚓ Maruyama finds a Bible at his bedside no doubt because his wife Miyoko and the founder of the Ogino Hospital—which always treated him—are Christians.

IN A MOUNTAIN FIELD—Japan's oldest poetry mentions burnt–over fields [*noyaki*]. This refers to the ancient custom of torching weeds, stubble, and straw to prepare for new growth. The controlled burning of grass and weeds in the fields also provides ash that fertilizes the growth of vernal grasses. By signaling spring's advent and the burgeoning of every growing thing, *noyaki* implies potentiality and hope. ⚓ The "Sailboat Song" [*Hobune no Uta*], then a popular ditty, relates neither to the work in the fields nor to Maruyama's interest in the sea.

IN MY PORTHOLE—For Ku–lang Hsü Island, ☞ BREEZES FROM LAND—FROM SEA.

IN PRAISE OF MORNING SUN—On the Japanese carpenter, ☞ NEW YEAR SEASON. ⚓ "Sol" registers *kami*, presumably the sun god*dess*, who in the West is masculine.

IN THE CORRIDOR OF OMAEZAKI LIGHTHOUSE—This structure stands on a promontory 120' above the sea on the southwest corner of Suruga Bay (☞ CHEERFUL BOOK) in Shizuoka. When Maruyama wrote this poem, nearby Omaezaki had a population of under 20,000. ⚓ 40 knots comes to ca. 45 miles; ☞ KNOT.

ISLAND—Braces—ropes connected to the ends of the yards (that hold sails)—allow changes in the angle of the canvas in response to a wind shift. "Tugging at braces" means a seaman adjusts or secures the yards. ⚓ Points refer to divisions of the compass; each equals 11.25°. Consequently, 3 points off starboard suggests about 34° (or roughly "1 o'clock" from the bow)——off the right side of the ship.

JAPANESE SKIES—Japanese celebrated Boys' Day (Festival) on May 5, now Children's Day. ⚓ Swimming carp refer to the *koinobori*, water–resistant paper or cloth streamers depicting carp [*koi*]. Japanese display these on poles set up in every home, ideally one carp for each male member of the household. ⚓ Ability to swim upstream [*noboru*] against swift currents makes *koi* good symbols of the courage, strength, and perseverance most parents desire for their sons.

JAPAN'S CONSCIENCE—During the war, the government required portraits of the Shôwa Emperor (Hirohito [1901–1989] who reigned from 1926) in every schoolyard across the land. Students were required to bow deeply whenever they passed the fire–proof structure housing the portrait. ⚓ Dewa is the ancient name of the area comprising all of present–day Yamagata and most of Akita Prefectures. ⚓ Gassan [literally, "Moon Mountain"], a volcano southeast of the city of Tsuruoka in Yamagata Prefecture, rises to almost 6,000'. ⚓ I have been told that powdery snow rarely falls in Iwanezawa; the snow there is usually heavy with moisture.

KATAKANA—The "square" syllabary resembles block printing and contrasts with the cursive syllabary, ☞ HIRAGANA, which is like longhand. Before 1946, schools taught *katakana* in 1st grade; after 1946, teachers introduce it in 2nd or 3rd grade.

KNOT—Refers to the following: (a) a division on the log line (☞ SLOW SAILING DAY) that measures the speed of a sailing vessel; (b) a unit of velocity; 1 nautical mile (each some 800' longer than a land mile, but the exact distance depends on latitude) per hour is ca. 1.15 statute miles per hour; and (c) 1 nautical mile. For navigation purposes, a knot stands roughly for 6,000'.

KOREA—As a little boy, Maruyama spent 3 years in Korea (between the ages of 6 and 9). His father served in Seoul as a high official with the Japanese peace–keeping (i.e., policing) agency. ♣ *Nukute* [*nwg–dai* in Korean] describes either the common Korean wolf or the red wolf, either of which is quite savage. Hunting in packs, they attack wild boar, deer, and sometimes even domesticated animals.

KOTO—The Japanese imported this zither–like "floor harp" from China well before the 9th century. Kneeling on the ☞ TATAMI at a right angle to the horizontal *koto*, the musician plucks the strings with 3 plectrums (separately attached to the thumb and the first 2 fingers of the right hand). The left hand dampens the strings to create sharps and flats. ♣ The usual *koto* has 13 silk strings, but may have any number from 7. Each string is drawn over an adjustable bridge that sits on a resonating "box" made of paulownia wood (from the Chinese figwort family). The chamber measures ca. 6' long, 9"–10" wide, and 3" deep.

LAMP AND ALBATROSS—☞ BARQUE.

LIFEBOAT DRILL—Cork fenders are bags of granulated cork that keep lifeboats from damaging (or being damaged by) the ship's sides. Semaphore flags enable daylight visual communication. ♣ The text of this poem in the *Works* contains a typographic error: *watashitachi* ni should be *watashitachi* wa (I:333, 3rd line in from the left). Mr. Haraguchi informs me that the particle *wa* correctly appears in the original collection. ☞ BARQUE.

LIKE MUSIC—☞ BARQUE. The chip log is a device that old–time sailing ships used with a timer to measure a vessel's rate of speed; ☞ KNOT (a) and SLOW SAILING DAY.

LINE FROM THE NORTH—☞ SEA OF OKHOTSK. For some reason, writers frequently depict horses or cattle feeding on beaches along the Sea of Okhotsk.

LIVING ALONE—An *irori* is a hearth open on all sides; a dangling spit allows one to hang a kettle over the fire. ♣ The hearth, a universal metaphor for family unity, is the sacred residence of the god of fire. ♣ It is bad luck (and poor manners) to drop anything into the ashes or put one's feet on the edge board.

LONELY UNIVERSE—As a boy in Seoul—when the old servant Mr. Han (☞ "Korea," page 95) told him local tales—Maruyama possibly heard stories about the Korean folk view that frogs are symbols of regret. ♣ Japanese folklore often depicts frogs as speaking or acting like humans.

LOVELY NOTION—The word "pond" registers *numa*, in this case a deep, spring–fed pool now a good deal smaller than when the poet lived in Iwanezawa. ⚓ Maruyama's "going deep into the woods" consisted of a short jaunt just over the hill from his room. ⚓ Note for contrast 2 Horiguchi Daigaku (1892–1981) works that Maruyama certainly knew. From one titled "*Ike*" [Pond] in a 1919 book: "The pond is my heart——/ so much sunk so deep within / on this chilled, this crystal winter day." ⚓ Another titled "*Hoshi o Tsuru*" [Fishing for Stars] appeared in a 1922 book: "Dropping a line into the dark pond, / I fish for stars. / If I grind them up and drink them, / I can write good poetry."

LUNAR CALENDAR—Widely used in the countryside, the lunar calendar still determines farmers' holidays and planting times. ⚓ A millennium of rural poetic tradition habitually holds sway in modern verse, too, as many poets educated in prewar days refer to the times of the year in terms of the lunar rather than the solar calendar.

MAGICAL COUNTRY—This title renders *Senkyô*, a place where hermits abide——a "pure" land isolated from the secular world. Japanese folklore treats such locations as enchanted or "magical" because extraordinary events occur in places not corrupted by the values of day–to–day living. ⚓ *Akebi* (Latin name, *Akebia ouinata*) is a deciduous viny bush native to hilly areas in East Asia. The *akebi*'s clusters of dull mauve or red flowers (shaped like 5–pointed stars) appear around April among 5–leafed twigs. Its fruit resembles fat, lilac–tinted, oval, thick–skinned sausages about 4" long. These mature in autumn and split open to expose white, sweet, semi–transparent meat. ⚓ Mountain boys gather unripe *akebi* and bury them 2"–4" in the soil. Depending on how hard the fruit was when picked, it should mature and become edible in 3–10 days. ⚓ For "button mushrooms" [*nameko*], ☞ HUNTING BUTTON MUSHROOMS. ⚓ *Shimeji* is an edible mushroom (a *matsutake* champignon); *maitake* [literally, "dancing mushroom"] is an edible shelf fungus of the *sarunokoshikake* [literally, "monkey chair"] class; *yamadori* (*sarunokoshikake* class): tasty, edible mushrooms that grow primarily in beech groves.

MAN WHO ENCOUNTERED A BEAR—One of Maruyama's favorite (and, I believe, one of his best) poems. He told me he'd heard of a man who confronted a bear on a mountain, so he used the idea for this work. ⚓ The source of his information could have been the novelist and sometime poet Ibuse Masuji (1899–1993), a *Shiki* [*Four Seasons*] colleague. In 1937, Ibuse published in *Shiki* the 8–line poem "*Nadare*" [Avalanche]. It describes a bear he had seen sliding down a mountain on the snow, "legs crossed / unruffled / .... / striking a smoker's pose." ⚓ On Maruyama's reference to time, note the resonance with T. S. Eliot: "But to apprehend / The point of intersection of the timeless / With time, is an occupation for the saint..." ("The Dry Salvages" V, 1941, 3rd poem in *Four Quartets*).

MEMORIES OF MASTS—Maruyama uses feet not meters because the Japanese navy imitates British naval terminology, even in these matters. ⚓ Mizzen refers to the 3rd mast of a sailing vessel. Originally mizzen referred to the forward mast on Italian ships; English sailors mistakenly applied the word to the aftermast. ⚓ The naval argot "head" (my addition) indicates a compartment with toilet facilities; Maruyama writes *shôben o shi ni iku* [go to pee]. ⚓ The jiggermast is the small mast near the stern, the last of the 4 masts on the training ship. ⚓ For other explanations of masts,

☞ BARQUE and FLAME.

MEMOS TO FACES—The ☆ exist in the original. ♣ MEMO (singular) appears in capital Roman letters in the Japanese title.

MINATO WARD, NAGOYA—MEMO ON THE ISE BAY TYPHOON—Minato means "port" or "harbor." ♣ The Isé Bay Typhoon (1959.10) caused tidal waves along the immediate seashore that devastated the area and took many lives. ♣ The Yomiuri Newspaper asked Maruyama to write a poem about this event (Toyohashi, where he lived, now a city of almost 310,000, lies roughly 45 rail miles east by southeast of Nagoya). ♣ Though discharged from the hospital on 1958.07.28, more than a year earlier, he had still not completely regained his health following an operation for intestinal blockage. His widow reports that he agreed to write the poem only if he did not have to view the disaster area in Nagoya. ♣ On Maruyama's experience with intestinal blockage, ☞ "Where Sky is No More" (page 246).

MOCHI—Japanese use a large wooden mallet to pound hot, steamed rice into a viscous mass. They make the sticky paste into balls or cakes used in various dishes or eaten separately. ♣ They convert *mochi* into confections and also toast it for inclusion in soups, etc. *Mochi* has long had special associations with New Year foods.

MONK HILL—The title "*Bôsan Yama*" could also be rendered "Bald Mountain." It indicates a hill that resembles the smooth–shaven pate of a Buddhist monk [*bôsan*]. ♣ Bamboo grass [*kumazasa*; Latin name, *Sasa albo–marginata*] belongs to the rice family; its narrow, whip–like stems grow to a height of from 1'–3'. The edible leaves dry up in late fall and turn chalky——another reason poets connect white hues with autumn. *Kumazasa* prefers hillside habitats, but people love to plant it in their gardens as an ornamental. ♣ Larks make their nests on the ground.

MONPE—Shapeless, ankle–choking slacks that females wore during the Pacific War.

MOON AND SATURN—Subtitled "For Recitation." ♣ 'K' stands for Kaneko Isao (born 1918), who then lived in Toyohashi. ♣ "Suburban pond" refers to Ôike [literally, "big pond"] in Mukaiyama. Kaneko, still an active astronomer, moved his telescope into the mountains northeast of Toyohashi. He has operated a private observatory for nearly 30 years. ♣ Maruyama's interest in the moon and Saturn goes well beyond his long–standing fascination with astronomy. For him, the sky and the sea represent similar symbolic dimensions of the psyche. ♣ Since ancient times, people have associated the moon with the mind. Notice expressions like "loony" (the mind off kilter) and "moon over" (infatuation being another kind of "craziness").
  Saturn, the 7th planet, is also a concept. Ancient Greeks saw Saturn as the symbol of time–creating space and human consciousness—i.e., man as an existential being. Note also that Saturn's "father" was Uranus—god of the sky and first ruler of the universe; ☞ MY WOMAN THE SEA. ♣ Both god and planet associate with old age, death, and restless activity. ♣ Miyazawa Kenji (1896–1933), an agronomist, wrote juvenile literature and poetry. Profound Buddhist faith informed much of his writing and all of his altruistic service to farmers in Tôhoku, the northeastern part of Honshû. ☞ MOON PASSAGE. ♣ An "equatorial mount" enables adjustment to 2 perpendicular axes to compensate for Earth's rotation: celestial latitude and celestial longitude. This

facilitates accurate tracking of a heavenly body.

MOON PASSAGE—At 70, Maruyama was hospitalized for an inflammation of the pancreas. ♣ The late Heian poetess Akazome Emon died in her mid–80s (ca. 1041). Her poem (quoted in 2 lines) reads: *Yasurawade nenamashi mono o sayo fukete | katafuku made no tsuki o mishi kana.* ♣ Lacking the headnote—which provides necessary context—these words do not make clear sense. ♣ Emon's lover had stood her up to meet another woman, so she wrote this waka as "revenge." Akazome bases the entire utterance on the conceit, entirely imagined, that the other woman had, in actuality, stood up the lover who had stood her up. ♣ It is, in short, the *other* woman the poetess describes lying awake late into the night and gazing, like Maruyama, at the moon. Professor Ben Befu provided this information.

The 2nd Apollo Mission took place between 1969.11.04 and 1969.11.15. ♣ *Hsi–yu–chi*, Romanized in various ways and meaning *Journey to the West* [of China], is a classic Chinese folk novel by Wu Ch'êng–ên (ca. 1505–1580). A Japanese translation of the *Hsi–yu–chi* has long enjoyed considerable popularity among the educated. ♣ Arthur Waley published an abridged English version titled *Monkey* (Grove Press, 1943), from which I take the rendering "Cloud Trapeze," the name of a spell. Having mastered this magic formula, the Monkey King could travel "a hundred and eight thousand leagues" in a single leap (page 26). I appreciate Professor Shirleen Wong's help in providing this information. ♣ Chapter One of *Monkey* contains death references echoed in "Moon Passage" (cf., the monkey's desire to "live forever among the people of the sky," page 14). ♣ For a related statement, ☞ "Within the Sun" (page 235). ♣ For data on Miyazawa Kenji, ☞ MOON AND SATURN. "Emperor Moon" renders *Gettenshi*.

MOORED IN AMOY—For Amoy (Xiamen • Hsia–men), ☞ DROPPING ANCHOR IN AMOY HARBOR. For Ku–lang Hsü Island, ☞ BREEZES FROM LAND—FROM SEA. ♣ Three thousand knots comes to ca. 3,500 miles; ☞ KNOT. ♣ "Sunrise banner" is the Japanese naval flag, a rising sun with scarlet rays radiating to the edges. ☞ OUR NATIONAL ANTHEM. ♣ "Square rigged" means the masts carry yards (spars) that hold "square[d]" (i.e., rectangular) sails; ☞ BARQUE.

MORNING WATCH—The poop deck, an area above the main deck at the stern, lies just behind the rearmost mast; ☞ YOUNG MEN SHOULDER THE SAIL. ♣ Watches designate the hours a sailor is on duty. They usually last 4 hours, changing at 12, 4, and 8. The 4–8 P.M. watch is split into 2–hour "dog watches" so no crew member will constantly stand the same watch each day; ☞ DOG WATCH. ♣ Head means toilet; Maruyama uses *benjô*.

MORTIFIED FIGURE—A photograph of a soldier killed in the Third Arab–Israeli War (1967.06.05–1967.06.10) evoked this poem. ♣ Maruyama believed publicly viewed or photographed corpses should be made up the way American morticians prepare bodies. Since the Japanese neither embalm nor prettify the dead, he specified that his remains not be displayed. ♣ "White face cover" refers to the custom of placing a handkerchief over the face of a person who just died. ♣ Maruyama's widow Miyoko followed to the letter the poet's instructions concerning his corpse. After she personally prepared it for cremation, a close relative helped her transfer the body into the simple pine coffin. They then nailed it shut so no one could view his corpse. ♣ For a muted reference to the shameful act of viewing the dead (published 2 years earlier), ☞ FACE WITH ANTS.

MOTHER'S UMBRELLA—The umbrella, which forces people to walk shoulder–to–shoulder, symbolizes togetherness. ✦ A common graffito in Japan is an umbrella with a boy's and a girl's name under it; this expresses an idea similar to "John loves Jane."

MOUNTAIN—The poet's family name means something like Roundhill. *Maru* means "round • rotund" and *yama* means "mountain • hill."

MOUNTAIN CRONE—Ms. Watanabe provides the following background: "*Tom–tom* bird" renders *pon–pon tori*; *pon–pon* is the sound that people in Iwanezawa associate with the song of the *tsutsudori* [literally, "barrel bird" or "pipe bird"], the Himalayan cuckoo. ✦ Though people of the North connect this bird's call with children at play, they feel its song sounds quite lonely. ✦ The *Waa–waa* bird renders *oao tori*, the green dove [*aobato*]. It is necessary to go quite deep into the mountains to hear this bird, whose call sounds exquisitely sad and lonely.

MOUNTAIN VILLAGE—☞ HIGH VILLAGE for Iwanezawa's elevation. ✦ Even mountain adults describe animals by their sounds (the way we might call a cow a "moo–moo"). ✦ Most Japanese associate the dove's coo with the sound *pôpô*. The wild dove has a thicker, lower call, which mountain folks hear as *tedeppoppo*. Perhaps his trouble with the local dialect caused the poet to mishear this as *dedepô*. ✦ Ms. Watanabe provided information on local customs.

MR. MOON—Children refer to the moon [*tsuki*] as *O–tsuki–sama* (the title of this poem). This may be akin to "Noble Sir Moon," which I simplify to "Mr. Moon."

MY JOURNEYS (i)—Maruyama's postscript notes, "From memos of an old trip." ✦ Tôhoku [literally, "the northeast"] includes 6 prefectures: Akita, Aomori, Fukushima, Iwate, Miyagi, and Yamagata (the location of Iwanezawa). ✦ Hokuriku embraces the 3 prefectures of Fukui, Ishikawa, and Toyama. Kanazawa (present population in excess of 300,000), the capital of Ishikawa Prefecture, remains the chief city of the area. ✦ The 1st stanza of Rilke's poem "The Panther" (☞ PANTHER) provides relevant information: "His vision from the passing of the bars / is grown so weary that it holds no more. / To him it seems there are a thousand bars / and behind a thousand bars no world." ✦ M. D. Herter Norton, translator, *Translations from the Poetry of Rainer Maria Rilke* (New York: W. W. Norton, 1962), page 159. ✦ For other references to Rilke, ☞ BLESSED and DREADFUL METHOD.

MY JOURNEYS (ii)—Abashiri, the northern terminus of the Sekihoku Line, abuts the ☞ SEA OF OKHOTSK (on Hokkaidô's northeastern coast). ✦ The poet Kitagawa Fuyuhiko (1900–1990), who met Maruyama at the Third Higher School in Kyoto, graduated from Tokyo University in French literature. He contributed to the movement for new–style prose poetry and is also remembered as a translator and movie critic. ✦ "*Uma*" [Horse] reads: "*Gunkô wo naizô shite iru.*" Maruyama replaced *shite iru* (progressive • stative) with *suru* (simple present). ✦ Hiroo, the southern terminus of the Hiroo Line, lies on Hokkaidô's southeast coast. To go round Cape Erimo (or Point Erimo), Maruyama took a bus to the southeast terminus of the Hidaka Line at

Samani (no railway connects Hiroo and Samani). ♣ From there he went to the northeastern terminus of that line at Tomakomai, on the Pacific Coast directly south of Sapporo. The last stanza describes a scene at Samani.

MY JOURNEYS (iii)—Shiretoko (the Japanese version of an Ainu place name) is a peninsula on Hokkaidô's northeast corner; it points toward the Kuril[e] Islands (Chishima Rettô). The ☞ SEA OF OKHOTSK stretches to the west, Nemuro Strait lies to the east. ☞ CORAL SEA. ♣ Most render *umé* [apricot] plum; ☞ PLUM TREE. *Umé* customarily bloom in late winter or early spring.

MY WINSOME WIFE—Miyoko was born in Arimatsu, Aichi Prefecture, the daughter of a wholesale dyer who was a *yôshi* (that is, adopted into his wife's family to carry on the business). Miyoko's family relocated to Chiryû just before she began school. ♣ After graduating from elementary school, Miyoko went to stay with grandparents living in Yokohama, where they'd relocated for family reasons. Miyoko's oldest brother worked in the area at a plant producing synthetic silk fiber, and the next older brother attended school in Tokyo. In Yokohama, she entered a mission school, Sôshin Jogakkô [Girls' School]. ♣ Her grandparents' sudden deaths in her 2nd year forced transfer to Kaneshiro Jogakkô in Nagoya, also run by missionaries.

After graduating from Kaneshiro, Miyoko entered the English course at Aichi Prefectural Higher Girls' School. A light case of spinal carries, contracted not long after entrance, forced withdrawal. ♣ Once she recovered, the owners of the Ôtaniya, a well-known Toyohashi drapery, invited her to come to the city to prepare for marriage——ostensibly with their only son, a friend of Maruyama. ♣ Heading to Kyoto, or for home in Tokyo, Maruyama regularly stopped off at Toyohashi to visit with this friend, with whom he shared a love for literature. That's how he met Miyoko, whose younger sister Kunié often came by the drapery during holidays. Kunié met and got along well with Maruyama. He fell for Miyoko, however, and actively pursued her hand. ♣ For more than 33 years after the end of the Pacific War, Miyoko served on the arbitration committee of the Toyohashi Family Court. In 1984, Jiji Tsûshin Sha published her 256–page book, *Manekin • gâru—Shijin no Tsuma no Shôwashi* [Mannequin Girl—Shôwa History (seen by) a Poet's Wife].

MY WOMAN THE SEA—Maruyama's choice of planets seems significant. In psychological terms, Neptune—god of the sea—represents the deepest (sometimes the stormiest) levels of the unconscious. ♣ Somewhat like Neptune, Uranus reigns over the unconscious, as well. Uranus as god of the heavens has a special relationship with ancestral memories and psychic latencies. ☞ MOON AND SATURN. ♣ The Chinese graph for *umi* [sea] contains the element meaning "[my] mother."

NEW YEAR SEASON—Japanese carpenters will not build unless Shinto priests have first used sacred branches to "purify" the site; this provides the referent for "exorcised by sacred leaves." ♣ Framing has traditionally been a matter of joining the members by notches and grooves rather than by nails. The carpenter in Japan has always used his chisel and mallet more than his hammer; ☞ IN PRAISE OF MORNING SUN.

NEWS FROM THE CAPE—Maruyama says this poem—which shows how he merges sea and sky—is purely a product of his imagination. He never went diving or snorkeling, much less harpoon fishing. ♣ Sea mussels renders *igai*, 6"–7" long, blackish–brown marine bivalve mollusks with tasty pearl–gray meat. ☞ ABALONE [*awabi*].

NEWS FROM THE MOUNTAIN—On "winter solstice squash" ☞ "Squash" (page 184).

NEWS OF RAIN—Maritime "folklore" regards dolphins (the class to which porpoise belong) as beneficial to humans since they predict rain storms, dangerous seas, etc.

NIGHT BELLS—People love to attach these small bells to pets; ☞ BELL SONG.

NIGHT TREES—Subtitled "For Recitation." ♣ I use *hinoki* [Japanese cypress] rather than repeat "cypress." These pictures Vincent Van Gogh (1853–1890) painted at Saint Rémy between 1889 and 1890. ♣ "Aspera," from the Latin name *Aphananthe aspera*, renders the Japanese *muku no ki*, for which I find no English equivalent. ♣ For Chagall, ☞ TREE VOICE. ☞ YUKATA, a light cotton kimono–like garment.

NOBUO WEATHER—LAMENT FOR TSUMURA NOBUO—Tsumura (☞ AGES) nicknamed people he liked; Maruyama's "Nobuo weather" reflects this penchant. ♣ Sengataki [literally, "1000 falls," i.e., very many] lies northwest of Karuizawa, a well–known summer resort in Nagano Prefecture. Many Westerners and Japanese own summer homes or villas in the area. ♣ Maruyama visited Tsumura at Sengataki from 2–4 August 1934. Tsumura thought his friend would enjoy taking a look at the falls, about 60' high. Maruyama says a sudden shower forced them to turn back. Tsumura claims in his diary that they waited till the downpour ended and then visited the falls. ♣ Crape myrtles—which Japanese call *sarusuberi* • "monkey slip" because of their smooth bark—bloom red and pink flowers during much of the late summer.

OLD POETRY COLLECTION—Refers to *Infancy* [*Yōnen*] (1935), which contains Maruyama's earliest poems. ♣ A *yen* corresponds to $1, a *sen* to 1¢. ♣ Together with countless other poets, Maruyama certainly believed Walt Whitman's claim that his collection "is no book. / Who touches on this touches a man."

ON THIS FOSSIL—The context of this poem is the trail–blazing 89–minute orbital flight of the Soviet spacecraft Vostek. On 1961.04.12, cosmonaut Yuri A. Gagarin (1934–1968) became the first man to observe Earth from space. ♣ A nova is "a star that suddenly becomes much brighter and then gradually returns to its original brightness over a period of weeks to years." ♣ Maruyama's list follows the order of the Five Agents in Chinese thought (*wu–hsing*; *gogyō* in Japanese): fire, wood, water, metal, and soil; these also designate the weekdays Tuesday through Saturday. ♣ The actual order of the planets from the sun is Mercury (water, which Maruyama skips), Venus (metal), Mars (fire), Jupiter (wood), and Saturn (soil); ☞ MOON AND SATURN.

ON THIS PLANET—Halley's Comet appears every 75 or so years. Maruyama saw it in 1910 when he was 11 and living in Matsué (☞ VISITING MATSUE); it next appeared in 1985. ♣ The British astronomer and mathematician Edmund Halley (1656–1742) first calculated its orbit and in 1682 predicted its reappearance.

ORIENTAL NOISE—On the priest, ☞ DISTAFF STONE BUDDHA.

ORISON—This title renders *kitôka*, "supplication" [literally, "prayer song"]. ♣ The crossjack (crojik) is the lowest yard (spar or crossbar) on the mizzen mast——3rd from the bow on a 4–masted sailing vessel.

OUR HOUSE—☞ CRANE for Maruyama's image of this bird.

OUR NATIONAL ANTHEM—The Japanese anthem, the *Kimigayo* ["Our Lord's Reign"], is a 31–syllable waka (tanka) from Book VII of the *Kokinshû*, an Imperial anthology dating from 905 A.D. ♣ The poem might be rendered: "Our Lord's reign shall last a thousand, no eight thousand ages——till pebbles turn to boulders thick with moss." ♣ Wishing for the Imperial family's eternal reign takes a poetic twist in the word "eight," a mystical or sacred number that appears in ancient descriptions of indigenous gods. ♣ Note that "8" (a folded oval) implies the endless, somewhat like a Möbius strip. Subjects hope for a reign as eternal as the wait to witness small pebbles becoming boulders; this hope extends to the life of the nation, as well. ♣ For "drunk as the sea," ☞ SEA WAS SOUSED (page 216).

OUR UNSHOD POOCH—Though distinctly marginal, this piece deals with more than mere sentimentality. Maruyama's concern for relationship frames his reaction to the dog; being a childless loner, he projects the wish for relationship on his pet. Combined with the acerbic hint that his spitz puppy promises to be as honest a friend as any human being, this frame drives the poem beyond bathos. ♣ Japanese live on straw mats (☞ TATAMI), so removing one's shoes before entering a house is a fundamental act of being human, of belonging to society. Average Japanese, at least in the milieu Maruyama depicts here, did not usually allow a dog kept in the yard to enter their living space. If they let a small dog into the house, they certainly washed its paws. ♣ The poet consequently finds himself prevented from more closely relating to the innocence, dependence, and loving acceptance that his dog symbolizes. These—rather than crude mawkishness—deeply move the poet.

PANTHER—Rilke's "The Panther" inspired this work. The 2nd stanza (☞ MY JOURNEYS [i]) describes the "padding gait" of the animal who turns "in the very smallest circle," much "like a dance of strength around a center in which / stupefied a great will stands." ♣ For Rilke, ☞ BLESSED, DREADFUL METHOD, and MY JOURNEYS (i).

PEOPLE OF THE NORTH—Those in Iwanezawa immediately think of cedar trunks that "grow lissome, straight into sky" as trees that tenaciously resist the weight of snow and gravity in their skyward reach from crags or steep ravines.

PERVERSITY—This title renders *amanojaku*, a cross–grained, cranky individual who willfully behaves opposite of what society expects, desires, or requires. Traditional Japanese regard an *amanojaku* as the ultimate trickster and rebel. ♣ An element of "perversity" existed not only in Maruyama's personality but in his artistic choice to exert intellectual control over intuition and feelings. ♣ On the mirror's significance, ☞ the early paragraphs of the Introduction (page 23). ♣ Similar perversity characterizes the wild boar [*inoshishi*]; ☞ HUNTERS AND I.

PICNIC—This work, which refers to a school outing, appeared in a publication for 3rd graders. ♣ Laver [*nori*, a type of *Porphyra*, is sloke • sloak] consists of thin sheets of dried, edible seaweed. Since the early 17th century, Japanese have grown this dark brown alga in sheltered shallows. After gathering the alga, they wash it in fresh water, then dry the thin sheets on frames. The modern mechanized process produces thin and brittle 7" x 8" sheets. ♣ Minnows registers *medaka* [killifish • creekfish • guppies], found in fresh or brackish waters. ♣ Eulalia translates *susuki*, usually rendered "pampas grass," though there are no broad, grassy plains in Japan; ☞ WHEN I WALK THROUGH FIELDS.

PLOVERS—AT THE DUNES ON NAKATAJIMA <II>—For Nakatajima, ☞ STROLLING THE DUNES. ♣ The plover [*chidori*, literally, "1000 bird"] has appeared in Japanese poetry since the *Man'yôshû* era (latter half of the 8th century). ♣ The plover is a white-breasted, plump shore bird found worldwide in ice–free lands. Its wings and roundish head are primarily dark brown; many types have strong black (some Japanese varieties have red) markings in the head and neck area. ♣ Medium–length legs allow plovers to wade through shallow surf along ocean beaches, in mud flats, or riverbeds, where they flock. They move in a zigzag course or appear to reel along in their search for food. Plovers make nests on flat ground, often among rocks with the same colors and patterns as their eggs. ♣ Haiku poets associate the plover with winter. Over the years poets have assigned these birds a variety of characteristic calls, none exactly like Maruyama's penetrating *piririiiii*.

PLUM TREE—The *umé*, apricot, is translated "plum," I presume, because plum scans better. ♣ This tree obeys the lunar calendar, which places the beginning of spring in February; thus it sometimes blooms in the snow. ♣ This significant harbinger of spring symbolizes virtue and beauty in women; traditionalists think females should strive to be as pure and strong as the *umé*. ♣ Moss sometimes covers the twisted, gnarled trunk and cracked bark of an aged tree; this adds considerably to its attractiveness and value. ♣ Japanese use India ink [*sumi*] in calligraphy.

POEM OF IDLENESS—Idleness renders *mui*. On one level, *mui* suggests inactivity, having no goals, or simply "vegetating." ♣ On another level, it resonates with the Taoist (and Zen) concept *wu–wei* [literally, "no do"]——the Chinese pronunciation of the same graphs as *mui*. Alan Watts (1915–1973) suggested rendering *wu–wei* "no sweat." ♣ This concept suggests the power of water to carve away mountains simply by being itself, not by willed or intentional activity.

POETRY—Candles symbolize purification of the soul, ward off darkness and evil spirits, and imply faith in rebirth. ♣ The butterfly symbolizes the human soul, attraction to light (enlightenment), and rebirth or new life (resurrection). It may, as well, signify love, intuition, frivolity, and vanity. ☞ TRACES OF A BUTTERFLY.

POET'S WORDS—Nakahara Chûya (1907–1937) died suddenly from acute meningitis some 5 years before this poem appeared. An idiosyncratic style did not prevent his association with *Shiki* [*Four Seasons*] poets. He became one of Maruyama's most congenial drinking partners. ♣ Aside from his own poetry, Chûya earned repute as a translator of French poets, particularly Arthur Rimbaud (1854–1891).

POND'S EDGE—In Greek myth, a wild boar gored the youth Adonis. Both Aphrodite (goddess of love and beauty) and Persephone (underworld queen and the goddess of fertility) loved him and wanted to claim him from Hades. ♣ Zeus allowed Adonis to spend the warm half of the year with Aphrodite above ground, the cold part with Persephone in the underworld. His life thus exemplifies seasonal change. ♣ Swan symbolism is exceedingly complex. Swans drew Aphrodite's chariot and the chariot of the sun. An early myth says Achilles strangled Cygnus (meaning swan), the son of Neptune, who then transformed him into a swan. Associations with death and resurrection follow. ♣ Aesop claims the swan—an emblem of poetry and the poet—sings only when it is about to die. This relates it to the tragic and melancholic; connections with music and prophecy further associate this bird with poets. ♣ The Greeks dedicated the swan to Apollo, god of music; the white swan was sacred to Venus, goddess of love. Others saw the bird as an androgynous god: its phallic neck masculine, its rounded body feminine——a harmony of opposites.

RECKONING THE COMPASSES—Maruyama registers *teruteru • konpasu* [telltale compass] in ☞ KATAKANA. Lacking graphs, a Japanese reader unfamiliar with this term could momentarily mistake *teruteru* for "fair weather" [literally, "(sun) shine–shine"]. ♣ "Telltale," meaning "informer," indicates an instrument for recording information. It also refers to a device that indicates the position of the rudder or helm. ♣ However self–indulgent, it seems unlikely that the captain might smoke in his bunk.

REMINISCENCES OF LAMPS—"Family Buddhist chapel" renders *butsuma*. Well–to–do families sometimes set aside a small room for Buddhist services. The chapel—the center for remembering family progenitors and honoring their spirits—faces north since that's the direction of the dead. ♣ "Bantam lamp" renders *mamé ranpu* [literally, "bean lamp"]. "Lantern" renders *kantera*; ☞ DAWN, where I translate the same word "tube lamp." ♣ Anzai Fuyue (1898–1965) was one of the poets who founded the influential quarterly journal *Shi to Shiron* [*Poetry and Poetics*] (14 issues between 1928.09 and 1931.12), which encouraged free verse using colloquial Japanese. This put Anzai among the vanguard of early Shôwa attempts (1926–1932) to modernize Japanese poetry. He then lived in Dairen, Manchuria, where he spent 15 years helping operate his family's saké business. He returned to Japan in 1933, following his father's death.

Anzai's 1st collection, *Gunkan Mari* [*Warship Mari*], appeared 1929.04. He produced several more collections and a book of essays. Anzai's compressed imagery and concentrated language bring Maruyama's early style to mind. ♣ "Portrait" renders Maruyama's *poutoré* (in ☞ KATAKANA). ♣ On Murô Saisei, ☞ TREE–LINED PATH. ♣ Before the days of electricity, Japanese frequently used acetylene lamps to illuminate stores. ♣ Prosper Mérimée (1803–1870), French novelist and translator of Russian writers, wrote that he enjoyed reading letters by starlight.

RETURN TO THE MOUNTAIN VILLAGE—Maruyama's visits to Iwanezawa in the early 1970s relate to setting up and dedicating a poetry stele to him on the grounds of the elementary school where he taught. ☞ "Unveiling Ceremony in the Hills" (page 290), the poem that follows this work. ♣ Stony Mountain Witch renders *ishi no yamauba* (or *yamanba*; Iwanezawa people call her *ubasama*). Villagers set up on a pedestal the statue of this fearsome–looking "witch" with sagging breasts——visible from the road leading into town. As a tutelary deity, she protects from danger, interlopers, or aliens. ♣ Somewhat like our "the bogey man'll get ya," villagers at times invoke the ugly *ubasama*'s wrath against uncooperative children.

RHINOCEROS AND LION—Japanese call a lion in the wild, in a zoo, or in a photograph of the actual beast, *raion* (based on the English word). Maruyama uses the word *shishi* in the title because, he told me, *shishi* sounds better with *sai* [rhinoceros] than *raion*. ⚓ *Shishi* usually refers to the statues of stylized pug–nosed Chinese lions (sometimes called *fu* dogs) guarding the entrances to temples (and sometimes shrines). The stylized likeness represented by these statues, incidentally, depicts ancient Chinese notions—based on reports—of what a lion looked like.

ROOF—"Gargoyle" again renders *oni*; ☞ SORROW.

ROOM WITH BIRD—The sudden shift in line 5 from an impersonal to a personal mood (a conceit that appears several times in Maruyama's work), reflects the language in the original. This merging of observer and observed conveys the impression that the poet's Self objectively describes its subjective behavior; ☞ THAT FELLOW WITHIN, "Autumn Dreams" (page 254), and WHITE MAGNOLIAS ON MY MIND (page 291). ⚓ Mrs. Maruyama explains that, despite the impersonal nature of the first 4 lines, this poem describes a family experience. Early in their marriage, the Maruyamas kept a pair of small birds. One night Miyoko forgot to put them back in the cage and they flew away. The couple never kept birds again.

SAILING DOLL—Mrs. Maruyama informs me she had to work the day the poet sailed, so she was unable to go to Yokohama to see him off. ⚓ The female admirer who brought the doll to which Maruyama refers was a beautiful young woman in her 20s. Years later, she told Miyoko that Kaoru was the only man she ever loved. ☞ BARQUE. ⚓ Crojik or crossjack (☞ ORISON) is the lowest yard on the 3rd mast of a 4–masted barque; ☞ also MEMORIES OF MASTS. ⚓ Six bells ring at 3, 7, and 11 o'clock (A.M. or P.M.); 6 bells in mid–afternoon thus signal 3 P.M.

SAILING THROUGH AUTUMN—☞ CORAL SEA.

SCHOOL FROM AFAR—These are recollections of the Third Higher School in Kyoto, which Maruyama attended from 1921 to 1926, when he was 22–27. He wrote the poem in 1939, about 12 years later. ⚓ In prewar days, such schools prepared students for the university. Japanese higher schools [*kôtô gakkô*], on a far loftier level than American high schools, imitated the German Gymnasium.

SEA BEAST—For a nautical mile (ca. 6000'), ☞ KNOT.

SEA BIRD—On a ☞ BARQUE, the windlass—a device for hoisting or dropping the anchor—is probably hand–driven like a ☞ CAPSTAN.

SEA COLORINGS—ON AN AUSTRALIAN FREIGHTER—Reference to colored pencils reveals Maruyama's penchant for sketching. ⚓ For fantail, ☞ BUBBLES.

SEA DARKENS—☞ CRANE. ☞ BARQUE.

SEA NEAR CHICHIJIMA—Chichijima ["Father Island"], in the main group of the Bonins (Ogasawara Guntô), corresponds to Hahajima Guntô ["Mother Island chain"] and lies north of Iwo Jima, some 700 miles due south of Tokyo. ♣ Richard Dehmel (1863–1920), German lyrical poet and impressionist, moved from supporting to opposing Naturalism. Good at evoking landscape and atmosphere, he tried to "spiritualize" sex, made competent translations of the poetry of Paul Verlaine (1844–1896), and wrote a verse novel, which may be Maruyama's reference in this poem. ♣ Boat deck refers to the level where the lifeboats are secured.

SEA OF OKHOTSK—On the northeastern edge of Hokkaidô, this sea is bounded on the west by Sakhalin (Kamchatka Peninsula) and on the east by the Kuril[e] Islands. Okhotsk, icebound from November through May, is notorious for its heavy fog. ♣ Maruyama rode the Hakodate Line north from Sapporo to Asahikawa, where the Sekihoku Line begins. This runs through Kitami and terminates very close to the Sea of Okhotsk at Abashiri. ♣ His Sapporo friend's name was Sarashina Genzô (1904–1985), a poet and local historian known especially for his studies of the aboriginal Ainu. ♣ Maruyama likely met Sarashina around 1946.

SEA WAS SOUSED—Paul Ambroise Valéry (1871–1945) was poet, philosopher, essayist, and critic. ♣ The "witty [shareta] French poem" is "Le vin perdu"——wasted or lost wine [ushinawareta bishu] in Horiguchi Daigaku's translation.

SEA WIND—Maruyama insisted that each line appear as a separate stanza. He was less specific on the pronunciation of the title. The Japanese reading [kun–yomi] of the graphs for the title is umikaze; the Chinese reading [on–yomi] is kaifû. ♣ I prefer umikaze because it sounds more mellifluous than kaifû. Maruyama said I could choose which I preferred. When he recorded this poem for me, however, he read the title kaifû. Both readings appear in the index of Japanese titles.

SHANGHAI—The source of Maruyama's information is Fujii Sôsen (☞ DISTAFF STONE BUDDHA), a Pure Land Buddhist priest who lived in Toyohashi. For a time Fujii was an auditor at a Shanghai school; he also traveled in Chekiang Province with the renowned interpreter of Zen Buddhism, Suzuki Daisetsu (1870–1966). ♣ "H" refers to Higashi Honganji (Temple of the Original Vow). In the 1st published version of this work, Maruyama spelled the name out. This temple belongs to a branch of Pure Land Buddhism that Shinran (1173–1262) established in the 13th century. Buddhist temples have long served as hostels. ♣ The italicized lines (quoted in Chinese) resonate with the first 2 lines of a famous Sung period quatrain. Chinese usually attribute this poem to Su Shih, more commonly known as Su Tung-p'o (1037–1101), one of the most celebrated poets of his era.

The 1st line Maruyama cites is identical with the Sung quatrain. The 2nd has been so altered, however, its author doubtless meant only to create a faint echo of the original. ♣ The original quatrain may be rendered:

> The mists of Lu Shan and Ch'ien–t'ang's tidal bore
> make you regret never having seen them.
> Once you've seen them, however, you find they are only
> the mists of Lu Shan and Ch'ien–t'ang's tidal bore.

This tidal bore (or eagre) on the Ch'ien-t'ang River in Chekiang Province has been measured at over 15', the highest known water level of any such wavelike inrush. ♣ One interpretation sees this poem dealing with the stages of Zen enlightenment, another with the nature of apprehending Truth. Mr. Bai Xiaodong helped me render these lines. ♣ Chekiang Province lies directly to the south of Shanghai. The rivers that cause the tidal flooding exit into the bay at or near Hangchow (Hang–chou), some 100 miles west by southwest of Shanghai. Tidal bores occur in September. ♣ Lu Shan [literally, Mt. Lu] refers to a conglomerate of wooded peaks (up to ca. 4500' high). Aside from spectacular waterfalls, the area is important for celebrated Buddhist monasteries and Confucian academies. Mt. Lu is located in northern Chiang–hsi (Jianxi • Kiangsi) Province near the Yangtze River port of Chiu–chiang (Jiujiang • Kiukiang), nearly 350 miles west by southwest of Shanghai. For much of this information I am indebted to the kindness of Professor Shirleen Wong.

SHŌJI—Sliding doors paneled with translucent paper, *shôji* allow entry from the living quarters into either interior hallways or the exterior corridors (☞ ENGAWA) on the southern exposure of traditional homes throughout Japan. ♣ Windows separating living space and interior corridors sometimes also contain *shôji* panels.

SLOW SAILING DAY—The log line is a braided rope attached either to the chip log (a device to measure a sailing vessel's speed; ☞ LIKE MUSIC) or to the patent log (a device to measure the distance a vessel has sailed). ♣ "Velocity" renders *funaashi* [speed, headway], measured in ☞ KNOTs (ca. 6,000 feet) per hour.

SNARES—Originally, Maruyama titled this work, "*SEXE ni tsuite*" [On Sex]. He first published it in *Shiki* [*Four Seasons*] in 1972.04. He subtitled this work "*Poésie paradoxale 2*"; for 1, ☞ GOLDEN CUB. ♣ The choice of the hyena may have no relation to myths about this animal. Notice, nevertheless, the mythological belief that hyenas have the magical ability to change their sex. After a female has mated, she can become a male hyena.

SNOW BUGS—Renders *kawagera* [stone fly], a blackish brown insect slightly over 0.5" long with light yellow–brown wings. It appears in late winter or early spring.

SNOWY FIELD—Maruyama's description of the instrument the boy uses to catch the rabbit (*také no wappa*, which I render "bamboo *wappa*") differs radically from the way one of his former pupils described this device to me in Iwanezawa. ♣ The poet doubtless had confused the *wappa* with the *wakka*, another "weapon" used for the same purpose. ♣ The standard *wappa* is a snare that consists of a wire noose set up on stakes sunk into the sides of trails that rabbits follow through the snow in their hunt for food. During the war, boys made nooses of supple bamboo strips because steel wire was unobtainable. ♣ Passing along the trail, the rabbit's neck catches in the noose; the stakes hold the rabbit fast so boys can catch it. Even if the rabbit pulls up the stakes, they impede it sufficiently to allow even a child to capture the animal.

The device Maruyama describes in "Snowy Field" is the *wakka*, a hand–launched instrument. It is made of bamboo fashioned into a circle some 30 cm. (ca. a foot) in diameter. A piece of black cloth is then fitted over the frame. ♣ Once launched, the hoop makes a wooshing noise. Because this presumably sounds to the rabbit like a diving hawk or kite, the animal feels an urge to escape. It stops running, tries to burrow into the snow so it can hide, and in the process makes itself vulnerable to capture. ♣ Ms. Watanabe and Mrs. Katakura helped gather this information.

SNOWY MOUNTAIN—Maruyama here describes a trip to the village of Tsurubé (☞ also

"Tsurubé" [page 164], which describes a small one–room school now shut down). Young people of that community had invited him to talk to them about poetry.

SOLITUDE—The names in this poem reveal a hierarchy that may contain symbolic significance: Hirô = "sun son • sunboy," Tsukirô = "moon son • moonboy," and Hoshirô = "star son • starboy." ♣ Kimono have no pockets, so sleeves provide storage space. ♣ Foochow (Fuchow • Fu–Chou • Fuzhou), is a port on the Min River delta and the capital of Fukien (Fujian) Province. Located in southern China, the city lies west by northwest of the tip of Taiwan.

SONG OF THE CRANE—This poem depicts the same scene as ☞ FOUNTAIN (ii). ♣ For Maruyama's image of this bird, ☞ CRANE.

SONS OF THE WINDJAMMER—Sailors make decks on sailing vessels watertight by filling the seams with melted pitch, a by–product of tar. ♣ The young men Maruyama refers to are midshipmen training to be officers.

SOOTED SKIES—Maruyama was an agnostic, his wife a Christian. His references to God and creeds at times seem cynical, for he could not grasp the idea of faith.

SORROW—"Gargoyle" (no connection with the waterspouts on medieval cathedrals!) registers *oni*, which means demon, fiend, imp, or ogre. I think gargoyle more graphically implies a visage fearful enough to scare off evil spirits. ♣ These decorative figures typically appear on the gables of temples or private homes. ☞ ROOF.

SPARKS—Akutagawa Ryûnosuke (1892–1927)—one of Japan's more celebrated modern short–story writers—committed suicide at 35 partly out of the irrational dread that he had inherited his mother's insanity and could no longer write. ♣ Maruyama bases his quote at the end of the 1st stanza on Item #8, "Sparks" [*Hibana*; literally, "fire blossoms"] in Akutagawa's *A Fool's Life* [*Aru Ahô no Isshô*]; this, his last work, he finished only weeks before he ended his life. ♣ William Peterson's translation of this section reads: "Though he considered all of human existence, there was nothing special worth having. But those violet blossoms of fire…to hold them, he would give his life" (New York: Grossman • Mushinsha, 1970), page 27.

SPRING (i)—☞ CRANE.

SPRING IN THE NORTH—Every villager knows the woman (Itô Mitsuru, born in 1938) who as a 3rd grader made this observation. Indeed, they introduced her to me as the girl who had said, "Teacher, the swallows are here." ☞ "Class Log" (page 179), where Mitsuru reports the swallows' departure in fall.

SPRING STORM—The haiku text reads: *Kami ni sasu kanzashi ayafuku / haru arashi* (Maruyama splits the customary single line into 2). ♣ In Iwanezawa, he actively participated in local poetry groups and wrote a number of haiku and tanka that people there have proudly preserved. ♣ Maruyama asserted to me emphatically in 1973, however, that he was absolutely *never* interested in traditional poetry.

SPRING TO SUMMER—☞ UGUISU, the Japanese bush warbler; *uguisu* sounds better than "bush warbler." ♣ For bamboo grass, ☞ MONK HILL.

SQUASH—This renders *kabocha*, which some translate "Japanese pumpkin." *Kabocha* are green and resemble small to medium–sized pumpkins. ♣ The citron [*yuzu*; Latin name, *Citrus junos*] is the Chinese lemon. In autumn this tart fruit exudes an extremely pungent odor.

STANDING BY THE GRAVE—Another poem responding to the death of Maruyama's sister–in–law, Kunié. ♣ I render the title "*No ni Tachite*" [literally, "standing in the field"] this way because I've been told that this quite ordinary Japanese can imply attendance at a rural internment. ♣ Mustard or rape [*na no hana*] is a hardy annual herb of the *Cruciferae* family (Latin name, *Brassica napus*), related to cabbage and the turnip. Its seeds are valued for their oil content and as components of bird feed. Its cross–shaped flowers are yellow. ♣ Vetch renders *genge*, a leguminous herb of the Pulse family. Its stems grow from creepers that farmers plant in their fields for fertilizer. Common vetch blooms in spring with purple or pink flower clusters; the stems measure 4"–12" high. ♣ This profusion of cheerful spring plants intensifies the contrast with the burial of a young woman who died in her springtime. ♣ The planet Venus—the star of either morning or evening—shines brighter than any object in the sky except the moon or the sun. Its complex metaphorical significance includes spiritual love and sexual attraction. ♣ Sheol renders the Buddhist term Maruyama wishes read *Meifu* (though more commonly *Meido*). This designates the realm of dead spirits reigned over by Enma, the Japanese equivalent of the Prince of Hades.

STARRY NIGHT—For "god" [*kami*], ☞ GOD WHO WEPT. ♣ Japanese folklore has long regarded the horse a sacred beast because it brought the gods [*kami*] to earth. Some Shinto [literally, "way of the *kami*"] shrines keep a sacred white horse for the deity or deities they serve. ♣ People believe that the horse will hear their prayers or confessions and thus unburden them of anxiety or guilt.

STARRY SKIES—As a boy, Maruyama's love for flying machines very likely urged him to try making models. ♣ Jirô means "2nd son," Maruyama's actual position in his family. He had been raised and behaved as the 1st son and primary heir because his mother's 1st son did not survive infancy. ♣ In his father Shigetoshi's family register [*koseki*], however, Maruyama was listed officially as the 4th son because of the 2 sons from his father's 1st marriage. Neither divorce nor death affects that listing.

STARS—Subtitled "For Recitation." ♣ "*Les Etoiles*" means "The Stars." ♣ On the site of Maruyama's residence in Iwanezawa, ☞ HIGH VILLAGE. ♣ Alphonse Daudet (1840–1897) began his career with a volume of poetry but gained fame in Paris for naturalistic tales of life in the city and the provinces. Some stories featured childhood experiences. ♣ In interviews, Maruyama expressed interest in Daudet's depressed boyhood and brief career as a teacher. ♣ Sirius: The Dog Star is twice as large as our sun and 20 times as luminous (but almost 9 light years away). Only the sun, the moon, and Venus are brighter heavenly bodies. ♣ Polestar: Polaris or the North Star has always been important to navigators. ♣ Scorpio: Scorpius (scorpion) shines in southern skies, a constellation in the Zodiac. It reaches its highest position during evenings in July. ♣ Cygnus: The swan, a constellation people since ancient times have seen as a bird, is sometimes called the Northern Cross (for the Southern Cross, ☞ AT SEA) because its 5 brightest stars form a Latin cross (the vertical ca. 2x as long as the horizontal axis). Highest point reached during evenings in September.

STREAM—TALE OF AN OLD HUNTER—Making water flow against itself was one of the magical powers possessed by the monkey protagonist in the Chinese folk tale, *Hsi–yu–chi* [*Journey to the West* (of China)]; ☞ MOON PASSAGE. ♣ "Stream" originally served as the preface to ☞ HUNTERS AND I.

STROLLING THE DUNES—AT NAKATAJIMA—Subtitled, "The Dunes at Nakatajima <I>." ♣ Nakata Island lies just off the mouth of the Tenryû River, directly south of the city of Hamamatsu in Shizuoka Prefecture. ♣ Strong prevailing winds constantly alter the configurations of the dunes and make the area an important tourist attraction. Nakatajima is one of the 3 largest dune areas in Japan. ♣ For the 2nd work on Nakatajima, ☞ PLOVERS. ♣ I preserve Maruyama's numbering. Though he actually published "Plovers" 1st, it appeared later in the collection, so he labeled it <II>.

SWALLOW (i) • (ii)—The swallow [*tsubame*], a migratory bird, is a joyful harbinger of spring; ☞ CLASS LOG and SPRING IN THE NORTH. Japanese feel sad when the swallow leaves in early autumn, the season of dying. ♣ Maruyama admired both the looks and the graceful flight of this bird.

SWALLOW ARRIVES—☞ SWALLOW.

SWALLOWS OF AMOY—On Amoy (Xiamen • Hsia–men), ☞ DROPPING ANCHOR IN AMOY HARBOR. ♣ Also, ☞ "Swallow" (page 179).

TATAMI—Mats woven from rice straw have for centuries been uniform in size—— roughly 3' x 6'; 2 *tatami* (6' x 6') make 1 *tsubo*, the traditional measurement of area. ♣ Japanese describe room sizes by the number of *tatami* they contain. A room of 6 *tatami* [*roku–jô*] equals a 9' x 12' rug (108 square feet).

TENTH FLOOR BAR IN THE 'Q' HOTEL—Maruyama uses a standard method of disguising names. He converts the 1st letter into the next letter of the English alphabet; ☞ ABALONE. The Q thus stands for P, which refers to the Palace Hotel in Tokyo. ♣ This hotel, facing the Imperial Palace in Chiyoda–ku, lies between Ôtemachi 1– chôme and Marunouchi 1–chôme. Maruyama stayed there when he visited Tokyo to confer with his *Shiki* [*Four Seasons*] colleagues.

THAT FELLOW WITHIN—This 1956.11 poem relates to January surgery when doctors removed 66% of Maruyama's ulcerated stomach (caused, his wife claims, by drinking bad saké). His surgeon came by 9 days after the operation and showed him what he had excised. ♣ Maruyama told me that since this eerie experience he's had the impression that body and mind exist independently of each other. He explores this idea more poignantly in ☞ "Autumn Dreams" (1957.10, page 254).

THOSE PEOPLE—*Katakago*, ancient name for the *katakuri*, is the adder's tongue lily or dog–toothed violet, which appears in the earliest Japanese verse. ♣ The name of the *amefuri* [literally, "rainfall," the dotted bellflower] derives from the ancient belief that picking its blossoms will bring on a rainstorm. Colorful regional names include *hotarubukuro* [literally, "glowworm–sack"] and *tsuriganesô* [literally, "hanging–bellflower"]. ♣ The poet had met laconic northern people a number of times before he decided to live in the snow country.

THOSE WHO STAND ON ICE AND SNOW—*Umé* is an apricot, which hardly sounds as poetic as plum, the usual rendering; ☞ PLUM TREE.

THOUGHTS ABOUT SNOW—Lashed cedar poles serve as racks (many 3 tiers high) for drying rice. ♣ The short growing season, the then inadequate distribution systems, and inability in those days to travel far in winter forced families to store more provisions than required of farmers living in a less severe climate.

TOUCHING YOUR TOMBSTONE—Mrs. Maruyama cannot conceive that her sister Kunié might have had or expressed the thoughts the poet ascribes to her in this poem.

TRACES OF A BUTTERFLY—Universally, not just in Japanese or East Asian folklore, butterflies symbolize the soul of a deceased human being. Because of the "miraculous" way a caterpillar transforms into a thing of beauty, butterflies also naturally associate with change, resurrection, and rebirth. ♣ This poem is one of the works Maruyama asked me to omit after he found it impossible to answer questions about the meaning of certain expressions. ♣ My reading of "Traces of a Butterfly" suggests, however, that it may hint at the poet's search for his far–off—and escape from his immediate—Self; that is tantamount to rebirth. This poem may also imply a sublimated wish for spiritual enlightenment. ☞ POETRY.

TRAINING BARQUE—☞ BARQUE.

TRANQUIL FESTIVAL—☞ MOCHI (glutinous rice), a New Year delicacy. ♣ "Spirit" renders *kamisama*; for *kami*, ☞ GOD WHO WEPT (*–sama* is an honorific suffix).

TREE–LINED PATH—MOURNING SHIKI—All those mentioned are famous poets associated with the magazine *Shiki* [*Four Seasons*] that Maruyama edited. He offers 2 listings, those who tragically died young and others (who lived to maturity); each he orders by year of birth. ♣ The tragic poets: On Nakahara, ☞ POET'S WORDS. For Tachihara, ☞ EERIE TREES—TO POET FRIENDS WHO DIED YOUNG. For Tsumura, ☞ AGES. ♣ Others: Hagiwara Sakutarô (1886–1942), the poet Maruyama most respected, was a frequent drinking partner and dinner guest. Critics widely recognize him as the "father" of modern free verse, the 1st to use colloquial Japanese successfully. ♣ The poet–novelist Murô Saisei (1889–1962) was a lifelong crony of Hagiwara. Murô, somewhat of an acerbic crank, once told Maruyama that he was too fat to be a poet. ♣ Maruyama's fast friendship with Miyoshi Tatsuji (1900–1964), a major lyricist, dates from their days at the Third Higher School in Kyoto.

TREE VOICE—Subtitled "For Recitation." ♣ Marc Chagall (1887–1985), born in Russia, spent many productive years as an artist in France, where he died at 97.

TSURUBE—Though its graphs mean "region of cranes," the name Tsurubé derives from local geological formations in the shape of the bird; ☞ CRANE. ♣ Yamagata, capital and chief city of Yamagata Prefecture, lies some 50 miles west of Sendai (☞ DEVASTATION). Young people in Tsurubé had invited Maruyama to speak to them about poetry; ☞ SNOWY MOUNTAIN (page 256). ♣ Officials long ago converted the quaint one–room classroom described here to other uses.

TWO MINDS—No doubt Maruyama refers to the poet Miyazawa Kenji; ☞ MOON AND SATURN (for his dates) and ☞ MOON PASSAGE.

UGUISU—Renders the Japanese bush warbler, which—because of its lovely chirping [*saezuri*]—some prefer to translate "nightingale" (despite the fact that the *uguisu* does not sing at night). ♣ The size of a sparrow and a most inconspicuous brown, the *uguisu* lives in forests or among tall grasses. Feeding primarily on insects, it spends much time on the ground, where it makes a plate–shaped nest.

UNVEILING CEREMONY IN THE HILLS—Occurred 1972.10.08; ☞ FAR FROM HUMAN EYES, the untitled work Maruyama wrote for his poetry stele. ♣ Six kilometers come to 3.72 miles. ♣ "In town" refers to Yamagata, the nearest major city (☞ TSURUBE).

VERDANT CLASSROOM—On *akebi*, ☞ MAGICAL COUNTRY. ♣ *Hitorishizuka* [literally, "alone serene"] suggests silent singularity. This spring plant grows in the shade of mountain trees. ♣ The top of each stalk (6"–12" high) sprouts leaves that surround a swelling from which emerge delicate oblong flowers with neither calyx nor petal. ♣ I refer to the bush warbler by its Japanese name, ☞ UGUISU.

VERDANT SELF—Maruyama's original title uses not the word for "self" but for "existence" [*jitsuzon*]. Because the self is at the core of one's existence, I take the liberty of changing *jitsuzon*. ♣ The subtitle of this poem reads, "Based on the biography of Rilke by Tani Tomoyuki." On Rilke, ☞ BLESSED, DREADFUL METHOD, MY JOURNEYS (i), and PANTHER. ♣ Yasnaya Polyana, the name of the family estate of Count Leo (Lev) Nikolayevich Tolstoy (1828–1910), is located near Tuly, a town some 115 miles due south of Moscow. Tolstoy was born, raised, and buried there.

VISIONS OF FLOWERS—Butterbur stalks [*fuki no tô*, bog rhubarb; ☞ DEEP IN THE MOUNTAINS, ¶ 2] appear in early spring when they poke up through thawing snow. ♣ Amur Adonis [*fukujûsô*; on the myth of Adonis, ☞ POND'S EDGE], perennial of the buttercup family, has yellow blooms and also associates with the new year. ♣ On *katakago* and *amefuri*, ☞ THOSE PEOPLE.

VISITING MATSUE—This is the chief city (castle town) in Izumo, present–day Shimane Prefecture (of which Matsué is the capital). Shimane lies along the Japan Sea due north of Hiroshima. ♣ The central government appointed Maruyama's father governor of the prefecture between 1908 and 1911; the poet thus lived in Matsué when he was between 9 and 12. ♣ Koizumi Yakumo refers to Lafcadio Hearn (1850–1904), an Englishman born in Greece who ended up a newspaperman in the United States. Hoping to escape America's crass materialism, he fled in 1890 to Japan. He couldn't be a Japanese citizen without a Japanese name, so when he was naturalized in 1895 he took his wife's family name Koizumi [literally, "Smallspring"]. ♣ A relative suggested for his given name the poetic designation, Yakumo [literally, "8 (i.e., many) clouds"]; this compound comes from the opening of a poem about the area (for "8" ☞ OUR NATIONAL ANTHEM). ♣ Cloudiness characterizes Matsué's skies. Yakumo also contains a double echo of Izumo, the ancient name of the region: the "umo" sound and the graph for clouds.

Hearn taught English at Matsué Middle School (well above American high–school level) in the early 1890s; he later lectured on English literature at Tokyo University. He died and is buried in Tokyo. Hearn is celebrated for his interpretative works on and short stories about Japan. ♣ Dabchick registers *kaitsuburi* (the small grebe), an aquatic bird related to the loon. Very poor at either flying or walking, grebes flock together in ponds or moats where they habitually float very low in the water. ♣ When boys toss stones at them, dabchicks sink lower and lower into the water, gradually submerging like a submarine. To force the birds to sink into the water was no doubt part of the joy of harassing them.

WATER'S SPIRIT—Hagiwara Sakutarô (☞ TREE–LINED PATH—MOURNING *SHIKI*) once praised this poem as marking a new direction in Maruyama's poetry. Ever since, editors invariably include it in anthologies of modern poetry or discussions of Maruyama's work. ♣ A Japanese poet–critic confided several years before his untimely death that he had to include this work or his editor would not approve the anthology he edited. Just as mechanically, critics insist that "Water's Spirit" is a "typical" Maruyama poem. Readers of *That Far–Off Self* can judge the accuracy of this claim. ♣ In interviews, Maruyama asserted this poem's main point is lack of centrality in the human heart. He wanted the lines to flow mellifluously, but I have found it next to impossible to convert this work into satisfying—much less well–cadenced— English. ♣ Water (or the sea) symbolizes the psyche; that is, after all, the matter from which life originated. Running water in particular relates to life and quickening; ☞ also POEM OF IDLENESS. ♣ For a similar basic image, ☞ "Dusk," page 77.

WHEN I WALK THROUGH FIELDS—Fall is the appropriate season to tramp through dried–up fields and enjoy under clear skies the crisp air. ♣ "Fish–scale clouds" registers *urokogumo*, cirrocumulus clouds; ☞ DREADFUL DREAM. ♣ The (Chinese) bellflower [*kikyô*] associates with purple hues and hilly areas. ♣ Valerian [*ominaeshi*] is a perennial herb with yellow flowers; Japanese use its roots medicinally (cf., the Vandal Root). ♣ Eulalia renders *susuki* (Latin name, *Miscanthus sinesis*——native to East Asia), generally rendered "pampas grass" (Latin name, *Cortaderia selloana*—— native to Argentina). ♣ The word *susuki* appears in Japanese poetry from very early times; Japanese always associate it with autumn and admire especially its attractive plumes. This ornamental grass grows more than 8' high; its highly–valued whitish or ecru–hued plumes, rising from a spurt of saw–toothed leaves, grow from 1'–3' in height. ♣ Moon viewing [*tsukimi*] refers to a ritual observed during the mid–autumn full moon. This moon is especially lovely because the air is dry and skies are clear (N.B., the harvest moon in the West).

WHERE SKY IS NO MORE—The subtitle, "My Intestines Twisted," reveals that Maruyama wrote this work after he underwent surgery for an intestinal blockage on 1958.05.01. He remained hospitalized till the end of July.

WHITE MAGNOLIAS ON MY MIND—For background, ☞ the 1940 poem, "White Flowers" (page 106). ♣ In the West, magnolias symbolize beauty, love, perseverance, refinement, and sensuousness. ♣ In Japan's snow country, their early blooming marks the end of the long and dreary winter. They thus represent the land's rebirth and the onset of new life (☞ "Spring in the North," page 189). ♣ Mrs. Maruyama reports that the poet loved magnolias, particularly the *kobushi* type seen in the snow country. This may be the hardy deciduous variety called the kobus magnolia (☞ FLOWER TREE, ¶ 2); it grows to heights of from 20'–30'. ♣ To the poet's chagrin, kobus were unavailable in Toyohashi. Instead, he had a regular magnolia planted in his yard. Coincidentally, white is the color of death in Shintoism. ♣ The verbs of the last 4 lines imply personal, subjective involvement; those of the earlier lines create an impersonal, objective effect (despite the fact that Maruyama describes his own magnolia tree). I have been unsuccessful in communicating this shift. ♣ On merging observer and observed, ☞ ROOM WITH BIRD.

WHITE PICTURES—Poems about the North in no way exaggerate the snow's depth, which reaches above the eaves of an average home. ☞ "Witch Hazels" (page 152).

WIDE RIVER—On the priest, ☞ DISTAFF STONE BUDDHA.

WINDS—☞ BARQUE. ♣ A yard, a spar horizontally intersecting a mast, supports a sail; ☞ MOORED IN AMOY. ♣ "Right on!" borrows the standard British naval term used in this context. Maruyama writes the word *yoroshii* [fine, good, all right] and adds the ☞ KATAKANA pronunciation [*rubi*] *raitoon* beside it.

WINTER—Maruyama loved going to the zoo to observe animals; most likely he is at the zoo in Ueno Park, Tokyo.

WINTER COMES—☞ MOCHI, a special New Year rice cake; ☞ TRANQUIL FESTIVAL.

WINTER DREAMS—For *akebi* vines, ☞ MAGICAL COUNTRY.

WITCH HAZELS—Large deciduous shrubs or small trees, *mansaku no hana* are native to Asia and related to the magnolia. They can grow to heights of 12'. Redolent, golden yellow, string–shaped petals appear before the leaves. ♣ Pulverized and pressed, leaves and bark produce witch hazel, an astringent liniment barbers once used for after shave lotion. In Asia, the bark provides a fragrant balm used in perfumes.

WITHIN THE SUN—In the late 1940s, Maruyama regularly visited a tuberculosis sanitarium where he counseled patients interested in writing free verse. ♣ He told me that "Within the Sun" clearly expresses his changing philosophy of life; this poem accordingly qualifies as one of his favorites. An increasingly strong awareness of life led him to believe that human consciousness—not the "soul"—is immortal. ♣ Maruyama pondered such problems because his wife Miyoko is a Christian believer who had spoken to him often about "being saved," the possibility of life after death, and the like. That Maruyama relished dealing with such issues illustrates his involvement in intellectual as opposed to purely emotional concerns.

WOLF PACK—Re another dog–wolf transformation, ☞ "Becoming Wolf" (page 63).

WORDS ON DRIVING RAIN—The star (☆) before each line exists in the original.

WORKING GIRL—People of Iwanezawa do not know of a "workshop at the foot of the slope," nor do they recall that one ever existed.

YOUNG MEN SHOULDER THE SAIL—The poop deck, above the main deck at the stern, lies behind the rearmost mast——the jiggermast on a 4–masted ☞ BARQUE. ⚓ "Poop" means the stern; as a verb, it refers to waves breaking over the fantail (☞ BUBBLES). ⚓ The mainsail, usually square, is set the lowest on the main yard; a large barque has mainsails fore and aft. On masts, ☞ MEMORIES OF MASTS.

YOUNG SAILOR—For an explanation of the capstan, ☞ CAPSTAN. ⚓ For tar (pitch), ☞ SONS OF THE WINDJAMMER. ⚓ "Departure flags" are coded pennants that signal while in port a ship's status or intentions (here, that the vessel intends to depart).

YUKATA—Aside from use as nightclothes or pajamas, Japanese don *yukata* in summer around the house. Hotels invariably provide their guests with them as nightwear, and they are the common garb at spas. ⚓ Near hospitals, one comes across *yukata*–clad patients strolling the streets or seeing visitors off on train platforms. Because Japanese unfortunately identify *yukata* with pajamas, it is also possible to find ambulatory patients so clad on the sidewalks or at train stations.

CHRONOLOGY

DATE	EVENT

1899.06.08   Born in Ôita, Kyushu, the 2nd son of Shigetoshi (born 1855), official in the Home Ministry (3 children by his 1st wife), and his 2nd wife Takeko (née Ichikawa, born 1869); named Kaoru after early June's balmy, fragrant breezes

1899.09.18   Kaoru's older brother Toshinobu (born 1896.09) dies of stomach inflammation

1900.10   Shigetoshi transferred to Nagasaki

1905.05   Family moves to Seoul; government assigns Shigetoshi to the peace–keeping (i.e., policing) agency

1906.04   Kaoru enters elementary school in Seoul

1908.02   Shigetoshi's kidney problems cause reassignment to Matsué as governor of Shimane Prefecture

.09   Kaoru transfers to grade 3 in Tokyo

1909.04   Family follows Shigetoshi to Matsué; Kaoru enters grade 4, develops close relationship with his male teacher

1911.03   Shigetoshi's kidney problems worsen so he enters Tokyo University Hospital; family back to Tokyo

.04   Kaoru enters grade 6 in Tokyo; visits Yokohama with his class for a flying–machine demonstration; because of rain, the class goes instead to the harbor where the blue eyes of Scandinavian sailors astonish; this incident stimulates an infatuation with the sea

.05.22   Shigetoshi dies at 57

.09   Family moves to Toyohashi, builds a new home; Kaoru transfers to grade 6 in Toyohashi

1912.04   Enters Aichi Prefecture Middle School

1916.11   Middle–school magazine publishes 6 of his tanka about the sea

1917.03   Graduates from middle school; takes the entrance exam to the Merchant Marine Academy [then called Tôkyô Kôtô Shôsen Gakkô, now the Tôkyô Shôsen Daigaku]; fails the exam but decides to re–take it; enters a preparatory school in the capital; reads books on the sea by such authors as Robert Louis Stevenson and Joseph Conrad

DATE	EVENT
1918	Passes test, enters the Academy (April); cannot tolerate heights, so can't climb up the rigging; legs swell, given a medical discharge (September)
1919	Desires then to be a lighthouse keeper; urged to enter the Third Higher School in Kyoto instead
.08.25	Father Shigetoshi's 1st son Shigeo dies
1920, Spring	Decides to study for the exam, but resolves not to become a bureaucrat like his father; passes
1921.04	Enters Kyoto school as a French major; reads the poetry of Hagiwara Sakutarô, modern French poets in translation, and stories by Oscar Wilde, Edgar Allan Poe, and the like; skips so many classes he must repeat his 1st year
1922.04	As a 2nd–year "freshman," he meets new students Miyoshi Tatsuji (born 1900) and Kuwabara Takeo (born 1904); both later become friends
1923.07	Kaoru publishes works in the Kyoto school organ that generate friendship with Kajii Motosaburô (born 1901) who admires Kaoru's poetry
1925.03	Miyoshi and Kuwabara—another lifelong friend—graduate, but Kaoru missed too many classes so he must repeat his 5th year; meets his future wife, Takai Miyoko (born 1907), while visiting a friend, heir to the family drapery business in Toyohashi
1926.03	Graduates from the Third Higher School
.04	Enters Tokyo Imperial University, Department of Japanese Literature; begins to dabble in modern poetry [shi]; later gathers some of these works in Yônen [Infancy] (1935); contributes steadily to literary magazines
1927, Fall	Proposes marriage to Miyoko
1928.02.28	Marries Miyoko in Toyohashi; shortly afterward, he drops out of the university to concentrate on writing; also continues his lavish lifestyle and quickly squanders his inheritance
.09	Begins to write more imagistic, internal poetry
1929	Having depleted his father's inheritance, Kaoru must locate cheaper lodgings in Tokyo; he moves to Toyohashi to live with Miyoko's parents; then returns to Tokyo to stay with her uncle
1931.07	Letter from Tsumura Nobuo (born 1909), a Keiô University student who admires Kaoru's poetry,

DATE   EVENT

	begins a close friendship; the Maruyamas move back to Toyohashi, then move to Kyoto and stay with Kaoru's mother
Fall	To make his mark, Kaoru feels he must return to the capital, join a poetry circle, publish a book; through a friend, locates employment for Miyoko at the Mannequin Club in Tokyo, a firm that places attractive women as models and product demonstrators in metropolitan department stores
1932.03	Friend Kajii Motosaburô dies of tuberculosis
.04	Miyoko's sister Kunié finishes girls' school in Toyohashi and comes to Tokyo; stays with the Maruyamas; the Mannequin Club hires her
.12.05	Publishes *Ho–Ranpu–Kamome* [*Sail–Lamp–Gull*], his 1st collection; claims he's unaware of writing "intellectual lyricism" or being under "modernist" influences; for the 1st time, meets the poet Hagiwara Sakutarô, who praises his work
1933.05	Hori Tatsuo (born 1904) publishes 1st issue of the new journal, *Shiki* [*Four Seasons*]
.07	2nd issue of *Shiki* appears
1934.10.15	Hori attempts to resurrect *Shiki* with the help of Miyoshi Tatsuji and Kaoru; 1st issue of 2nd phase of the magazine
1935.05.05	Publishes *Tsuru no Sôshiki* [*Funeral of the Crane*]
.06.15	Publishes *Yônen* [*Infancy*], which later wins the 1st *Bungei Hanron* Poetry Prize of ¥30
1936.01	Sister–in–law Kunié, afflicted with pulmonary tuberculosis, returns to Toyohashi
.03.29	Kunié dies at 24 from TB
.09.15	Kaoru publishes *Ichinichishû* [*Day by Day*], which includes a substantial section of verse dealing with Kunié's death
1939	Given a spitz puppy, which becomes the subject of several subsequent poems
.04.06	Father Shigetoshi's 2nd son Yoshichika dies
1941.02.10	Publishes *Busshô Shishû* [*Images*], poems that feature attachment to concrete, impersonal objects
.05.24	Leaves on the naval training barque Kaiô Maru [Neptune] as a special correspondent for the *Chûô Kôronsha*, publishers of the *Central Review*
.07	Returns from visiting ports in China, etc.

DATE	EVENT
1942.02.25	Publishes *Namida Shita Kami* [*The God Who Wept*]
.05.11	Hagiwara dies; later, Tsumura Nobuo contracts Addison's disease
1943.09.20	Publishes *Tentô naru Tokoro* [*Hear the Ship's Bell*]
1944.06.27	Tsumura dies at 35; last of 81 issues of *Shiki* (since 10.1934) appears
.10	Publishes *Tsuyoi Nippon* [*Strong Japan*], a collection of children's verse that Maruyama later repudiates (presumably because of the pro–war nature of some of the verse)
1945.04	To escape the air raids, Maruyama takes a teaching job in Iwanezawa, Yamagata Prefecture; begins teaching grade 5
.05.29	Firebombs destroy his Tokyo house in Nakano; learns of loss 2 June from visitor to Iwanezawa
.07.01	Leaves Iwanezawa; finds Miyoko near Toyohashi
.08	1st issue of *Shiki*'s 3rd phase appears on the 5th
.10	To Iwanezawa with Miyoko; teaches grade 3
1946.07	Mother arrives in Iwanezawa at month's end
.09.09	Publishes *Kitaguni* [*North Country*]
.10.24	Mother Takeko dies in Iwanezawa at 77
1947.04.30	Resigns post; remains in Iwanezawa to write
.12	*Shiki*'s 3rd phase ends with the 5th issue
1948.03.31	Publishes *Senkyô* [*Magical Country*]
.05.10	Publishes *Aoi Kokuban* [*Blue Chalkboard*]
.06.20	Publishes *Hana no Shin* [*Flowercore*]
.07.07	Back to Toyohashi, hoping for early return to Tokyo
1949.04	Becomes visiting lecturer in modern Japanese poetry at Aichi University, a private school in Toyohashi
1951.05	1st chair of the League of Poets in Central Japan
1952.08.15	Publishes *Seishun Fuzai* [*Lost Youth*]; takes his 1st lecture tour in Hokkaidô
1954.11	Receives the Fifth Toyohashi Culture Prize for "contributions to regional literature" (the reason for the prize baffled the poet)
1955.07.07	Leaves Yokohama (listed as ship's purser) on the freighter Yamashita Maru for a 2–month voyage to the South Seas and Australia
.09.15	Returns from the cruise
1956.01.03	Enters the Ogino Hospital in Toyokawa, a suburb of Toyohashi; 66% of severely ulcerated stomach

DATE   EVENT
_____

	removed on the 7th
.02.22	Released from the hospital
1957.05.03	Receives Fifteenth Central Japan Culture Prize; delivers a lecture entitled, "Poetry and Science"
1958.05.01	Operated on for intestinal blockage
.07.28	Discharged from the Ogino Hospital
1959.04	Promoted to Visiting Professor at Aichi University
1962.01.29	Father Shigetoshi's oldest daughter Toshi dies
.11.20	Publishes *Tsuresarareta Umi* [*Hostage Sea*]
1964.04.05	Long–time friend Miyoshi Tatsuji dies
1966.01	1st of many trips to Tokyo to discuss *Shiki* and the possibility of re–publishing it
.12	Decides with others to reissue *Shiki*
1967.12	1st issue of the 4th phase of *Shiki* appears
1969.11.23	Inflamed pancreas fells him following a lecture in Sendai; again enters the Ogino Hospital
1970.04.29	Discharged but continues out–patient therapy
1971	Jointly responsible for editing the works (in 6 volumes) of Tachihara Michizô (1914–1939), a congenial young poet and fellow editor of *Shiki*
1972.09.01	Publishes *Tsuki Wataru* [*Moon Passage*]; old friend Kuwabara Takeo avers that it contains the same lyric impulse as his earliest verse
.10.08	Dedication of poetry stele on the grounds of the elementary school in Iwanezawa; inscribed with his poem "*Hitome mo Yoso ni*" [Far From Human Eyes]
1973.05.30	Publishes *Ari no Iru Kao* [*Face with Ants*]
1974.05.23	Hardening of the arteries forces hospitalization; spends half of each month in the Ogino Hospital
.10.21	Dies at home of a cerebral thrombosis
.10.23	Funeral, which most *Shiki* colleagues attend
.12.07	Memorial service in Toyohashi's Citizen's Hall
1975.05.20	Last issue of *Shiki* (17th issue of its 4th phase) dedicated to Maruyama
1981.10	Erect poetry stele in Toyohashi, inscribed with the 1946 poem, "*Utsukushii Sônen*" [Lovely Notion]
1990.04.04	Citizens in Iwanezawa open the Maruyama Kaoru Kinenkan [Commemorative Museum]

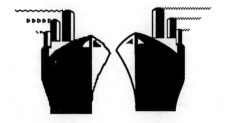

COLLECTIONS

The information below I extract from the *Works*

『丸山薫全集』　角川書店

[*Maruyama Kaoru Zenshū*] (Kadokawa Shoten, 1976–1977)
All 410 poems in Maruyama's fifteen
collections have been rendered.

The following lists only new works included in each of the collections; I do not re–list works published in earlier books. By "new" I mean works published for the first time in any one of Maruyama's fifteen books; these may have appeared in a magazine or newspaper but not in an earlier poetry collection.

Roman numerals after titles give the volume numbers; Arabic numbers offer the pages of each collection in the *Works*. All publishing houses are in Tokyo unless otherwise noted.

To differentiate poems with identical titles, I add (i), (ii), or (iii). Maruyama added numbers only to the two early poems titled "Bar Song" and to a pair of later works dealing with Nakatajima. The designation (p) follows the title of any prose piece or a prose poem [*sanbunshi*].

*　　　　*　　　　*

1. **SAIL–LAMP–GULL** [*Ho–Ranpu–Kamome*], I:11–59
   Daiichi Shobô, 1932.12.05—34 new poems
   『帆・ランプ・鴎』　第一書房

   PART 1 (8 poems)——Estuary, Anchor, Song of the Sail, Song of the Lamp, Song of the Gull, Pain of Parting, Lamp and Albatross, Glimpses of the Circus

   PART 2 (12 poems)——Wind, Gun Emplacement, Fragments, Crane (i), Dirge, River (i), Mist, Dark Sea (p), Street, Twilight (i), Twilight (ii), Twilight (iii)

   PART 3 (8 poems)——Spring (i) (p), Spring (ii) (p), Sea Lion (p), Fountain (ii) (p), Eaves (p), Naughty Tarô (p), Words on Driving Rain, Memos to Faces

335

PART **4** (6 prose poems)—Mountain, Winter, Daybreak, Elephant and Shade, Bullets' Path, Evening Skies

2. **FUNERAL OF THE CRANE** [*Tsuru no Sôshiki*], I:61–105
   Daiichi Shobô, 1935.05.05—31 new poems
   『鶴の葬式』　第一書房

   PART **1** (9 poems)——Dawn, Lamp, Night, Voices, Shadows (i), Supper, All Day Long, Drinking Bout, Nostalgia

   PART **2** (8 poems)——Wings, Palisades, Episode, Sundown, Waves and Foam, Bar Song I, Bar Song II, Cove

   PART **3** (13 poems)——Spring (iii), Summer, Mountain Pass, Autumn (i) (p), Dusk, Sorrow, Earth and Heaven (p), Roof, Fire, Our House, Song of the Crane, Funeral of the Crane, Water's Spirit

   PART **4** (1 work)——Reminiscences of Lamps (p)

3. **INFANCY** [*Yônen*], I:107–140
   Shiki Sha, 1935.06.15—18 new poems
   『幼年』　四季社

   Troubled Yard, Fabrications, Crow, Fisher, When Lightning Strikes, Infancy, Monk Hill, Lion, By Train, Training Barque, Views of the Harbor, Panther, Father, Brothers (p), Ship's Captain (p), Two Behinds (p), Tale of the Butterfly (p), Deep in the Castle

4. **DAY BY DAY** [*Ichinichishû*], I:141–188
   Hangasô, 1936.09.15—35 new poems
   『一日集』　版画荘

   MORNING SUN (8 poems)——In Praise of Morning Sun, City Awakens, Rose, Doves, New Year Season, Orison, Bedroom, Day–Long Dreams

   SUN TO LOVE (2 poems)——Sun to Love—Flower to Love, Journey on a Cloudy Day

   SUNSET (10 poems)——In Sunset's Glow, At the Beach, Afternoon, Light's Path, Traces of a Butterfly, Early Spring (i) (p), God, Song of the Spring Bird, Autumn (ii), Myths

STARRY NIGHT (6 poems)——Starry Night, Joys of Snow (i), December Twenty Fourth, Making a Living, Sacred Flame, Dreams

UNLUCKY DAY (9 poems)——Camellia, Cherry Blossoms, Beloved Tomb, Her Remains, Standing by the Grave, Bell Song, Elegy, Crane (ii), To a Pine

5. **IMAGES** [*Busshô Shishû*], I:189–252
   Kawade Shobô, 1941.02.10—28 new poems (total: 84)
   『物象詩集』 河出書房

   JAPANESE SKIES (20 poems)——Japanese Skies, School from Afar, Old Poetry Collection, Our Unshod Pooch, Loner's Dog, On the Road, Depressing Scene, Mining, The God Who Wept, Mud–Colored Painting, Dog and Old Man, Digression on a Solar Eclipse (p), Into Clouds on the Hill, Dog Watching Horizon, Sea Wind, Sea Darkens (p), Touching your Tombstone, Calmer than the Flower, Rhinoceros and Lion, Korea (p)

   DAY BY DAY (15 previously published poems)

   FUNERAL OF THE CRANE (3 new poems among 11 works)——Perversity, Decade, Night Bell

   SAIL–LAMP–GULL (2 new prose pieces among 23 works)——Self–Righting Lamp (p), Autumn Impression (p)

   INFANCY (3 new poems among 15 works)——Joys of Snow (ii), Drifting Penguin, Swallow (i) (p)

6. **THE GOD WHO WEPT** [*Namida Shita Kami*], I:253–278
   Usui Shobô, 1942.02.25—9 new poems (total: 30)
   『涙した神』 臼井書房

   PART 1 (5 new poems among 17 works)——Dazzling Spring, Spring Scene, White Flowers, Horse at Dawn, Into the Future

   PART 2 (4 new pieces among 13 works)——Be a Tiger! (p), Steam Launch (p), Dreadful Dream (p), Freight Cars (p)

7. **HEAR THE SHIP'S BELL** [*Tenshô naru Tokoro*], I:279–372
   Ôka Sha, 1943.09.20—34 new poems

   『點鐘鳴るところ』　桜華社

   Like Music, Winds, Waves, Birds (i), Helm, Feet of Sailors,
   Sons of the Windjammer, Cruise Duty Chart, Slow Sailing
   Day, Daytime Sea, A Poet's Words, Five Minutes Till Sun-
   down, Blossoms in Southern Seas, At Sea, Young Men
   Shoulder the Sail, Memories of Masts, News of Rain, Sea
   Travelers, Dolphins' Visit, Catching Bonito, Lifeboat Drill,
   Morning Watch, Apples, Sea Impression, Watching a
   Whale, Island, Reckoning the Compasses, Capstan, Moored
   in Amoy, Swallows of Amoy, Breezes from Land—From Sea,
   Sea Bird, Back in Port, In My Porthole

8. **NORTH COUNTRY** [*Kitaguni*], I:373–430
   Usui Shobô, 1946.09.09—25 new poems

   『北国』　臼井書房

   Deepening Snow, Tranquil Festival, Themes, Mr. Moon,
   Mountain School, Ages Back it Seems, Winter Dreams, Liv-
   ing Alone, White Pictures, North Country, Witch Hazels, Vi-
   sions of Flowers, On a Morning in Spring, Tracks, Fox, High
   Village, Wild Cherries, Above Our Village, Those People,
   Spring Night, Verdant Classroom, Grosbeak, Lovely Notion,
   Fate (i), Mountain Crone

9. **MAGICAL COUNTRY** [*Senkyô*], I:431–493
   Sapporo: Seiji Sha, 1948.03.31—25 new poems (total: 50)

   『仙境』　青磁社

   Magical Country, Hunting Button Mushrooms, Birds (ii),
   Living in Remote Mountains, Mother's Umbrella, Valley
   Trail, Thoughts about Snow, Japan's Conscience, Lunar
   Calendar, Prairie, Tsurubé, Rainbows, Early Spring (ii),
   Spring in the North, Snow Bugs, Beckoning Spring,
   Balmy Weather, Swallow (ii), New Buds, Flowers and a
   Goat, Rocks Roll Downstream, Climate, Snow Patch, But-
   terfly or Bird, In Rice Paddies

10. **BLUE CHALKBOARD** [*Aoi Kokuban*], II:9–86
Nyûfurendo Sha, 1948.05.10—30 new poems (total: 34)

『青い黒板』　ニューフレンド社

SPRING (7 new poems of 8 works)——Blue Chalkboard, Pictures and Chinese Graphs, Chorus, Ball, In a Mountain Field, Song of the Bird, A Swallow Arrives

SUMMER (10 new poems)——Sea Flags, Clouds Billow on the Offing, Summer Butterflies, Scenes Become Clouds, Cherries, Even in the Mountainous North, Spring to Summer, Deep in the Mountains, Polar Bear, Rainy Day

AUTUMN (7 new poems)——Twilight Clouds, Far Mountains—Near Mountains, When I Walk through Fields, Hands, Working Girl, Mountain Village, Winter Comes

WINTER (6 new poems of 9 works)——Mornings, Telephone Pole, Page One, Squash, Straw Boots, News from the Mountain

11. **FLOWERCORE** [*Hana no Shin*], II:87–186
Sôgen Sha, 1948.06.20—43 new poems (total: 47)

『花の芯』　創元社

FLOWERCORE (16 new poems among 17 works)——On Adolescence, A Youth and a Horse, Nobuo Weather, Flowercore, Swan, Rainbow, Concertinas and Trains, Sailing Doll, Ages, Vaguely, In a New Age, Poets' Friends, Carossa and Rilke, Like a Lamp, Unspoken Love, Remembering Mother

LONELY UNIVERSE (12 new poems among 15 works)—— Ears in the Sky, Lonely Universe, Summer Day on the Mountain, Child in a Dream, Death of an Unfortunate, Fate (ii), Devastation, Wolf Pack, Dog Watch, Weighty Baggage, Lad, Sea Birds

DREAMING NORTH (15 new poems)——Snowy Field, On the Way, Dreaming North, People of the North, White Valley, Those Who Stand on Ice and Snow, Flower Tree, Girls, My Feelings as Well, On a Mountain Path, Evening Mist, Foxfire, In Town, Spring Storm, Children's Song

12.   **LOST YOUTH** [*Seishun Fuzai*], II:187–312
      Sôgen Sha, 1952.08.15—49 new poems (total: 80)
      『青春不在』　創元社

      PART 1 (44 new poems)——Verdant Self, Dreadful Me-
      thod, Blessed, Sparks, Things that Bud, That Much, Im-
      pression, World, Night Journey, Aroma, Day of the Storm,
      Atomic Balm, Hands and Bread, Fireplace, Within the
      Sun, Things that Flutter, Efforts, My Winsome Wife, Un-
      familiar Locale, By a Pond, Bird Crossing Blue Skies,
      Greenfinch, Crow Flock, Herons, Alley Heaven, Sooted
      Skies, Into Chaos, "X," Tree Voice, Night Trees, Stars,
      Awakening, Free Flight, Moon and Saturn, On This
      Planet, Black and Gold (p), Zone of Collapse (p), Sea Was
      Soused (p), Bubbles (p), Wide River (p), Solitude (p), Ori-
      ental Noise (p), Distaff Stone Buddha (p), Shanghai (p)

      PART 2 (5 new poems among 33 works)——Handicaps
      Like These, News from the Cape, With But a Few Words,
      Flame, Sea's Eyes

13.   **HOSTAGE SEA** [*Tsuresarareta Umi*], II:313–338
      Chôryû Sha, 1962.11.20—11 new poems (total: 73)
      『連れ去られた海』　潮流社

      I. ESTUARY (14 previously published works)

      II. SONS OF THE WINDJAMMER (32 published works)

      III. SELF–RIGHTING LAMP (15 published works)

      IV. HOSTAGE SEA (11 new poems among 12 works)——Sea
      Colorings, Coral Sea, Sailing through Autumn, Illusion in
      the Reef, Hostage Sea, My Woman the Sea, Vision, Young
      Sailor, Sea Beast, Line from the North, Sea of Okhotsk

14.   **MOON PASSAGE** [*Tsuki Wataru*], II:339–406
      Chôryû Sha, 1972.09.01—22 new poems
      『月渡る』　潮流社

      MY JOURNEYS (8 poems)——Pond's Edge (p), Bird Talk,
      Heartrent..., Sea Near Chichijima, Dreams I See in the
      Sea, Captain 'S'—An Album of My Cruise, Reef and
      Waves, My Journeys (i), (ii), (iii)

SUCH SCENES (6 poems)——Such Scenes..., Strolling the Dunes, Plovers, In the Corridor of Omaezaki Lighthouse, Early Spring Sea, Horizon

AESTHETICS OF THE SEA (4 poems)——Aesthetics of the Sea, Mermaid and I, Abalone, Golden Cub

HUNTERS AND I (3 poems)——Hunters and I, Man Who Encountered a Bear, Snares

ESQUISSE [Sketch] (1 prose poem)—Moon Passage

15. **FACE WITH ANTS** [*Ari no Iru Kao*], II:407–442
    Chûô Kôron Sha, 1973.05.30—16 new poems
    『蟻のいる顔』　中央公論社

Face with Ants, Mortified Figure, Gray Bear, Afterimage of a Picket Line, Lovers' Whispers, On This Fossil, Mallards (p), Minato Ward—Nagoya, Autumn Dreams, Snakes, Stream—Tale of an Old Hunter, River (ii), Waterfowl, Our National Anthem, Tenth Floor in the 'Q' Hotel, Room with Bird

NOTE

Maruyama chose to include exactly 34 poems in his 1st, 7th, and 10th collections. That is the same number he selected for *Strong Japan*, the 1944 children's book he repudiated, ostensibly because of the pro–war attitudes that dominate some of the verse.

His 4th collection contains 34 poems and one prose poem. His 11th collection contains 43 new poems (34 backward). It is difficult to imagine that these several repetitions of the number 34 are fortuitous.

The number 34 comes, I believe, from the name of the poet's wife, Miyoko. The Chinese graphs for her name are "3," "4" (born on the 4th of March, the 3rd month), and "ko" (the common feminine suffix).

三四子

Given Maruyama's extremely secretive nature, he predictably never mentioned to Miyoko this subtle way of honoring the many years she single–handedly supported him so he could work on po-etry.

Over more than 40 years of marriage, Miyoko never saw him undressed. Indeed, if he ran out of soap in the bath, he'd simply reach his hand out the door to get a bar from her.

ENGLISH TITLES

The Roman numerals following each entry denote the volume number of *Maruyama Kaoru Zenshū* [*Works*] (Kadokawa Shoten, 1976–1977); Arabic numbers refer to the page(s) in each volume. Parentheses enclose the first known date of publication, giving year and month. A year–month–day sequence doubtless indicates that the poem first came out in a newspaper.

Maruyama uses the numbers I and II to differentiate two versions of "Bar Song" and two poems about Nakatajima. I add small case Roman numbers (i), (ii), and (iii) [there is one (iv)] to distinguish works with identical English titles.

Maruyama first published many poems only when he issued the collection in which they appear. In such cases, the listed date registers when he issued the collection. If nothing follows the date, the work did not appear in one of his collections; some he put out in anthologies.

The Arabic number (preceded by a #) after the date indicates the number of the collection (from #1 through #15) in which the poem first appeared. The title of the collection in italics follows the number. Details on the fifteen collections and the new (i.e., never before collected) poems they contain appear in COLLECTIONS (page 335).

*   *   *

JAPANESE TITLES

Maruyama uses the same title for several poems. Only twice does he add a number to distinguish works with identical titles. To differentiate such poems, I add to the translated titles small–cap Roman numerals in parentheses: (i), (ii), and (iii); in several cases, context allows using the singular for one, the plural for another title. In the listing below, I add the year of publication (in parentheses) to identical Japanese titles.

A number of poems have two entries because it is possible to read their titles in more than one way. Alternate readings appear in square brackets. In alphabetizing, I ignore long vowels.

The English version of each poem as I render it in *That Far–Off Self* follows the Japanese title; space limitations often require an abbreviated version. The source of the poem I indicate in parentheses (volume and page from the *Works*). See page 335 for the publication data and the contents of each collection.

Maruyama sometimes created his own Chinese compounds, so certain words in his titles may not appear in dictionaries.

*   *   *